THE TOUGHEST MAN ALIVE

GENE LEBELL

with

BOB CALHOUN

HNL
PUBLISHING

*This book is dedicated to my father Maurice LeBell and my mother
Aileen LeBell Eaton.*

*From my dad I inherited my athletic ability and my sense of humor and from
my mother I received my business sense and red hair. Both of them were
truly brilliant individuals so I guess that in my case,
brilliance must slip a generation.*

*With love
Gene
May 7, 2003*

ACKNOWLEDGEMENTS:

First and foremost we would like to thank Noelle Kim for her tireless efforts in making this book happen. Without all of her good work and advocacy of all things Gene LeBell, this epic autobiography would not exist today.

We would also like to thank: Steve Kim (the North Korean Fighter Pilot), Paul Power (www.paulpower.com), and George Foon of CFW Enterprises for all of their time and assistance in tracking down and scanning the numerous photos throughout this book. Dana Parso for driving the ghost writer down to Los Angeles on several occasions and Greg, Tigger and Felina Franklin, Scott May and Jacqueline Calhoun for putting the ghost writer up at their residences - without all of them this book would have been a lot more difficult to realize. Many thanks also go to Benny Georgino, Gene's daughter Monica, Gokor "The Armenian Assassin" Chivichyan, Mando Guererro, Midge LeBell and everyone else who helped to jar Gene's memory and thus fact check this volume. And lastly, Gene LeBell would like to thank all of the wrestlers, stuntmen, his family and friends as well as the people he loves and the people he hates.

First published in Hardback in 2003

ISBN: 0953176673

Published by HNL Publishing

e-mail: hnlpub@hotmail.com

FOREWORD

I remember my first workout with Gene almost 35 years ago. I was a young karate competitor and I was trying to extend my knowledge so I went to train with Gene LeBell. To say that it was life changing experience is an understatement because every workout with Gene is a life changing experience - if you live through it that is. When I first went into his dojo, Gene said, "I'm gonna' teach you the proper way to apply a choke hold, but before I teach that to you, you've got to know what it feels like to be choked out."

"I do," I said and he told me that I did. I had no choice so I said, "Okay," and he proceeded to choke me out. I woke up soon after to see a flurry of faces looking down on me and so I got my experience of being choked by Gene LeBell and it was, to say the least, the first of many.

I remember another time when Bob Wall, Richard Norton and myself were working out with Gene and he grabbed Richard in a wrist-lock. Richard's wrist was bent back about 180 degrees and Richard later said that it hurt so bad that he couldn't say, "It's breaking! It's breaking!" He said that he was just in shock. At the time I was looking at it and I was thinking that Gene was going to break it, but of course he didn't. Still Richard felt like he did. After that, Gene grabbed Bob and twisted Bob's head sideways. I could see the veins in the side of Bob's neck sticking up while Bob's legs were going crazy. I thought that I was next and I wondered which leg Gene was going to grab a hold of Fortunately, he was pretty nice to me that night.

One thing that I would never want to do is get Gene mad. I've seen him mad one time in 35 years. It was at the Olympic Auditorium and some wrestler came in who had been drinking and he got into Gene's mother's (Aileen Eaton's) face and got pretty obnoxious. I looked at Gene and his face turned red. Gene grabbed this guy, who weighed about 250 pounds and picked him up over his head and threw him on Main St. I knew then that I would never want to get Gene mad at me.

Gene LeBell is my mentor and he is a very, very special man to me. All of these years of working out with Gene have been an incredible experience.

Chuck Norris
Glendale, Calif.

April 12, 2003

INTRODUCTION

The first time that I stepped into Gene LeBell and Gokor's Judo School on Sunset Blvd. in Hollywood, California, Gene proceeded to pull my hair, tug on my ears and told me that biting was a perfectly legitimate grappling maneuver. He then had some of his top students put me in a series of excruciatingly painful leglocks that made me fear for my ability to walk freely. After he was done with that, he tried to demonstrate some finger breaking techniques on me but I quickly reminded him that I needed my fingers to type up the manuscript to his autobiography. Begrudgingly, he gave up on pulling my fingers out of their sockets and moved on to show me a whole host of moves that I had never seen in all of the time that I had spent earning a blue belt in Brazilian Jiu-Jitsu but you could still tell that he really wanted to twist my digits.

All of this finger busting and hair pulling would have made me turn tail and run never to return if it wasn't for the first time that I met Gene LeBell in person. I live in San Francisco and Gene lives in Los Angeles so the early days of working on this book were done over the phone and through email and faxes. After two months of taping interview sessions using the very finest in Radio Shack phone recording equipment, I finally decided to drive down to Los Angeles to meet the voice at the other end of the line and discuss his autobiography in person.

Gene met me in front of his San Fernando Valley townhouse and ushered me into a nearby parking space. I got out of the car and we exchanged greetings and then Gene told me to come around the side of the house with him to his garage. I followed Gene to his garage which was was crowded with an oversized Honda motorcycle, a red Cadillac, boxes of his grappling books and several jars filled with assorted nuts. Gene grabbed a handful of walnuts and went out to his driveway and all of a sudden a couple of the pigeons and squirrels that make their homes in a palm tree adjacent to his property made their way down to the ground to pick nuts out of his hand. He seemed to have names for all of them: there was Nibbler and Mrs. Nibbler (the squirrels) and Spot the pigeon and a whole host of others. Gene only stopped feeding his makeshift pets to occasionally chase off a curious alley cat, but then he resumed with his feeding session. "I really want to get Spot and Nibbler to both eat out of my hand at the same time," he told me. I almost have gotten them to do it but something always breaks the deal."

That was the first time that I had met Gene LeBell and there he was, the toughest man alive and a self-described sadistic bastard, wanting nothing more than to make peace between the pigeons and the squirrels.

Bob Calhoun
Pacifica, California
May 14, 2003

PROLOGUE

THE SAVAGE CHALLENGE

It was the early 1960s and I owned a judo school around the corner from the famous gates of Paramount Studios. America was just becoming aware of judo, karate and the other martial arts and popular stars like George "Superman" Reeves and Elvis Presley were starting to train in them for self-defense and exercise. One day in 1963, Ed Parker, the man who founded American Kenpo Karate and gave Elvis his black belt, came into my dojo with a rolled up copy of the latest issue of "Rogue Magazine." "Rogue" was a class magazine with thick paper and a lot of cartoon drawings in color. It was a competitor of "Playboy" and was just as popular at the time. In this particular issue, there was an article called "The Judo/Karate Bums," which was illustrated by a cartoon of a slant-eyed, Japanese guy with a judo suit on. Jim Beck, who wrote this article, offered $1,000.00 to any judo man that he couldn't beat. I saw big signs – dollar signs.

Ed Parker showed me the story and said, "I want you to fight this guy."

"Why me?" I asked.

"Because you're the most sadistic bastard I know," he replied.

Of course for a thousand dollars I said I would fight my grandmother but then again, she could whip me. A thousand dollars was a lot of money back then and with any side bets that I placed on myself, I could come out of this thing with a good chunk of change. You have to remember that you could buy a very nice car for only $2,500 back in 1963.

I had my lawyer write a letter to Beck saying that if it wasn't just a publicity stunt, I was game. There were a lot of sarcastic letters back and forth and contracts to sign. I tried to get the fight in Los Angeles, where I come from, because my family ran the boxing and wrestling cards at the Grand Olympic Auditorium. I knew there were over 10,000 seats for screaming fans to fill the Olympic and we could charge ten dollars a head winner take all. We would be too rich to talk to anybody.

But the California State Athletic Commission, which was a dominating factor, classified the fight as a duel and wouldn't sanction it. So we went back and forth and the bout ended up being scheduled for December 2, 1963 at the Fairgrounds Coliseum in Beck's hometown, which was Salt Lake City, Utah. Also, instead of fighting a mouthy magazine reporter, I was going to fight a guy named Milo Savage who was rated the #5 light heavyweight contender in Ring Magazine at the time.

Now since boxing was like a family business for me, I had seen Savage fight before. He was a cut-up, imposing fellow with an intimidating face. He was the kind of journeyman boxer that top ranked contenders and champions feared to face because he was good enough to knock out any fighter on any given night.

When I saw him fight at the Hollywood Legion Stadium on Hollywood Blvd., he walked into the ring and just cold-cocked his opponent at the opening bell. After he hit the guy he just turned around like he knew it was all over with. He didn't hover over his opponent at all. No, Savage knew it was over. It was like when Barry Bonds hits one out of the park and he just watches the ball clear the fence before he circles the bases. Savage had iron in both of his fists.

I arrived in Salt Lake City about a week before the fight to get used to the weather and the altitude. Accompanying me was Larry Coughran who was my first judo instructor and the lawyer who helped me negotiate this fight. I was in pretty good shape back then and I prepared for match by focusing on my cardiovascular conditioning. I hit the cold Utah streets and did my roadwork while carrying a heavy log behind my shoulders. I also did thousands of pushups and sit-ups but didn't really focus on judo drills. It wasn't like I was going to master any new holds that I already didn't know with only a few days before the fight, but keeping my wind up was what was going to make the difference because a car that's out of gas isn't going to win the race.

I went to this Salt Lake kenpo karate school and the students there told me that Milo Savage had visited about a month before. Savage came into the school and told them that a boxer could beat any man wearing his pajamas (which was his way of referring to a karate/judo uniform). He then put on a pair of boxing gloves, hit the instructor, knocked him out in ten seconds and sent the guy to the hospital with a broken jaw. "You've got to watch this guy. He fights dirty," the karate students told me.

Now it wasn't that Savage fought dirty: he was just a boxer and he happened to be a damned good one. The kenpo students also told me that Milo Savage was in the barn training with Gene and Don Fullmer. Gene Fullmer bore the distinction of winning a 15 round decision over the great Sugar Ray Robinson in 1957 to gain the middleweight championship of the world. Sure, Sugar Ray got his title back but to win even one round against Robinson made you a cut above let alone being good enough to take the whole fight from him. Don Fullmer was also a championship quality contender himself and these were the guys that Savage was using for sparring partners.

I also went around to these different pool halls because I used to shoot pool, billiards and snooker just to kill some time. Everybody was talking about this fight. I didn't tell anybody who I was and I would join in on the conversation. I would say, "Wow! Sounds good. What's going to happen?"

"Don't you know who Milo Savage is?" they would come back. "He's going to kill this guy." Milo was a pretty big hero up there.

A couple of days into my stay Larry told me that this local sportscaster wanted me to be on his television show. I forget the guy's name now but he was the big local, muckety-muck and he was kind of commentator that was very good but very insulting. That's how he got listeners I guess. I was listening to him announce before I went on and he was insulting this guy and insulting that guy. I didn't really think anything of it.

They called me on. The host looked me up and down and said, "You don't look tough and I can tell you're not tough. We'll see how tough you are when you're laying on your back out cold. This guy Milo Savage is going to break every bone in your body just like he did when he went into that karate school and broke the teacher's jaw and sent him to the hospital."

"Why do you want to die?" He asked me.

I was listening to him and played it straight but then at that time I was a wrestling pro. The idea of a pro is you put people on with jesting, joking, and teasing. You know, saying things like, "I'll annihilate, mutilate and assassinate you! You pencil neck geek!" A pro would use words to that effect to put more people in seats and get them to buy extra hotdogs. A bigger house makes the cash registers ring.

The guy stepped in closer and asked, "Well what do you think you're going to do?"

"Well, I wasn't planning to come up here and with this kind of weather," I answered. "I am going to wait until it snows and when it freezes, I am going to hit Milo Savage into the ground. And when he's frozen like a Popsicle and sinks into the ice, I'm going to wait until summertime and thaw him out and stick him in a 350 degree oven for an hour."

"You know something -- you're crazy!" the sportscaster said and he was probably right because I was speaking total nonsense.

"How are you going to beat the guy?" he questioned again.

I said, "I am going to use the secrets of the orient and put him to sleep."

"How are you going to do it?"

"I can't show you. It's a secret," I answered.

So the guy gave me a shove, not hard, and said, "Put me to sleep. Go ahead! Put me to sleep!" Since it was his show, I had to do what he told me so I reverted back to being a sadistic bastard and I grabbed the guy quite rapidly and put him out with a sleeper hold while he was standing. Then I dropped him and his head slammed into the floor. The cameras followed him down and one of the two camera guys in the back started laughing hysterically.

While the host was out I picked up the microphone and said, "Well now this is the Judo Gene LeBell program! You go to the matches tomorrow at the arena and it starts at 8:30. Be there, but if you've got a weak stomach, then don't show up. I have to go now because I'm hungry."

On the day of the fight, Larry and I got to the arena early to get warmed up and hash over the rules of the bout. Believe me, the problems associated with drawing up a good and fair set of rules for a fight like this is nothing new to Ultimate Fighting or any of these other get tough contests. There have always been problems with coming up with a set of rules for a boxer vs. wrestler match or for a judoka to take on a karate man. In the end, the only person who is ever truly satisfied with the rules for these fights is the guy who won the fight and sometimes even they find a way to complain.

Savage's manager, who was also the manager of the Fullmer brothers, came into our dressing room with some lackeys and said, "Here are the rules: you're not allowed to kick like they do in football." I assumed he was referring to karate.

Back then; everyone was a lot more worried about karate kicks than they were about a judo chokehold. "What am I allowed to do?" I asked.

"All of that judo crap," he answered flippantly.

I had a little judo book that I wrote and it has all of the throws and pins and all of the chokes. I showed it to Savage's manager, flipped through the pages in front of his face and said, "Can I pick him up and twirl him over my head and slam him down and then jump on him like a cat and demonstrate the secrets of Orient?"

I was just talking and putting him on at this point and I could tell that Larry was getting kind of annoyed with my behavior, which, of course, just egged me on. "I will just put him to sleep," I told them.

"This guy's a psycho," the manager and his cronies said laughing back and forth.

The more that they said I was a psycho the more I started teasing. Larry Coughran started shaking his head and said, "Okay Gene, that's enough!"

"How long?" I asked knowing that the fight was supposed to be 10 rounds.

The manager replied, "It's until the first guy is laying on his back unconscious and that's the rules and if it goes 50 rounds it goes 50 rounds." They were figuring that the first time Savage hit me it that it would be all over with.

"Well I don't care how long it takes," I said. "I'm just going to take my time and wait until my opportunity comes."

Other rules agreed on were that I was to wear a full judo gi (judo suit/kimono) and no gloves or shoes while Savage was to also wear a judo gi but his hands were to be covered by 8-ounce sparring gloves and he could wear boxing boots. I was also told that I couldn't do any leg locks and leg locks are one of my specialties. If you do a leg lock, it's long way from the hands. It's harder to counter a leg lock than it is an arm lock. You go for an arm lock and there's his other arm, which is right there and easy to move. I usually go for a heel hook, a half or full Boston crab, a knee crank, or whatever, but this fight was going until one man was out cold so to win this thing I was going to have to put him to sleep anyway. A joint lock would have incapacitated him quite nicely, but under these rules, it wasn't going to win me the fight and I was there to win. Was it for the glory? Hell no – it's the money that fills your stomach.

Things got a little more serious after Savage's people left and I confessed to Larry that an old injury of mine had started flaring up. I had a dislocated shoulder at the time and it was really killing me.

"Hey, why don't you pass on it and wait a couple of months?" Coughran said full of genuine concern.

"You've got to be kidding, I can beat the guy with one arm." I said with a young man's confidence or maybe it was stupidity. I was confident in myself and also confident in everything that my teachers in judo, wrestling and boxing had taught me.

So after agreeing on the rules and the length of the fight Larry and I went into Milo's dressing room to inspect him and make sure that he was living up to his end of the bargain. Trainers and managers will check on their fighter's opponent before a fight to make sure that they aren't using too much or too little hand wrap or that that fighter's trunks aren't pulled up higher than they ought to be so us checking on Milo wasn't seen as anything out of the ordinary.

First, he didn't have a judo gi on but did wear a karate gi -- but only the top part of it. A karate gi is smoother than a judo gi and doesn't have as many handles on it for throwing and choking. On top of that, this karate top was covered in Vaseline and I mean grease, so the handles that were there were all slicked over making Savage almost impossible to grab a hold of.

Also, instead of the standard, eight-ounce boxing gloves that we agreed on, he was wearing brass knuckles covered in leather. It looked liked they tried to disguise the brass knucks as a leather glove but you could see that they were what they were. I mean the guy wasn't taking any chances.

My lawyer said, "You're not going to fight him with these irons on his hands are you!?!"

I said, "He'll need the brass knuckles because when I hit him there'll be two sounds: one when I hit him and two when he hits the ground." I was in full pro wrestling shtick mode and I was putting Larry on at this point. Seriously though, you're not going to exchange punches with a guy with brass knuckles.

Our last order of business before the fight was to select a referee. Now I ran into a couple of pro wrestlers who were out there in Salt Lake betting on me to win the fight so of course I wanted them to ref the match but Savage's people nixed that idea.

"No. We have the doctor referee" Savage's manager informed us. Their man was a boxing referee and he was also a doctor -- not that that means anything. I was on such an ego trip trying to be modest that I figured that Milo was going to need a doctor.

Finally, the fight was about to begin and I made my way out to the crowd. In pro wrestling, I was always told that they've got to either love you or hate you to be a drawing card and in Salt Lake City that night, they were booing me pretty heavily. So when they booed, I blew kisses to the crowd and was just hamming it up. But Larry was pinching me on the way to the ring and he said, "Straighten out and stop messing around! This is your life –you can get killed here!"

I had a world of confidence. "The guy is not going to hit me," I said. In addition to my judo and wrestling training, I grew up at the Main St. Boxing Gym in Los Angeles. I knew how to keep away from the guy, but another rule that they imposed on me was that there were no tackles. Now the best takedown in the world is a football tackle. You get the best karate guy or boxer in the world and if he's hit by Mean Joe Green or Ronnie Lott he's going to be on the ground – I don't care who he is. And when they're on the ground it's going to be the best wrestler who wins the match. When I say the best wrestler that includes Brazilian Jiu-Jitsu, Judo, and grappling. That's all part of wrestling.

The bell rang and the match started. He hit me once and I hit him once. I stayed out of the way of his punches just out of common sense. I grabbed him and took him down and I got on top of him. Now if I get on top of anybody, they're not going to get up, but with the grease on his gi he just slipped around and I couldn't get a hold of him. The bell rang. There were rounds, which is a bad way for a judo guy or a grappler to fight. You go 15 minutes, 30 minutes, whatever until you get a finishing hold, but with rounds, you only have three minutes at a time to get your hold on the other guy and then the bell rings and they stand you up again which gives the boxer another chance to connect with his knockout blow.

After hitting me again, I decided that it was time to put him to sleep before he knocks me into the nickel seats. I knew how he, being a well-trained boxer, would react to certain things. I put up my right guard and dropped my left hand to bait him into throwing his over hand right, which he did. Once that power punch started to fly, I ducked under it, grabbed him, and spun him into the corner. I grabbed onto his lapels and attempted to choke him while keeping my elbows up high to protect my face. If he connected with my head he would have knocked me into tomorrow land. I could barely grip his gi because it was saturated with Vaseline. Savage started to rip shots to my body as I held on as tightly as I could. Some of these shots were so hard that my conditioning was the only thing keeping me standing.

Then something happened that I had never seen before or since. Those body shots that Savage was pegging me with actually broke off a piece of my black belt. I swear, he connected with my midsection and a 6-inch piece of my belt just broke off and fell to the mat. It wasn't even like it was sliced off like by a knife, it was more like it was frayed away by the sheer power of his punch. You couldn't hit that belt a thousand times and never break it the way that he did.

When the round ended, I couldn't wait to get back to my corner and tie my belt again. I found the piece of belt on the ring floor and threw it to the crowd and started blowing kisses to them again. I was just showboating and Larry exclaimed, "Gene stop screwing around and get to work!"

At the beginning of the fourth round, I grabbed him and threw him into the ropes. When he bounced back, I lifted him on his toes and threw him with a left-sided thigh sweep like a hip throw. I landed on him in an effort to knock the wind out of him. Then I got behind him grapevined and hooked his legs with mine so I could control his body. I went to slip a winding choke on him, which is where you grab one of the collars, go under the armpit and around the back of his head. Savage must have known what was coming because he grabbed my hand and he put it in his mouth and he bit down hard enough to start to draw blood. I brought down my arm and gently nudged him with my elbow above his eye hard enough to raise a mouse there. "Milo," I said, "I'm going to take your eye out if you bite me!" I was serious too. I was fighting for my life now and at this point it was anything goes.

Milo let go with his teeth and I grabbed his left collar with my right hand, and then pulled it tightly across his neck. Then I switched the grip to my left hand and held it with my palm down. I put my right hand on his shoulder and scissored my forearms from behind while spreading my elbows and keeping my wrists straight. I had what you would call a rear single-lapel tourniquet choke cinched in and I wasn't about to let go of it until they declared me the winner. The referee, despite being a practicing M.D., didn't have any idea what was happening and he just stared at us. I was fighting for my life and at that time, I was pretty nervous because the referee wasn't doing a damned thing but staring at us like a curious fan. Then he picked up Milo's arm and it just fell down limp. The ref then walked around to the other side to check on Savage from that angle with me still holding the choke on.

Usually it takes three, four or five seconds to choke a guy out if the tourniquet is applied correctly and I've put a lot of people to sleep and not always by telling them jokes, because I can do it in seminars. People actually want me to choke them out these days. I held onto that choke longer than I think I had ever done before. He was out. Now choke is a crude word. When you choke a guy: what you're doing is slowing down the blood supply to the head so he doesn't get enough oxygen to the brain. This makes him go to sleep. You don't cut the blood completely off because there's always a little blood that gets in there. If you held it on for a long time, you would eventually cause serious injuries.

You have to remember that these people who put on this fight had an attitude. They wanted to kill me going into the ring. I had to win. The truth was that I was not only fighting for my life but I was also fighting for the reputation of all of the martial arts and that was the attitude that I had going into that fight. With everything that went on with the greased down gi and the hidden brass knuckles it was very easy to hold onto that choke. After lifting up Milo's eyelids while I still was still applying my hold, the referee finally gave me the match and said, "Okay, it's over with!"

I stood up with my arm raised in victory and as I crossed the ring back to my corner I stepped on Milo Savage. I didn't step on him very hard. It was more like when you are playing with a kid and you step on them very lightly to scare them a little, but Milo was still out cold at that time so he wouldn't have felt anything even if I laid the boots in on him. But to the audience it looked like I stepped on him hard when he was down. A few moments later, he was still unconscious and people started coming into the ring. The doctor was trying to revive him but he didn't know how, so I wasn't going to be keeping my appointment with him. Then his manager came in the ring and the rest of his entourage followed.

The sold out crowd, upset that their hero had lost and I had stepped on him, started throwing chairs into the ring and a near riot broke out. Don Fullmer, seeing what was going on and attempting to allay the situation, entered the ring and raised up his hands so the people would see him and stop hurling bottles and seat cushions. It slowed the melee down a little bit, but it didn't really stop it.

Things were going pretty crazy and I went to get out of the ring to go hit the showers and get the hell out of there. As I stepped down the ring steps and onto the arena floor, a guy had a knife and he jammed it right towards my stomach. I jerked to the side and he missed me. I fought my way to the dressing room as fast as I could. Those fans wanted to lynch me.

When I got to the dressing room, I showered and cleaned up. It was a big dressing room with a big shower. Milo came in and he was sort of being helped a little bit. He kept on saying, "I'm all right." I went to shake hands with him and he was, you know, nude. With my hand outstretched, he blacked out again. His knee straightened out, slipped out from under him, and he just went down and out and hit his head. My lawyer and this other guy said, "Let's get out of here." His handlers picked him up and that was the last time that I saw him. It turns out that Milo Savage was unconscious for almost 20 minutes in the ring. The doctor/ref and his trainers didn't know what to do and it took my coach to give him a katsu, which is the technique that you use to revive somebody after they have been put to sleep judo style. This was also Savage's last professional bout.

On our way out of the arena, a crowd from the fight spotted us and actually followed us back to the hotel, which made getting out of Salt Lake City a major chore. We had to sneak out of there. When we got back to the hotel it was time to leave so I climbed out the window making sure that nobody saw me while Larry squared our bill. The next morning, we arrived at the airport to catch our flight to Los Angeles and I spotted one of the Salt Lake City newspapers. The headline read: "SAVAGE WAS TAMED!"

CHAPTER 1

THE BEAUTIFUL

Now this book is going to be a lot of meat without very much in the way of potatoes if you know what I mean. I never knew where and when my father and mother got together or the why's and how's of it all. I guess that I never found those sorts of details to be very interesting or nobody ever bothered to tell them to me. I do know that my father was born in New York and my mother is from Canada and they met in Los Angeles the melting of Canadians and New Yorkers. On top of all of that, a lot of information on my father was withheld from me until very recently for reasons that I will never fully understand.

I was born in Los Angles, California in the shadow of Hollywood and I have lived most of my life here. My mother Aileen LeBell was a serious woman with a mind for business and she became a bigger force in the Southern California sports world than I ever was. My father, Maurice LeBell, was a Hollywood chiropractor and a doctor to the stars of the golden age of Hollywood in the 1930s. He had black hair and blue eyes and was often described as a handsome Clark Gable type, so I definitely didn't get my looks from him.

He had an office somewhere in Hollywood and I would visit him there as a kid. There was a chart on the wall, which showed the skeleton on the right side of the body but not the left. I asked him why it didn't have a bone in the arm on the left side.

"Everybody's right-handed," he teased, "so you don't have a bone on the left arm."

Now I have always liked to tease people myself but everyone who knows me knows that I'm only teasing. I don't try to make a man or a woman feel bad. When I tease, let's say, during a judo class, it's because I like to make people part of a family. I'll hug them or something like that just to let them know I'm having a bit of fun and to make a person feel good. Maybe I inherited this from my father's side of the family. I can only speculate but there is an awful lot of evidence to support this idea.

My grandfather on my dad's side of the family also liked to pull my leg. "I'm a war hero," he told me and then he claimed that he single-handedly defeated the Germans in World War I using only his tongue as a weapon. He explained that he caught the German soldiers with his tongue (which must have been over a block long), wrapped them up and squeezed the life out of them from around the corner so he wouldn't have to look at their bodies. It was very strange but he was so convincing to me when I was five years old that I actually had nightmares about some Germans attacking me when my grandfather wasn't there to take them out with his tongue.

I used to ride my bike to visit my grandparents' house on Crenshaw whenever I could just to see their little brown dog named Andy Rooney and hear my grandfather spin some yarns. "You know your name's LeBell and that's because of me," he once told me. "LeBell in French means 'the beautiful,' and they named a town after me in France." He pulled out a map and the only thing that I could read at five years old was my name. He spotted the town on the map and circled it and said, "This town was named after me! Vive Le France!" He was fluent in about five different languages so he started speaking in French. "We are French you know," he said with a flawless accent. Okay, I was convinced, and for over sixty years I was French. How did I find out that my grandfather wasn't French? Well read on -- read on.

My father was very athletic. He held the record for the fastest mile on a bicycle and he was also an excellent swimmer. On the weekends he often took me to the beach, but one trip in particular ended in tragedy. He must have been doing a forward roll in a wave when he hit his head on the bottom and he broke his neck. There was a big crowd gathered around him and I went to see it. I made my way through the people and saw him lying in the sand. He wasn't moving. "Somebody else will drive you home," he said, but I don't remember how I got home that day.

The next time I saw him he was in the hospital in traction with a brace around his neck. He had a broken neck; he was paralyzed but he was always upbeat when I was in the room. "When are you coming back?" I asked him because as a small kid I didn't know any better.

Still, he had me stand up on his shoulders and tried to do all of the things that fathers do with their sons under normal circumstances. They didn't have the trauma centers back then that we take for granted today and there just wasn't as much that the doctors of the time could do for him. He lived for about a month. Before he passed away, my grandmother visited him and he told her, "I've had a good life, and I want to move on."

After that my mother parted ways with my father's side of the family and I was never told why. I asked my mother why I couldn't see my grandfather anymore and nothing was said. She just shrugged it off and didn't say anything. When I was about 10 years old, I hopped on a bicycle and went to their house. The front door was locked and I started to go around to the backdoor. The next-door neighbor stopped me and asked what I was doing.

"Well, my grandmother and grandfather used to live here about five years ago," I said.

"Oh, they're dead," he told me. I then asked about the dog Andy Rooney. "He's dead too," the neighbor fired back, "and you'd better leave."

So I left and I was heartbroken and to this day it still bothers me. I wanted to tell them that I loved them. They gave me shirts to wear, fed me and my grandfather told me stories. It was all a one-way street with them and was the way people should treat their grandkids. It would have been nice if my grandparents and my father could have seen me win judo tournaments and do stunts in the movies. It would have been nice.

When I was six, I was sent to the California Military Academy in Southern Los Angeles. My mother handled public relations for the school and she got me in at a discount. Now the biggest thing that you learn in military school is how to behave, but in my case what I really learned was how to get my butt whipped. Maybe behaving was just a lesson that I learned temporarily because it really seemed like I had to relearn that one over and over again. I got my butt whacked by a belt and my hindquarters whacked by a paddle designed for maximum pain with holes in it. I was what you would call too soon old and too late smart and as a result of that I probably was in the Guinness Book of Records for getting my behind whipped more than anybody else back then.

I got to go home a lot at night or on the weekends but sometimes I had to live at the academy. My bed was in a barracks style room with rows of beds in it where a bunch of other students slept too. In that room was a closet or armoire that was about five feet high. I couldn't resist climbing up to the top of it, leaping off of it and doing a pancake onto the mattress. One night, I jumped off of the closet with the lights out. Right in the middle of my dive, the lights went on and this giant teacher caught me. Why is it that every time that I was caught doing something I shouldn't have been doing in military school, it was by a mammoth male teacher with a paddle, a strap or a cat o' nine tails and not by some little old lady who would feel sorry for me and let me go? I don't remember who it was but he whacked my backside and made me stand in the hall all night long facing the wall. In the morning some-body nudged me awake and asked if I was okay. The man who pun-ished me just left me there by myself and I must have laid down and gone to sleep right in the middle of the hall.

The head boss, or commandant, or principal of the school was named Mr. Brick. Everybody there used to just call him Mr. Brick but I called him Stubby Brick or just Stubby for short because he was a short, portly fellow. I have always come up with nicknames for people because I find it is way easier to recall a nickname than it is someone's real name. I don't remember if I ever called him Stubby to his face but it wouldn't surprise me if I did from the amount of times that I had to visit his office and taste his whip.

His office stank of cigars. When he used to whip me with his belt, he pulled it out with his left hand like he was unsheathing a sword, but then when I looked around, he would beat me with his right. I found out later that it was mandatory in dress uniforms to tuck your belt in on the left side where it comes out on the right. Stubby might have been a sadistic bastard but then again, I probably deserved some of the whip-pings that I got.

Stubby had his own nickname for me as well. "Hey Mr. Looking for Trouble," he would say as he passed by me in the halls. The school had a dog for a mascot and they had a contest among the students to name the pooch. You won some kind of hero button if they chose the name that you came up with and of course I turned in the name "Trouble." The mess hall had a microphone and Stubby used to make announcements during mealtime. "One of the guys wanted to name the dog trouble," Mr. Brick announced, "and it shouldn't be too hard to guess that it was Gene LeBell who wrote that." They didn't name the dog Trouble though, and they instead gave him some kind of ridiculous name.

At the military academy, we had to attend services but we got our choice of what religion we were. My mother was never a very religious person so she didn't give me that much direction in choosing a faith, but she didn't want me to grow up to be a heathen either. Now I couldn't be Jewish because synagogue was on Saturday and that was the day that I went to the movies to find out if the hero made out okay in all of the old cliffhanger serials. At first, I was a Catholic because their services were only two hours long, but later I found out that the Christian Science church ended in a half hour so I ended up with that as my religion. When I found out that Christian Scientists didn't go to doctors when they were sick, that ended my time as a Christian Scientist. Now when you get sick or hurt, I believe that God will let you get an expert opinion.

The only teacher there who didn't whip me was this Russian Cossack who was the head of the horse stables. He had a dark complexion, wore a handlebar mustache and he had a wind-beaten, chiseled face. He always carried himself in a very dignified, very Russian manner. When he walked, he always walked with his head up high and you would think that he had a broken neck because he wouldn't turn it around. He had an image you know and in his life he had to live up to it. He could walk from here to Chicago and there could be 100 nickels on the ground along the way but he held up his head so high that he would never pick one up or even see one.

I used to skip class and hide out in his stables and he never asked me what class I was running away from but he wouldn't hide me from

Stubby Brick or anyone else who was hunting for me either. I used to jump from one stack of bales of hay to another and he never told me to stop, but he did say that a piece of hay was going to stick in my body sooner or later. He then took out a potato and shoved a straw right through it to scare me, which is a gimmick that you can do.

The Cossack really took the time to teach me. "This is the most important thing in your life," he told me because he was a fanatic at horses. He taught me how to ride and whether it was a snaffle bit or a spoon bit. I learned the parts of the English saddle, Western saddle and the army saddle from him. When we were tested for the blue ribbon in horse riding, I passed because I always knew what questions he was going to ask and how he wanted me to hold the reigns. He even taught me how to ride bareback, which really came in handy later when I worked as a stuntman playing Indians in so many Westerns.

Like with my grandfather, I had good communication with the Cossack and he told me tales. He told me that he was a bodyguard to the Czar and in Russia they used to fight duels with swords. He said that he went on military charges and cut peoples' heads off.

I once asked him how many people he had killed in the wars. "When you're a Cossack," he said, "that is your life. You don't count how many people you have killed – it's bad manners."

I look back at his stories now and realize that he might have stretched the truth just a little, but all of his stories were very believable to me when I was seven or eight years old. His elevator might not have reached the top floor or maybe it just came down to my level.

The first time that I choked a person out like we do in judo or jiu-jitsu competition was at the military school. We were marching in a parade in front of a whole grandstand full of parents and teachers and Stubby Brick's son started pushing me. "You're out of time," he said, and then he shoved me to make sure that he was right.

"I am not out of time, you're out of time," I fired back but he wouldn't stop and I was struggling to keep in step. We started arguing back and forth and he got so me so irritated that I pulled off my belt like it was a sword just like his father Stubby Brick used to do. I wrapped the belt around his neck and got him in what we call a bear claw or half bear claw in judo which is kind of a like a bow and arrow. I was pulling one side of the belt and pushed the other side into his neck and slowed the blood supply to his brain. He passed out unconscious and dropped down on the grass, all the while the parade was still going on and the rest of the marchers just stepped over or around him. I put my belt on as quickly as I could so I wouldn't lose my pants and/or my place in the parade.

His father came and picked him and carried him off the grounds while he was still out. He came too shortly after that and he sat down in a chair and watched the rest of the parade go by. Of all of the people the people that I happened to get in a physical dispute with, it had to be Stubby Brick's son because I knew that the judges would be prejudiced in his favor. Of course nobody would believe that Mr. Brick's son could have been in any wrong and have started the whole thing and that "Mr. Looking for Trouble" could be right so I got my butt whipped about a dozen times or so. At the time, I had no idea what I was actually doing when I choked that kid out. It wasn't until I learned chokeholds in judo and jiu-jitsu that I realized what I had actually done. I got whipped the first time that I choked a guy out. Now in judo I get trophies for it because chokeholds are legal in judo competition, which is now an Olympic sport.

CHAPTER 2

THE GRAND OLYMPIC

On the beach at Santa Monica there's a quarter mile stretch consisting of thousands of boulders. A man known as Mr. Garbutt imported these enormous rocks on barges from Catalina Island decades ago. Mr. Garbutt, I was told, was worth over 91 million dollars in the 1930s and 40s, which was real Bill Gates money at the time. I never knew his first name (maybe he didn't have one). My mother always made sure that we showed him the proper respect and you just didn't call people with that kind of money by their first names back then. Garbutt was an oil magnate and he was a driving force that made Los Angeles into the metropolis that it is today. He was also an amateur sports fanatic and he took the LA Athletic Club model and expanded it into a Southern California chain, which included the Hollywood Athletic Club and the Deauville Athletic Club in Santa Monica, and, most importantly to my family, he was major player in the building of the Olympic Auditorium.

The Olympic was finished in 1926 for the 1932 Los Angeles Olympics, and it later became the Mecca of boxing and wrestling on the West Coast. It was an imposing concrete structure and it was a class place in a nice part of town. There were no hoodlums or graffiti. It was safe to park there at night and the parking lot would be filled with luxury cars for the big fights. When I went there as a kid, the cops all looked like they were eight feet tall and the ushers wore perfectly pressed uniforms. The women wore evening gowns and high heels and were taller than the men while the men all smoked cigars. There was never as much cigar smoke in there like you see in the movies though, because the Olympic had big ceiling fans that blew it all away. It was the largest auditorium on West of the Mississippi for years and seated over ten thousand fans, and there was nothing even close to its size on the West Coast of the United States back then. For the really big fights, the place would be packed with gamblers, glamour girls, actors and starlets. You had rowdies pouring beer on each other and looking to start riots in the upper deck and the ringside seats were taken by high-powered politicians and top-flight celebrities, but sellout crowds were the exception and not the rule when my mother first came into contact with the place.

Times were tough for my mother after my father died, but they started to get better after she took a job as Mr. Garbutt's secretary. She was actually a little more than just a secretary. She wrote all of the checks and managed Mr. Garbutt's business at the Olympic and his other enterprises. When I wasn't off at the military academy, I was often at the Olympic hanging around my mom's office sharpening pencils and probably getting in her hair. One day when I was seven, she sent me to the Los Angeles Athletic Club. The professional wrestlers worked out to keep in shape and she thought that I should go watch them and try to learn some mat holds. I didn't know if it was to keep me busy or to get her out of her hair for a few hours.

I rode my bicycle down to 7th and Broadway in downtown Los Angeles where the L.A. Athletic Club was. The building was seven stories tall and they had an Olympic-sized swimming pool on one of the upper floors where gold medal winning athletes used to train for swimming and diving. They also had a banked running track with a corked surface, a boxing ring, various weights, and even juggling equipment and of course the mat where wrestlers sharpened their skills. The first time that I went there, world champion Ed "Strangler" Lewis was holding court.

"Strangler" Lewis ranked with Ruth, Dempsy or Ty Cobb as one of the towering figures of the golden age of sports in the 1920s. I used to watch "Strangler" wrestle and he did this side headlock that would put his opponent to sleep. There was even a publicity shot of him grabbing a 75-pound sack of wheat with that hold, and his grip was so strong that the bag burst from pressure and a stream of kernels leaked out of its bottom. When I first saw him, he seemed to tower over everyone. He weighed over 300 pounds at the time and he was about 6'2". He looked like a barrel that walked like a man. He would flex his arms and say, "Feel this," and of course his biceps were as hard as steel.

I stepped onto the mat and introduced myself as his new student when he came up to me. He hovered over me like a black cloud and blocked out the light from the ceiling. "I want to be tough like you," I told him. "I want you to show me your strangle hold."

He then snatched me up by the head and neck and jerked me off of the ground. It felt like I was swinging from the gallows. Now he was used to wrestling full sized men so when he did that it was the first time in my life that I heard every bone in my body crack all the way down to my spine and it wasn't a sound that I cherished. When he put me down I started to have second thoughts about learning that strangle hold. If I was smart (which I'm not) I should have gone to a movie instead of trying to learn how to wrestle.

My neck and back hurt me for a couple of days but I didn't tell my mother because I was macho or at least I was trying to be. He really did hurt me though, but that didn't stop me from coming back to train with him again the next week. The next time I worked out with him I told him what he did and he said, "You know if the frying pan is hot, stay out of the kitchen." In other words, if you want to wrestle you have to take the consequences and one of those consequences was pain. There's no easy way to success in any vocation or avocation and you're going to get your hands dirty.

I took his advice to heart and I was persistent. I kept returning to the L.A. Athletic Club to learn whatever he and other pros would teach me. Now I wasn't much of a workout for The Strangler and his sadistic buddies and I am sure that they wanted to practice holds on people their own size, but they still showed me a few things anyway when they weren't busy dishing out real pain to one another. All of the wrestlers knew and respected my mother so I doubt that any of them wanted to be caught bouncing her kid around too hard.

One time when I stepped on the mat to work out, Lewis asked me, "You want to roll?" The first time that I heard that I thought it was something to eat, but to roll meant to roll around and wrestle. After having a laugh at my expense, "Strangler" asked what kind of wrestling that I wanted him to teach me. I wasn't aware that there were different kinds of wrestling when I was seven years old, but Lewis took the time to explain the different styles to me. "I can teach you the Greco-Roman wrestling," he said calmly, "which means that you can only attack your opponent above his waste, or freestyle wrestling, which is a full body contact wrestling where you can attack above and below the waist..."

He then broke off almost in mid-sentence and paused. His voice got deeper and louder and his face became distorted and he said, "or I can teach you GRAPPLING."

"What's grappling?" I asked seizing that last word waiting for the bogeyman to jump out at me.

"That means you can do anything and everything. You can do Greco-Roman, freestyle, you can also bite, hit, kick, punch, or whatever – anything goes," he told me.

What seven-year-old could resist that? "I want to learn grappling," I told him and I've been learning it ever since. Sixty years later, I wrote a book called "Gene LeBell's Grappling World: The Encyclopedia of Finishing Holds," which became one of the best selling martial arts instructional books and it all started with a man that they called "Strangler."

Even with name wrestling attractions like "Strangler" Lewis and a host of world champion boxers and top ranked contenders competing there, boxing and wrestling weren't drawing all that well at the Olympic. My mother thought that the different people that Garbutt had running the fight cards weren't really doing enough with publicity and she told Mr. Garbutt that she could do better.

"If you think that you can do any better then you're the promoter," Mr. Garbutt told her and that was the start of a career that not only changed her life but my life as well.

But times were different back then and women weren't even supposed to be working at all, let alone promoting boxing for a living. In 1942 it was completely unheard of for a woman to promote professional boxing and wrestling matches. Some members of the salty, old guard that ran boxing at the Olympic rebelled at the idea of a woman being in charge. A 5'7", 350-pound, cigar-smoking matchmaker named Babe McCoy lead the charge. "I'm not taking orders from a lady," he said to anyone who would listen, "I was in this business before she was born."

Mr. Garbutt, however, was in my mother's corner. ""If you don't work for her," Garbutt told McCoy, "then you don't work." After that, Babe and my mother got along fine and they made a lot of money together.

My mother had to be tougher than the tough guys and able to con the cons. She was only 5'2" with flaming red hair but she could be a very hard woman with a hard personality and she didn't take any mouth from anybody. If somebody said a swear word in her office, she stopped everything and told them to leave. "Come back when you have a clean mouth," she would say. Even the crustiest characters in sports didn't dare to curse in front of her. She wouldn't allow it. Imagine trying to negotiate a contract worth thousands of dollars and having her just end the meeting and slam the door on you. She demanded respect and she got respect.

At home I called her mom, but at the Olympic I had to call Mrs. LeBell (later Mrs. Eaton) just like everybody else. It was an honor or to call her by her first name. If you jumped the gun and call her Aileen without her letting you know that you had that privilege she would look at you in the same way that I would look at you if you called me "schmuck."

My mother could sense when somebody was trying to con her. She always went along with the con at first, but in the end she always negotiated results that were in her favor. I remember one time when this fight manager tried to put one past her. This guy was a cigar chomping, Damon Runyon character and he came into her office and tried to sell her on this fighter from Mexico for a main event. Now this guy's fighter was what you called a catcher and I don't mean a baseball catcher. I mean that he took a lot of punches and had cuts above his eyes. "My fighter is 81-2 down in Mexico," the manager said, "and we want to get him in a main event."

No matter how his fighter did in the fight, this manager was going to make some money. You made 1500 dollars for fighting a main event at the Olympic back then and the manager's take was always at least a third of that so he didn't necessarily care if his guy won or not.

My mom started going through her cabinets while she was talking to him, nodding and stringing him along. She then pulled out the stat sheet on the fighter and started to read from it. "Let's see," She said, "He's had his license suspended due to cuts and has had to go in for neurological examinations."

"I'll tell you what," she told the manager, "We can use him next Thursday, but since there's no fights on Thursday would your fighter like a job sweeping up?" The guy nearly choked on his stogie. She played it completely straight and that guy knew that he was caught with his hand in the cookie jar.

While my mother was negotiating with fighters and managers and putting together fight cards, I was doing just about everything else at the Olympic Auditorium and a lot of that consisted of things that I wasn't supposed to be doing. The head of maintenance at the Olympic was this older black man named Leland and he used to let me change the light bulbs in the rafters. To do this, I had to climb up 50 feet above the arena floor and walk along this nine-inch metal railing that was covered in bird droppings and feathers. One misstep and it was a long way to the ground. Every 12 feet there was another light bulb that I had to replace and there were a lot of pigeons up there had to be shoed out of the way. There was no safety net or safety line for this job so none of the other maintenance crew wanted to do it, but I never had a problem with such things. One time my mother caught me up there and yelled at me to get down. She made me stay in her office for a while, but when she wasn't around, I climbed right back up there when the opportunity presented itself.

I was put to work doing just about every little job you could do at the Olympic. I not only pushed a broom but I also pushed a paintbrush. I sold boletos, which is Spanish for tickets. I sold programs with the names, numbers and pictures of all of the players. I parked cars and helped with security. I worked concessions and sold soday pop ("tastes like champagne if you're thirsty!") and hotdogs ("Chicken in a bun!"). I used to take boxers to get their physicals and I took them to the gym and drove them around. None of the fighters there ever gave me any attitude no matter how famous some of them were because I belonged there. When you're the barnyard dog, you belong in the barnyard. I was young back then and I had a lot of energy and enthusiasm but it was all a good experience from top to bottom.

Before they cemented the parking lot around the arena, there were tunnels underneath the streets. I used to crawl through these tunnels and I was told it was old Olivera St. I found old bottles: purple bottles, green bottles and I would break them. I later on realized that they were valuable antiques but I was just a kid and I didn't know any better. I also found tomatoes down there. I told Leland and he just laughed at me. "That was from the runoff from the outhouses," he told me. Before the Olympic was built Olivera St. was filled with stands where they sold everything from produce to jewelry. It as kind of like a flea market and there were several portable toilets there for the shoppers to use. For years, I ate those tomatoes until I was told where they came from. After Leland informed the origins of those tomatoes, I never used ketchup on my hotdogs at the Olympic because I never be sure where it came from.

As I got a bit older, Babe McCoy, the boxing matchmaker ended up playing an important part in my life. Babe was a very interesting man and he made a lot of fighters, but despite his gruff exterior, he could be a soft touch. All of the fighters used to gather at his apartment house on 3rd St in downtown L.A. They would all have their hands out for money and he would give it to them – even the guys that were too old or too banged up to fight anymore. I got kind of close to Babe McCoy. He liked me because I wasn't adverse to a little sweat and he always treated me like a grownup. He changed my life when he started me training at the famous Main St. Boxing Gym.

The Main St. Boxing Gym was an old time, dirty, stinky gym located on 3rd and Main in old LA. It had two rings and dressing rooms that smelled like urinals. The guys that trained there just whizzed in the shower and I was one of the only guys that wore shower slippers. The walls were cluttered with pictures of boxing greats that trained there and two color posters announcing fight cards past, present and future. You had to go up a flight of stars to get into the place where you would be met at the door by a guy who would charge you 50 cents for a work-out. Howie Steindler ran the gym, but he never charged me to spar there. Steindler was always very nice to me but he was a little man with a big ego and he insulted a lot of people. If you insult enough people, somebody's going to get the fur up on the back of their necks and then you're in trouble. Steindler ended up being found murdered in the back of his car on the Ventura Freeway in 1977. No suspects were ever identified and the case is still unsolved.

I started training at the Main St. Gym when I was around 11, but I kept up my boxing training even after I started in judo. You can call it the beginning of my cross training although we didn't have a name for it back then. I believed then and I believe now that everything compliments each other. My work in boxing helped me in the judo and wrestling. If I skipped rope, that helped me keep my wind up which helped me in every full-body contact sport that I went into. If you train in a martial art (and I consider boxing to be a martial art) and you take away even one move from that art and add it to your repertoire, then that training was more than worth your time.

The Main St. Boxing Gym was the facility of choice for champions when they visited Los Angeles for a big fight. When I was working out there it wasn't unusual to see greats like Ike Williams, Harry Armstrong, Archie Moore or even Sugar Ray Robinson sparring or training on the heavy bags.

Howie Steindler said that Sugar Ray Robinson was the best pound-for-pound fighter that ever lived and a lot of people agree with him. I remember that Sugar Ray was always flanked by his entourage. When he walked down the street there were always two people behind him and two people in front of him. If he stopped suddenly, two or three of his hangers-on would go three inches up his derrier. Still, Robinson had an air of class about him that not too many other fighters can lay claim to. Even after sparring his hair was immaculate and he was always a sharp dresser.

One day, I went to the Main St. Gym and Sugar Ray walked in and looked around impatiently. "Sugar Man's sparring partner didn't show up," Howie Steindler announced to the room, "Does anybody want to spar with the Sugar Man?"

"Is it okay if I get in the ring?" I asked as I jumped into the ring. Howie just smirked at me and put the gloves on my hands.

Somebody rang a bell and Robinson moved and danced around the ring and threw combinations at my head. It didn't hurt a bit because he wasn't really trying to hurt me but his hands were so fast that by the time I went to counter him his hands were gone and he was in another place.

After he knew that I couldn't catch up to him, he stuck his chin out and said, "Hit me." I threw punches at both sides and he stayed in one place until the last moment and then just moved effortlessly to the side to avoid my blows. In a three minute round, I never touched him once and he must have hit me 300 times. I was lucky that we didn't go two rounds because the punch stats would have read: "Sugar Ray: 600. Gene: Zero." He was practicing throwing quick combinations. He'd throw a flurry of four or five fast punches and then move out of the way. It wasn't like he was fighting. It was just an exercise to him.

The whole time I was in the ring with Robinson, I was just trying to touch him – to lay one glove on him. In an actual boxing match, I wouldn't have lasted 20 seconds with the man. After it was over I joked, "I hope I didn't hurt you champ." Howie Steindler told me not to quit my day job but I was just a kid in school at the time.

Babe McCoy sent me on all kinds of boxing errands. I was just a kid and could barely tie my shoes and he had me make a hung over Lauro Salas get out of bed and do his roadwork. Salas was a talented fighter from Mexico and he won the lightweight championship of the world in a stunning upset over Jimmy Carter (not the president but a very good boxer) at the Olympic in 1952. "The guy drinks a lot," Babe informed me. "You have to go over to his place in the morning and get him out of bed and do roadwork and he'll be hostile because he's drunk."

Lauro Salas lived in the Echo Park district of Los Angeles. It wasn't the worst neighborhood in the world but it wasn't the best either. His apartment was on the bottom floor of a rundown building. I went to his room and the door was open. It was a dirty place with beer bottles strewn about all over the place and Salas was passed out on his bed, asleep with his clothes still on from the night before. I shouted at him and tried to wake him up but he barely responded. He was a dinky guy back then and probably only fought at 118 pounds so I picked him and dragged him outside. He started to struggle and muttered at me in Spanish. The fumes from his breath could have KO'd any opponent at that moment.

"You're going to run your five miles," I said, "Or else I am going to strip you down and make you do it naked." He then shrugged me off and gave in. I moved him along and we ran around the park two times, which was maybe about four miles. After that, we returned to his apartment and he went in and laid down and as soon as he did that, he was out cold again.

I called Mr. McCoy and told him what happened and that Lauro had done his roadwork. "Can you do it again tomorrow," he asked and of course I did. Babe used to pay me five dollars for making Lauro Salas run which was big money for a kid back then. Salas' sparring partners probably didn't even make that much money.

By the time I was dragging lightweight prospects out of bed to do their roadwork, my mother had turned around the boxing and wrestling business at the Olympic Auditorium. She promoted weekly boxing shows there and they started to become a staple of the national boxing scene every bit the equal of what was going on in New York at Madison Square Garden. When something is nothing and you want to build it up, there's only one thing that will do it and that's publicity and my mother had a talent for it. She got me into military school with her knack for public relations and she made the Olympic into the West Coast Mecca of fisticuffs with those same skills.

She started by making sure that all of the LA newspapers (and there were a lot more of them back then) ran the results of her fights to create a buzz about the Olympic and what was going on there. Not every promoter got the results of their fight cards into the sports pages, but she did. She greased the sports writers a bit and made things easy for them. She gave out a free meal here or VIP passes there. She gave some reporters a bottle of good booze. She had ringside seats reserved for the press and supplied them with a typewriter and a phone so they could call in their stories. My mother rolled out the red koiet for the media and they showed up.

She was a good judge of what would draw and what wouldn't

draw. She built up fights and she built up fighters. She would take a local Mexican boxer and build him up until he became a star and won a championship belt in his weight division. Mando Ramos, Bobby Chacon, Danny "Little Red" Lopez, Carlos Palomino, Alberto Davila, Jaime Garza, and Lauro Salas benefited from her promotional expertise and became champions in their respective weight divisions. While one of her fighters would be on his way up, they wouldn't draw anything for weeks and the promotion would barely break even. But after she finally established a buzz about a fighter and put together a big fight for him, she would clean up. She was very good at pitting East Side against West Side. She had the locals fighting each other and made a lot of money doing it. It was her idea to cater to the Latino audience a long time before the entertainment industry decided that it was fashionable to do so. By building up Latino fighters my mother had Mexicans coming up from Tijuana to the Olympic see their heroes battle for championships in the fights that she promoted.

When Art Aragon and Lauro Salas got into a drunken brawl in a bar my mother made sure that the story made it into all of the papers. She then turned around and promoted their boxing match at the Olympic as a "grudge fight" when no one had ever heard of a "grudge fight" before. Sure enough that fight did sellout business and the Olympic had to turn people away. Lauro entered the ring with a big sombrero and my mother had a guy there who played "The Brave Bulls" on the trumpet for his entrance music and the crowd just went crazy for it. Aragon and Salas fought toe-to-toe for ten brutal rounds with Lauro losing the fight but I believe that Art actually came in the ring 15 pounds heavier for that fight.

But my mother was only part of a team and she had a lot of help from a lot of people. Four boxing matchmakers come to mind here: Babe McCoy, George Parnassus, Mickey Davies, and the Great Don Chargin. All of the matchmakers were outstanding but Don, with the help of his beautiful wife Lorraine, was the best. Chargin was the matchmaker at the Olympic for over twenty years. On paper, don worked for my mother. I say he worked not for her but with her. As far as I am concerned, in the fight game, Don and Lorraine walk on water.

My mother also cross-promoted the fights at the Olympic with famous movie stars. When Frank Sinatra needed publicity for a new record or movie that he had done, my mother got him to attend a fight card at the Olympic and made sure that the newspapermen and newsreels were there to get plenty of pictures of Ol' Blue Eyes sitting in the front row. That way Sinatra got the publicity he wanted and my mother picked up some press for her fight business as well.

By the time that television hit in the late 1940s, anybody who was anybody started coming to the Olympic Auditorium to watch the boxing matches. The weekly fight cards that my mother put together with help from her matchmakers were made into a network TV show that aired nationally. The show was sponsored by Acme Beer. I don't think that they've made that in years but their slogan was: "Acme! Acme! The beer with a high IQ. Acme! Acme! The beer with a mellow brew." Movie stars started coming down there to sit in the front row and be seen on television. Bob Hope was a regular and so were George Burns and Jose Ferrer. You name them and they were coming to see and be seen at the fights.

Jimmy Lennon, Sr. was the Olympic Auditorium's ring announcer for both boxing and wrestling for over 40 years and both sports benefited from his stylish introductions. He was the first announcer to roll the R's for the Spanish fighters' names and his announcements built up the intensity preceding a fight.

The wrestling cards at the Olympic were also given a boost by television. Both boxing and wrestling were easy to produce. All you needed were one or two cameras and an announcer and some action in the ring and you had a show and television in its early years needed programming more than anything. The wrestling show out of the Olympic, which first aired on channel 5 in Los Angeles, ran for nearly 25 years and was syndicated in several different markets coast-to-coast. Programming directors for independent stations in different cities picked up our show because it was produced in Hollywood, which was the entertainment capitol of the world. This gave the stars of the Southern California territory national recognition at a time when the top wrestlers of other territories were only known locally or regionally.

Around this time my mother took a brown-haired wrestler named George Wagner and made him one of the first big stars of television. Wagner was a very good technical wrestler and even Lou Thesz thought highly of his skills, which is really saying something, but as a draw he was mired in the mid-card. One day, he was hanging out in the booking office while my mother was leaving for a hair appointment. She saw him sitting there with nothing to do and hatched out an idea. "George, why don't you come with me to the hair salon and have your hair styled?" she said to him. Now George, being a macho wrestler, probably didn't want to go to a ladies' hair place, but you really didn't say no to my mother. They got to the salon and my mother had the women there give George the works. They dyed his hair and put it up with curlers. When they were done, George Wagner emerged with little ringlet curls and platinum blond locks. My mother took one look at him and exclaimed, "You're gorgeous, George," and that's how a wrestling legend was born.

George took the gimmick and ran with it. He made his ring entrance to "Pomp and Circumstance" and had his valets spray the ring with perfume. He played the effeminate, arrogant villain to the hilt. Since the wrestling shows from the Olympic were carried nationally, "Gorgeous George" not only became a huge wrestling star, but was one of the biggest television stars of the 1950s. Ever since then, pro wrestling has always had a blond-haired pretty boy from Buddy Rodgers to Ric Flair. Many people have claimed credit for Gorgeous George's transformation over the years, but I am here to put my two cents in for my mother.

With all of the success in boxing and wrestling, my mother started to have parties at her house and where famous people were regular guests. We had this piano and Al Jolson regularly showed up with some songwriter friends of his and he sang all of his hits like "Mammy" and "April Showers," while his friends accompanied him on the keys. Jolson was the first American pop star. At that time he was on the level of an Elvis or a Sinatra but I remember him just crooning at get-togethers at my mom's house. A lot of very famous songs were written on that piano of my mother's. One time Jolson took me to the movies to see

"The Jolson Story" with Larry Parks playing Jolson and Al handling his own singing. Jolson bought me two bags of popcorn, but about halfway through the movie he just couldn't take it anymore and we got up and left. I asked him what was wrong as we made our way out of the theater. He turned to me and said, "Lousy acting but great singing."

One of the men that my mom worked closely with was a California State Boxing Commissioner named Cal Eaton who she later married. Cal was a balding gentleman and he was 5'6" or 5'7" at the most. He had an air of respect about him but he liked to put people down. Although he was a great man, this wasn't a quality that I condoned. Every time that I saw him he would insult me just to make himself feel good. When he did it in front of my brother, my brother laughed at me. You know, there was no reason for that.

After they were married, my mother did most of the work while Cal took most of the credit, which was actually an all too common arrangement for successful women in business back then. While my mother was at work at the Olympic, he was busy playing golf at the Riviera Country Club (which was also built by Garbutt by the way). The posters for the boxing and wrestling cards at the Olympic often read "A Cal Eaton Promotion," but everyone in the Southern California sports world knew that the "Redhead" Aileen Eaton was the real power behind the throne.

Still, despite all of that, Cal Eaton had some very influential friends and after he and my mother were married our family's parties were attended by very powerful California politicos in addition to the movie stars, sports heroes, and jazz singers. Governor Earl Warren was a frequent guest at our house and so was Lieutenant Governor Goodwin Knight. Cal Eaton's son (my stepbrother) Bob Eaton married one of Goodwin Knight's daughters and two nice girls came out of the marriage. After Eisnehower picked Warren to be the Chief Justice of the U.S. Supreme Court in 1953, Knight became the governor.

Governor Knight was always really nice to me like a salesman. He always said the right things to the right people, and that is what made him good politician. Knight believed very strongly in fortune telling, palm reading and astrology. Once at my mom's house in the early

1950s said that he would tell me my future. He just looked at me and then wrote his forecast down on a piece of paper.

"In April of 1954," he told me, "your whole life is going to change."

"What's going to happen?" I asked.

"You will just have to wait and see," he answered.

"What if I'm dead?" I asked.

"You won't be dead," he assured me.

He then handed me the piece of paper with the date "April, 1954" scrawled on it. I folded it up neatly and tucked it away in my wallet and didn't really think too much about it.

CHAPTER 3

FANATIC

Back when I was in junior high school (in California it would be the 7th grade I guess) you didn't have to have a driver's license to ride a scooter or motorcycle. It was legal for you to operate one at the age of 12 and of course I could hardly wait. Some of the kids who had rich parents got a car when they were old enough to drive but I wasn't so fortunate. I worked all of those odd jobs selling sports programs, hot dogs and everything else at the Olympic and the Los Angeles Coliseum just to save up every dime that I could to buy motor scooters. By the time that I was 13, I had already bought a Cushman, a '41 Powell and a Whizzer. The Whizzer consisted of a gas-powered engine attached to a regular bicycle that turned the rear wheel but it wasn't as fancy as the Powells or the Cushmans.

My grandmother on my mother's side liked me a lot because I was a hard worker. She lived with us until she passed away and she really loved to play poker at the Gardena Card Club (poker was legal in Gardena, California back then). Since she didn't drive she bought me a three-wheel Motorette motor scooter so I could drop her off to play cards. The bike wasn't like a sidecar three-wheeler – it had two seats side-by-side. It had two wheels in the back and a ten horsepower motor. It had a battery and a horn, didn't go into reverse and was probably the most dangerous vehicle that money could buy. She was 75 years old and she rode shotgun on that Motorette from our house to the card club, which took a half hour. I dropped her off and picked her up about four hours later and drove her home. This was all before the helmet law and we had some pretty close brushes, but close only counts in horseshoes.

It gave my mother fits that I drove her mother to gambling houses on that three-wheel scooter. My mother advised my grandmother not to talk to me and lectured the lady on the sins of gambling and the dangers of driving that scooter around the greater Los Angeles area, but my mother's admonitions fell flat. My grandmother loved her games of chance and if I dropped her off at the card tables, she had a little bit more money to place bets with than if she took a taxi and when she won, she gave me money for gas. But her big gamble was not at the poker table, was riding to and from the clubs on my motor scooter.

After collecting a few scooters, I soon stepped up and got a 1936 Harley Davidson VL with a suicide clutch. The 1936 VL Harley had you operate the gearshift with your left hand while the clutch was on the floorboard on the left side. That means you had to take your hands off of the handlebars to shift, which made that bike even more dangerous than that Motorette and is also how it got to be called a suicide clutch. Now you shift all motorcycles with your foot so you can leave both of your hands on the handlebars.

With the suicide clutch, you could put it in gear after you would kill the motor so it wouldn't roll. One time I made a mistake and I put it in gear and then I pulled out the key. The bike fired up again and went up the side of the garage and busted a window. The glass from the shattered window cut me and I had to have five or six stitches right above my eye. I couldn't tell my mother that my motorcycle went through the wall of the garage so I had to sort of nail it up in the hopes that she wouldn't notice. I went to the emergency hospital on one of my motor scooters to get sewed up. It wasn't as fast as the Harley but I had to live with that for a while because that incident was the demise of my Harley Davidson. My mother found out about the damage to her garage a couple of weeks later and actually tried to make me walk all over town but I just snuck out with my scooters when she wasn't watching.

Later on in life a man came to me and told me that my grandfather owned the first Harley Davidson dealership in Southern California on 10th St. in downtown Los Angeles where they sold both Harleys and bicycles. He said that he used to work for my grandfather way back in 1906 when he was a kid and that he had a couple of pictures of my granddad and his shop. I called him back a couple of times, but I guess that I wasn't persistent enough because I never got my hands on those photos. But still, that story is proof positive that bikes have always been in my blood.

One day I rode my scooter over to this body building gym in Burbank to pick up some dumbbells and weights. The gym was owned by a strongman named Van Rose and was equipped with barbells, benches, and other weightlifting equipment but it also had a small mat area in the back where judo was taught. As a kid, I had studied judo during and after World War II and I wasn't really that impressed with it. The classes that I had encountered taught mostly rudimentary hand-to-hand combat and were usually taught by some guy with a wrestling background that was a Marine Corps instructor or something like that. They taught us things like a chop to the neck that was supposed to send your opponent down to the ground like in the movies but as I got older, I realized that it didn't really work. Of course this technique always worked for Captain Kirk in "Star Trek," but remember that Kirk had more strength than a mere mortal. You get that strength when you travel to different planets. But despite my reservations, Van Rose, who was kind of a hustler, convinced me to come back and take sport judo.

The classes at Van Rose's gym were run by Laurie Coughran who did amateur wrestling and then studied the Osaki system of judo in Oakland and San Francisco under Professor Ray Law so he had a much better background than usual. Laurie later Americanized his Irish name to Larry so that people would stop thinking that he was a girl. When I met Coughran, he was a private detective who was studying to become a lawyer and he later accompanied me to the Milo Savage fight. The system that Coughran taught was heavy on sport judo and we did knife defense, club defense, defense against multiple attackers, some striking and of course throws and some chokes.

The first time that I went to Larry's school, I thought that I was pretty tough because I could beat the guys in my grade and maybe a grade or two above me with everything that I had learned from the wrestling pros at the L.A. Athletic Club and the boxers at the Main St. Gym. I was pretty good in any schoolyard fights that I got myself into. Larry matched me up with a brown belt that was my height but he was a man and I was just a kid. "He's going to throw you with a hip toss," Larry told me and motioned his student forward.

Remember I thought that I was tough and I honestly believed that I would be able to keep him from throwing me. The next thing that I knew, I was up in the air and on the ground. I asked him to try it again and with Larry's approval he sent me to the mat a second time, but that was good because the competition was on. It was a challenge for me to get better at judo and be able to throw him around. He didn't know it but I did. He regularly threw me around but I kept on getting closer. Finally, after about six months, I was able to toss him at will but maybe it helped that I gained a few pounds during those six months.

At first, in those postwar years, you couldn't even get a gi so we used to wear old, green army fatigue jackets to practice with. They were strong but they would rip. Finally, after Japan recovered from the War, they started importing kimonos again and you could buy them. I used to go all over the place on my motor scooter wearing my gi. It was a way of life and I was a fanatic. When I was in high school and junior high, I went down to the boxing gym in the morning, then I sneaked out of school at lunch to go to the LA Athletic Club and worked out with the pros, and then after school I went to the dojo (a gymnasium for judo practice), which started at 8:00pm. Every chance that I got, I studied some kind of fighting art and added different techniques to my repertoire.

When you're a fanatic, it is like being an alcoholic. Now I've never had a drink in my life. I've never gotten high in my life. I've never taken dope. I don't even eat broccoli or turnips (oh God I hate those things), but the reason that I didn't smoke was because of my allergies and the smoke turned me off. As far as drinking goes the only thing I have in my home is vodka and the reason for that is that I put it in a spray bottle and use it for shoe stretch. I got high on judo, wrestling, boxing, and motorcycles. I didn't need drugs, booze, cigarettes, broccoli, or turnips.

I even hopped a freight train to Chicago to learn different techniques because I didn't think that my motor scooter would make it that far. There was a teacher there who had a couple of terrific throws and I wanted to study with him. I only had enough money for a one-way ticket, however, so I had to hop the train to get there and paid my way to get back. If my mother had known that I was hopping trains like a hobo to learn judo she would have been on me like white on rice.

One time, all of the self-defense techniques that I was learning from Larry Coughran came in handy. I was at the movies and this man was told by this little usherette to move out of the loges because you had to sit forward and make room for other moviegoers. After he wouldn't budge, the usherette pointed her flashlight at him and he took it away and hit her right in the face with it. Then he stood up and pushed her down and when he did, I was sitting kind of close and I went and grabbed him from behind with a winding choke and put him to sleep. He had a big overcoat on which made him look bigger and it was just like working with a judo gi or karate suit. It was ideal and he probably had no idea what was happening to him as he went under. I dragged him out into the lobby and told the manager what had happened. I had just gone over this particular choke the night before in class and it sure did work because this guy was asleep in seconds. He was a big man and the manager said, "Just hold him until the police come."

It was awhile before he came to and I didn't have anything to tie him up with so I held him in what we call a surfboard with his face down and his hands behind him and me sitting on his back. If you want a closer look at this move, try buying my DVDs or one of my instructional books. The police came and they took him away. The manager said, "Anytime you want to see a movie, you can come here for free," but for some reason I never went back to that theatre.

After I told Larry what had happened he taught me katsu, which is the art of reviving. If you want to learn how to do this, you should go find a good judo or jiu-jitsu school or teacher.

After my first sensei Larry Coughran was accepted into law school, he didn't have time to teach the classes anymore, so a man named Jack Sergil took over the judo lessons at Van Rose's gym. Sergil taught kodokan judo, which was sport judo that was developed by Professor Jigoro Kano in 1882. Kano took what he felt were the best aspects of jiu-jitsu and streamlined them into what is known today as sport judo and it is now an Olympic event.

Sergil was a tall man and he acted in a lot of westerns under the stage name of John Holloran. He was a Caucasian but he played a Japanese heavy in the James Cagney World War II movie "Blood on the

Sun" in 1945. Before there was even such a thing as a "martial arts movie," Cagney and Sergil staged one of the best judo fight scenes ever in this film. The more that time goes by, the more I appreciate this fight scene because it is actually very realistic. Cagney studied judo under Sergil and both men used actual techniques in their fight scene, which ends with Cagney finishing off my sensei with a winding choke from behind.

James Cagney was what I would call a real triple threat as an entertainer. He could sing and dance, play a serious dramatic role, handle comedy and be menacing as a gangster. You don't have that many actors with that much variety today. One time Sergil took me to work out with the man. "Just take falls and don't hurt him because he's an actor," Sergil told me. I worked out with Cagney and I took falls for him just like my teacher advised. Cagney was very nice and he kept on telling me how good I was but I just couldn't figure out how he could know if I was any good or not when I wasn't allowed to fight him. I was still very competitive minded back then but I learned an important lesson because over the years I have gotten more from losing a fight than I ever have from winning, but I will explain that more later.

When I went to Hollywood High School, they didn't have wrestling as a sport in California so I went out for the basketball team instead but the coach never played me. I had a half court and a hoop in my backyard and I practiced my foul shots and free throws for hours after I got back from the dojo but it didn't seem to matter to coach Guy Wrinkler. I wasn't as good as the first four or five guys on the team because basketball wasn't my sport, but I weighed 150 pounds and I could move and I thought that I could do more than warm the benches. Coach Wrinkler even tried to discourage me by pitting me against one of his first-stringers. "I can tell you who's the best athlete by who could do the most pull-ups," he said. His top player only did 18 or 20 but I kept going until I did 100, which was considered a lot at that time. This didn't matter though and the coach made it some kind of point not to put me in a game. Maybe this was all because I was so eager to tell him what I could do. Since then, I've learned to keep my mouth shut because a closed mouth catches no foot.

One night they had a big game on the same night that there was a judo tournament. I couldn't resist judo competition and I knew that Wrinkler wasn't going to let me play so I went to the tournament instead. The next day I went to basketball practice and the coach asked me where I was the night before.

"I went to the judo tournament," I said and I showed him the first place trophy that I had won. "They played me and you wouldn't have played me would you?"

His face turned red and he started to stutter. "Probably not," he said and then he told me to turn in my gear. That was the end of my basketball playing and I was kicked off of the team. That was okay though because basketball practice was during the last period of the day in high school. They stuck me in a homeroom, which gave me another chance to sneak out and work out even more.

I was very competitive and I probably bounced some of my fellow judo students around a bit. A lot of these guys that I was training with were just trying to learn some self-defense or get in shape, but I was there for so much more. After Van Rose moved his gym across the street to a bigger place with a larger mat area, I was working out with a couple of paying students and I landed them pretty hard. After seeing this, Van Rose tossed me out of his school. "We don't want you here," Van Rose told me, "and never come back."

To me, I was the school's hardest working student but to Van Rose, I was just killing his cash customers so maybe he was right. But I was beside myself because judo was my life so I went to Larry Coughran and asked him what to do.

"There's only one thing left to do," he said, "and that's to go to the Japanese School."

Larry took the time out from studying law to take me to Hollywood Dojo, which was in a big, old garage with a sawdust mat. There were no signs or anything to let you know that it was a judo school. You just went behind a house and there was the school. It had a benjo (a bath) and a pretty nice shower but it was very old you know. It was probably built in the 1920s or before and it was an all-wooden shack like a barn. From the looks of it, it probably held horses at one time, and the place was so low key that you could easily mistake it for the Buddhist temple that was right next door.

The instructors were Frank Kucuchi, Art Emi, Frank Emi, and Shig Tajima and they spoke nothing but Japanese although they all knew English. They called the techniques by their Japanese names, but it was their sport and all over the world the judo moves were referred to in their language. I was the only Hakujin there, which is the Japanese word for Caucasian. It wasn't derogatory; it was just their word for white Europeans. I was only about 15 and this was right after World War II so nobody there was overly friendly towards me. A lot of the Japanese at the Hollywood Dojo were held in internment camps like Manzinar during World War II and frankly they didn't cotton to Hakujin, which was understandable.

The way that you learned there was by getting the hell beaten out of you, and after that, you got the hell beaten out of you again. When you had completed that first and second lesson, you got the hell beaten out of you for a third time just to make sure that you got everything. When I first went there, some of the teachers just tried to throw me around but my wind was good and they often got tired of throwing me before I got tired of being thrown. I was the first one there every night and the last one to leave and after proving myself, they really accepted me.

They didn't teach the way that we do nowadays. They started by warming up and doing the duckwalk and falls. Then they had you randori, which was free sparring with no real class instruction. Occasionally the older teacher would demonstrate a technique, but you mostly learned by watching other good players in a contest. Then once a month, they had an in-dojo tournament where you competed. The school lined up according to ability. If you beat the guy to your right, you would be to his right. If he beat you would be at his left. That's how they did it and you fought to move up that line.

The Hollywood Dojo belonged to the Nanka Yudansha Kai, which was the Southern California Judo Association. When I was going for my black belt, some of the professors in Nanka Yudansha Kai didn't want to promote me from brown belt. In other words if you beat five black belts it's supposedly was an automatic promotion, but they wouldn't promote me no matter how many black belts I had beaten. I was in one tournament and they put me against one first-degree black belt and two second-degree black belts. I beat them all one at a time but I still didn't get moved ahead in their rankings. A couple of those guys even got promoted ahead of me when I was the one who won the matches. I guess that I started to have sour grapes.

Oftentimes, I threw my opponent down and they wouldn't give me the win or I got on top of the guy where he couldn't get up and the official tell me to stand-up. In other words it gave the other guy a chance to stand up and run away until time ran out so I wouldn't have a chance to pin him. Some of the tournaments that I went into, the judges and referees made it difficult for me but I didn't care. I just wanted to do it. That was and is just part of playing any sport and believe me, I have seen plenty of questionable calls in national and international competition in boxing, wrestling, jiu-jitsu, football – you name it. Some of it is because referees make decisions and they have their styles and what they like. Some like the boxer and some like the slugger. What kind of referee do you have? Does he like the technician or the animal that eats people up through brute force? Other times though, I could swear that the ref wasn't seeing the same match or game that I was looking at.

At one of these tournaments, I went against one of the top competitors from Japan and he had just gone against this fellow named Fuji Nazawa. Fuji Nazawa was the best judo man that we had in Southern California back then and him and me were really close. At that tournament, they had these worn out, canvas mats that were filled with horsehair and they were not covering the floor evenly. During their match, Fuji got his leg tangled up in the mat cover and he busted his ankle really badly after the Japanese judo player threw him. The move twisted Fuji's foot clear around to the other side to where it almost looked as if his foot was pointing behind him. They had a chiropractor turn Fuji's foot back around but I really thought that they needed an orthopedic guy to look at it. Fuji didn't say a word while that chiropractor pointed his foot forward although it must have been very painful. That was just the kind of guy that Fuji Nazawa was. He translated the Japanese words for me in my first judo book and he is one of the good guys in martial arts.

I was the Japanese competitor's next opponent and in just a matter of moments I threw him down, which I thought should have been a win, and I ended up pinning him. In judo if you pinned your opponent for 30 seconds, it was a win. The referee was Kenneth Kiniuki who was a good judo man a but he threw in the beanbag and said, "Time's run out, it's a draw." After a ten second match that's really stretching the time limit but at that time they demanded a lot of respect and you didn't make waves. They didn't want one of their champions to lose face and the Japanese were very big on issues of losing face. You were taught to thank your sensei for the honor of letting you sweep up the dojo. You just didn't smart off and that was out of respect. You learned a lot of respect there, which is a good thing. In the Japanese dojo, I never had to lock up my wallet or my other valuables but at the local YMCA, I even had my underwear stolen.

Still, maybe I was a little too American and too competitive because I wanted the win. The Japanese man that I went up against was better than me at that time, but everybody at that tournament had to know that I had thrown him. If Kiniuki had just had us just start over and let my opponent get back up on his feet, he probably would have tossed me into the nickel seats.

Ishikawa, who was the All-Japan Judo Champion, came up to me, patted me on the back and said, "Ichi bon." Ichi bon means number one. He was a round-faced guy with big round glasses. He was the best in the world and he was calling me number one. I was really touched at that moment. It made me feel that it was all worth it and that the referee's decision to stop the fight and call it a draw really didn't matter. Afterwards, Ishikawa taught me his favorite throw, which was really an honor for me to learn.

Although the instructors and students of the Hollywood Dojo became friendly to me, deep down some of them still carried an animosity towards the Caucasian because of World War II. Eventually, I did get promoted but some of them were very cold to me. After we got to know each other better, we became very friendly because time heals most wounds. Years have gone by and I have wondered what made them change. When I represented Hollywood Dojo, I was a fanatic's fanatic. When we competed in different tournaments with other schools, we would win and I picked up a few of those victories representing the school. I had to work even harder than everyone else to prove myself because I had entered a world where people from my background previously weren't accepted.

I became closer to most older judo teachers because they were the fathers that I never had. In my whole life, I worked out every day. I could hardly wait to go down to schools like the Hollywood Dojo. Everybody needs something. While my buddies were out stealing cars and getting drunk, I was at the dojo. I got pretty close to teachers such as Coughran and Sergil at my first dojo and Shig Tashima at the Japanese School. Shig was my big sparring partner and boy did I ever learn a lot from him. I felt that these teachers were interested in my well-being. You feel very comfortable when somebody gives a damn about you.

One time Larry Coughran came into the Hollywood Dojo and decided to work out. He hadn't sparred in a long time, and I was training everyday. He used to beat me up and throw me around when I was 14 and 15 years old and I always wanted to throw him because he was really good. That day, I went against him and I threw him very high. After he came back down, he said, "Gene, that's the last time I'm working out with you," and then he laughed He must have beat me up 500 times or more and I only got to bounce him once.

When Nanka Yudansha Kai finally relented and promoted me to black belt, Kucuchi-sensei (the head teacher) had me line up the class. After the class was lined up, I was supposed to say "keosuke," which means "attention" and then I was to say "rei" with a rolling r to get the class to bow. Now I had heard my senseis say "keosuke" for years but I had never paid attention to the actual pronunciation and I've got a tin ear. I never broke it down into sounds and syllables, so I mangled it pretty badly as I screamed out, "kitski!" The whole class started to laugh at me and I didn't have any idea why. I looked over to this old teacher who never smiled and all I saw were his teeth and eyeballs as he was busting a gut trying to keep from laughing in my face. I turned to his main understudy and asked, "What are they laughing about?"

"It's not 'kitski,' it's 'keosuke,'" he said holding back the tears that were at my expense. Now "kitski" didn't really mean anything. It wasn't like I was going before the class and saying a dirty word or something, but it was like I was the sensei or the teacher and I couldn't say, "Good morning ladies and gentlemen" without messing it up.

I must have turned redder than my hair because I tried to just get up and run out of the place. There was only one way out into the dressing room and the bigger guys in the school blocked it off. I grabbed every one of them and I didn't let any of them go until I worked with everyone of them in a manly attempt to stifle my embarrassment. I came back the next week and got it right and said "keosuke," but the Japanese made fun of me for years about that. Art Emi and his brother Frank used to call me "Mr. Kitski" after that. When I walked into the dojo, they would say, "Hello Kitski! Hey Kitski!" It was then that I knew that I belonged.

CHAPTER 4

THE NATIONALS

In the 1950s it was the law that when you turned 18 and got out of high school that you had to sign up for the draft. The Korean War was on for the first few years of the decade, but even after that you could still get drafted because the U.S. was always worried about those Soviets jumping over that Berlin wall that they built and taking over the rest of Europe. Now even Willie Mays ended up getting drafted so I was looking for a way to avoid the draft. I was told that if you signed up for the reserves and you were in college that you wouldn't have to go into the service full time and maybe whatever the hassles were would be over with by the time that graduation day rolled around. I joined the Coast Guard because I thought that nobody ever got shot in the Coast Guard and that they just stayed in their boats which shows you how much I knew. Once I signed up for the Coast Guard, they activated me two or three times. All of this active duty and serving my country was having a negative impact on my studies so I finally had to go down to their recruiting offices and tell them that I was still in college because they can't activate you until you finish school.

After high school, I went to Pierce Agricultural College and studied animal husbandry if you can believe that. Now in high school, representatives from all of these colleges showed up and tried to recruit you so I went out and visited a couple of them. I checked out Pierce, which was out in Woodland Hills. When I was there, I saw a guy with a straw hat throwing corn or whatever it was to the chickens. My mother said that I had to go to college and I thought that she would never know that I was just tossing corn to the animals and I could also arrange my schedule so I could work out because they said that you made your own schedule there. When I went to high school they assigned you certain subjects you know and you were pretty much stuck at the place the whole day, but college would be different.

When I signed up for Pierce the guidance counselors asked me what I wanted to take. "Feeds and feeding," was my answer because I really believed that all I would have to do was wear that straw hat and throw grain at the poultry. Instead they made me buy this book and it must have been about, without exaggerating, four inches thick and it weighed at least five pounds. I didn't understand it. It might as well have been in Greek. That book was loaded with math and formulas. I never imagined that feeding cattle would involve so much algebra but it did. Let's say that you're feeding cattle for example and you have a steer that is three months old. You had to figure out how to get the most weight on the thing for as cheaply as you could. All of the feeds like milo, wheat germ, corn, and barley changed prices every day so you had to figure out how to get the most feed for your money so you could maximize your profits. It was very difficult. I didn't like it a bit but I was committed. I did arrange it so I had a morning class and an after-noon class so at noon instead of eating I would go to wrestle or exer-cise. After my afternoon feeding classes were over, I went to judo.

At Pierce, they had what they called the branding day, which was where all of the upper classmen grabbed the underclass guys and basi-cally hazed them. If you were unlucky enough to get caught, two or three of them would jump you and drag you into the barn and they would beat you up along the way. Once you were in the barn, they poured the pancreatic juice from dead cows on you. It wouldn't come off and it was the worst smelling bile that you could ever imagine. If they were low on pancreatic juice, they settled for dragging your face in the manure and shoving it in your mouth.

On my particular branding day, I was just out of the gym and walk-ing across the football field just past the bleachers and three guys jumped me. I was already a black belt in judo then and I beat the hell out of two of the guys really quickly and smashed them down. These guys had no idea what a sadistic bastard I was and that I loved to stretch bigger guys who rubbed me the wrong way just to take the fire out of them. The third one who was left standing must have been about 6'4" with me being 5'11". Once he saw what I had done to his buddies, he started to run away. He ran across the field where they were building this arena. I came close but I couldn't catch him and then he started to pull away. I did five miles of roadwork a day back then, but I just couldn't catch up to that guy with those big, long legs of his. I never knew what happened to the other two guys but I hurt them and they were on the ground when I left.

About a week later, I went into the cafeteria. The tall guy with the long legs that I couldn't catch was there but I didn't even recognize him. I just wasn't really thinking about him anymore. He was carrying a tray filled with food. I bumped into him and he said something but I still didn't recognize him. I asked him if he was talking to me and he turned around and got one good look at me. He turned as white as a sheet and threw his tray up in the air and ran out the door. His lunch was splattered all over the place and got all over some of the students there who were just innocently trying to eat. I tore off after him again but I still couldn't catch him. Those long legs worked for him again. Now that I think about it, I never saw him after that and the good news is, is that I never did get branded.

The whole time that I studied feeding cows at Pierce and was in the Coast Guard Reserves, I kept up my schedule of tournaments. There were still the small inter-dojo and in-dojo contests, but judo started to become more recognized by the amateur sports community. The Amateur Athletic Union sanctioned the first Judo Nationals in the United States in 1953. That same year, I entered the California State Judo Champion-ships, which was also an AAU sanctioned event. It was an elimination contest with no weight divisions or belt rankings. You just went into the tournament and competed. I represented Hollywood Dojo and I took the top spot that year and I won a pretty big trophy too. I liked that trophy a lot until I found out that it wasn't real gold.

In the Coast Guard Reserves, you had to spend two weeks out of the year back at boot camp. After I had already won the state judo championships, they sent me out to Alameda for another round of basic training. Alameda is this island in the San Francisco Bay next to Oakland, California. There was an instructor there who was showing unarmed self-defense. The guy said that he was a brown belt in judo but I didn't let on that I was the state champ. He studied a system that used a lot of katas (dance forms) and he demonstrated a lot of moves that I knew wouldn't work in a real street fight. I tried to keep my mouth shut, but he threw out an open invitation to the class. "If anybody wants to fight me," he said, "they can." A couple of guys got up and he dispatched of them very quickly.

"You proved that stuff works on spastics," I said jokingly, "but does it work on real men?" He motioned for me to join him on the mat. He made me put on a judo jacket and gave me a belt and I acted like I didn't know how to tie it, but I was a black belt in kodokan judo so of course I knew how. He got impatient and tied it for me. We began and I threw him in five seconds. He was stunned and believed it was just beginner's luck so we went at it again with the same result. I threw him down and just sat on him.

"Now what are you going to do?" I asked looking down on him. "That stuff doesn't work."

He finally gave up after I got him in a neck lock. I let him back up and he asked if I had ever taken judo or jiu-jitsu before. "I've had a week or two of it," I told him putting him on. The judo world was made up of a very small fraternity back then so it was only a day before he found out who I was by asking his sensei. I wonder what he must have looked like when found out that he was trying to school the state champion? The next day, everybody had to go on a grueling six-mile hike with full packs on and he said that I didn't have to go because he wanted to work out with me and we couldn't work after that hike. I was the only guy that didn't have to go but I had to show him some of these moves that I knew. He made me a lot of good deals and we trained together at Ray Law's school in Oakland, which was where Larry Coughran got his start in judo.

It was because of incidents like this that I was never too braggadocios. I didn't go into that class with a big sign on my head that I had been in 1,000 matches or that I trained with Lou Thesz or won any championships or anything so he had no idea how good I was. That Coast Guard instructor didn't know me from Adam and I caught him totally by surprise. You think or might even know that you're good, but it's always a smart move to keep it to yourself. Nobody likes to hear a conceited bastard, but it's okay if you're a sadistic bastard.

Because the Coast Guard kept insisting on calling me up, I decided to sign up for active duty when I graduated from Pierce with my two-year degree. I just wanted to get the whole thing over with so I served my two years. The way that things were going, the Coast Guard would probably still be calling me up to this day if I hadn't.

My first duty station was in San Pedro, California, which is located in the Los Angeles harbor area. There was a big televised wrestling show at the Olympic Auditorium one night and my mother left a message for me to call her that said: "Gorgeous George's second, who sprays the perfume around the ring to purify the air before George starts to wrestle is sick. Can you do that bit? Try to get here."

I was really excited to do the show so I asked for permission to leave and Commander Pollack, who was the top brass at the base, said, "No you can't have a pass. You have to stay on base."

"There's nobody here," I said almost pleadingly. "It's a small base. There's only like 30 people here and it's no big deal."

"That's tough. You've got to make sacrifices in the service," he replied in a sarcastic way that I didn't particularly care for. Now this commander had the habit of hopping into his car on base and speeding through the guard's gate and cutting the corner really fast like he was in a race. He was the officer in charge so there was nothing that any enlisted personnel like myself was going to do about it. We all called him Barney Olefield who was an old time auto racer. I waited for him to leave and once I heard his tires squeal around the corner I knew that it was all clear. As the sun started to go down, I went over the fence, walked a half-mile to my car, and went from San Pedro to the Olympic Auditorium almost as fast as my commanding officer would have. I had more fun spraying that ring with perfume as Gorgeous George antagonized that crowd than a barrel full of monkeys. Right after the match was over, I went back to the base and went over the fence before the sun came up. A couple of guys on guard knew that I had gone over the hill, but we were buddies and I had looked the other way for them on more than a few occasions.

The next morning at the start of the day, everybody lined up to receive the duties of the day. At that time I was taking down names of all of the ships that came in and out of the harbor, where they were

coming from, what countries they were from and where they were
going to. We lined up that morning and Commander Pollack was giving orders and then he stopped and said, "By the way we have a captain's mask."

A captain's mask was when somebody screwed up bad enough for
it to be a court-martial offense. If you were convicted of such a thing,
you went to jail for sure. I looked out into the yard and only a short distance away I could see the penitentiary at Terminal Island and I wondered who had messed up this time. I thought that it was probably
another drunken sailor caught without a pass or something along those
lines.

"Well I never watch television," the commander said looking back
and fourth over the row of men standing at attention, "especially professional wrestling on television." My eyes opened up and I began to
perspire. Some people would call it sweating like a dog and if that's
what it was, I was doing it. "I never watch wrestling but I was flipping
through the channels and Mr. LeBell, I saw you there last night on television, but I couldn't have – you didn't have a pass so you had to be
here."

He moved in closer to me and I knew that he had me dead to
rights. "You came to me and asked to be relieved of your duties so you
could go off for that evening and I specifically remember denying that
request." He stared at me and I wanted to jump out of my skin.

I don't know where I came up with this, but I quickly said, "Sir,
Commander Pollack, Sir, that was a kinescope taped three months ago
Sir." Kinescopes were how they used to store old TV shows back in the
1950s for posterity's sake and, of course, reruns.

He looked at me and said, "I knew that," and then he just kept on
going down the line like nothing had happened.

I could just feel the perspiration running down my face and back
and I turned to one of my buddies who knew that went AWOL. He
grinned at me and whispered, "Well you got away with this one."

Now I never went AWOL in high school like all of the other kids
did. I never took these phony holidays. I never did anything that was
out of order. In the service sometimes I did things. I remember when a

bunch of guys went AWOL, and they were caught on the Long Beach Pike where all of the funhouses, bars, and whorehouses where. At the same time, I snuck out to the dojos to work out. When I came back the other guys were caught drunk with no pass and they got thrown in the pokey. I never saw them after that but I heard that they got a couple of years for going AWOL. That's what I was told and I had been sneaking off of the base without a pass just to work out. That was the last time that I did anything wrong. I told my commanders that I could represent the Coast Guard in the 1954 Judo Nationals if I had more time to train and they actually bought it.

I was soon transferred to the downtown LA Recruiting Office and I got liberty every night and every weekend so I could train for more competitions and bring more medals to the Coast Guard. That's all I did was work out. That was my life. Everything was going great, but the guy that was the head of the office didn't like jocks like me because we got special duty. I remember once, I came back from winning a big tournament and I had a bunch of newspaper clippings announcing the results with my picture in them and everything. I spread the papers out on my desk and showed them to the head of the recruiting office and said, "Look at these papers! Isn't that terrific?"

He took one look my papers and handed me a different kind of papers and said, "Here's your papers. You're going on the Minnetonka for weather patrol." The Minnetonka was a 255-foot cutter and weather patrol would have put me out to the middle of the Pacific for a month where it was rough and you got seasick and I wouldn't have been able to work out or anything.

I didn't want to go but I had to. I loved my country and orders were orders. I got in my car and headed down to Pier Baker in Long Beach. I don't know if that pier is there anymore. There was a hill above the docks where you could park your car. I saw the Minnetonka. Smoke was coming from her chimney and I could see the sailors going back forth and doing their little shtick. I had about an hour to get down to the ship. It was about a five-minute walk from the hill down to the pier and I had all of my gear ready to go. In other words, I had 55 minutes and it would only take me three or four minutes to get to the ship. I was watching the vessel and I knew that I didn't want to go because I couldn't work out for at least thirty days or longer. My God, I would get all flabby. I was in the best shape of my life and I would have lost it all that month out at sea. As I watched them pull up the anchor, pretty soon the whistle blew and the ship's crew started pulling up the gangplanks and throwing in the lanyards and the ropes. I kept on telling myself that I didn't want to go. But I must go. It was for my country and it was the right thing to do. Slowly the ship turned around and headed out towards the mouth of the harbor.

Before it got out of site and just past the breakwater, I hopped in my car and I sped down to the Captain of the Port. I was in a panic by the time that I got to him.

"My boat left without me Sir," I said practically tugging on his uniform as if I really wanted to get aboard that ship. "Get me on a plane and fly me out there! I'm supposed to be there with my shipmates! Here's my papers!"

The officer was trying to calm me down and I said, "I missed the boat! I tried my best but they left without me! I'm supposed to be on the Minnetonka!"

"Calm down, calm down, it will be all right," said the Captain of the Port.

"I can't." I said, "My buddies are leaving without me."

The Captain apologized to me and said that they didn't have a plane or helicopter or anything like that. He kept on assuring me that everything was going to be alright and he even complimented me on my devotion to my duties and my shipmates. He then stationed me back at the local recruiting office in Los Angeles, which was only about 10 minutes away from the Hollywood Dojo. I could work every night and had liberty on the weekends. I really was crushed that I wasn't going to be on weather patrol for a month in the middle of the ocean.

When the Minnetonka finally returned a month later, I went down to the shipyards to greet my buddies and they called me every name in the book. "I missed the boat," I said, "Can I help it?" I told them that if they wanted to reenlist that I was at the LA recruiting office and I would be happy to help them. If looks could kill, I wouldn't be telling you this story today. Oh man, they were unhappy – very unhappy.

I still represented the Coast Guard during the spring of 1954 and the AAU sanctioned the second ever Judo Nationals at Kezar Pavilion in San Francisco. The nationals were my chance to compete against the best in the country and maybe the world. Just about everybody who entered this contest would be good or even great.

Larry Coughran was my coach and he told me to go into the heavyweights even though I weighed maybe 170 pounds with a sopping wet gi on. Still, I regularly worked with very skilled pro wrestlers who weighed in at over 250 pounds, so I thought that I could step up in weight. Coughran's reason for moving me up in weight class was that there were only three great heavyweights and about six or more great judo players coming into the contest at 180 pounds and under. This all sounded really good to me but one of the men who was entering the nationals as a heavyweight was maybe the best in the world and his name was Johnny Osako.

Johnny Osako hailed from Chicago and everybody wanted to see him. He didn't enter the first nationals in 1953, but he was already the Pan-American Champion and was a legend in the world of judo. All everybody at Kezar in San Francisco talked about was Johnny Osako this and Johnny Osako that. He had lined up 30 black belts and had beaten them all one after the other. He was a big man who was fast. He was a masterful technician.

The first time that I saw him, he was handsome enough to be a movie star. He was a very distinguished Japanese man in a double-breasted suit and when you looked at his face you could tell that he owned the world. You knew that he had confidence in whatever he did and he was like a god. That first time that I saw him, he was leaning up against the brick wall of a drugstore and he was surrounded by surrounded by a crowd of hero worshippers and he was puffing on a cigar.

"He can't be that good because he's smoking," I said to a judo teacher standing next to me.

The guy laughed at me and said, "What happens to you when you smoke?"

"You get tired," I said, "your wind isn't that good. You get out of breath."

The teacher laughed at me again and said, "His matches don't only go about ten seconds." Everybody within earshot of that conversation joined in and laughed at me like I was stupid.

Kezar is nestled against Golden Gate Park and it is encompassed by big, Pacific Northwest redwoods and oak trees. The Haight-Ashbury district, which was famous during the 1960s for all of the hippies and free love, runs right into it. There is an outdoor stadium there where the 49er football team used to play right next to the indoor pavilion, where the nationals were held in 1954. Kezar Pavilion was an old, wood and brick municipal building with bleacher seating and a waxed hardwood floor. They regularly held basketball games there and other events.

There were four weight divisions in the nationals that year. There was 130 pounds and under, between 130 and 150 pounds, between 150 and 180 pounds and 180 pounds and over made up the heavyweight class. There were 29 competitors entering the heavyweight division. All of the heavyweights lined up and Osako strolled up to the front of the line. I stayed near the back of the line. Hell I was in the back of the line. Next to me, was a brown belt that I thought that I could take easily to give me an easy opening match when the time came.

In Osako's first match, he went against a big Caucasian guy who was very good. Johnny bowed and the match began and he immediately spun into a throw. It was so fast that it was like a blur. I couldn't tell if he did a right or left-sided throw. I wasn't sure what kind of throw it even was -- if it was an uchi mata between the legs or a bent knee throw or an o goshi hip throw. Osako's opponent went straight up into the air and he was vertical. The throw was so fast it was like this 220-pound guy was on an air ram or a nitrogen ratchet. Osako's opponent went very high in the air and came down like almost as if he had jumped and he landed fast and hard. The match was over before it had even started, and after the officials had given Osako his assured win he bowed like it was something that he does for fun in his spare time like chewing gum.

"Oh my God," I said to myself, "What did he do?"

You could hear everyone in Kezar Pavilion whispering among

themselves saying "Did you see that? Did you see that?" I looked over at the brown belt next to me and I could tell that he was scared to death. I was sure that when the line got to me, that I was the odd man and I would get to go against that brown belt. In the 1954 Nationals, you had to lose twice before you were eliminated and with guys like Osako in that contest, I needed every easy win that I could get. I knew that I would beat that brown belt easily.

The way the tournament was run was on a five point system. You lose once in the middle of the mat and it was three points against you. If you lost a decision, that was two points against you. If you won a decision (as opposed to a victory on a throw or a pin) and it was one point against you. If you won the match straight out, you had no points against you and the guy that lost the match had 3 points against him. The whole object was not to get eliminated on points. The guy next to me had three points against him already. I believed that he was my next match or maybe I would even get a bi being number 29 -- the odd numbered man in the heavyweight division.

The voice of the announcer blasted through the loudspeaker. "The next competitor is Johnny Osako from Chicago," it said. You could hear a pin drop at first, but as he strolled up to the mat, people started to cheer his name. He gave the crowd a short nod like he had heard it many times before. Then, as if it was in the distance, I heard the voice from the loudspeaker echo, "LeBell, Los Angeles." I wanted to see this Osako go at it again and I was waiting for this LeBell guy to get up there.

Guys started bumping me and going, "Go, go, go, you're on."

"Who me?" I said and then I went to stand up and I just couldn't stand. My legs wouldn't move at all. I froze. Osako walked out there and people were cheering and I tried to get up and my legs still wouldn't work. Finally I got to my feet and my legs were numb and I was out of breath. I was basically scared to death and I think that was the only time ever in my life that I was scared of an opponent. When I was ten years old, Frankenstein and the Wolf Man in the movies scared the hell out of me, but Johnny Osako froze me dead in my tracks just by being as good as he was.

Larry Coughran was the only guy there who was cheering for me. "Easy pickings," he said as I finally got up and slowly made my way to the mats where Osako was standing almost as if he was at attention. Larry was the bravest coach in the world and it was like he was sending his lamb to the slaughter.

It must have taken me three minutes to walk the length of that basketball court. We bowed and the match commenced. The matches are five minutes in judo tournaments today but they were ten minutes back then with an overtime period if needed.

The first thing that Osako did was he spun in for this throw. I went way up in the air like his first opponent, but I flipped around and landed back on my feet. I don't know how I did that but I did and it saved me from losing the match early. After that, I was broken in and the numbness in my legs had disappeared. I could actually continue with the match and compete with Johnny Osako.

The match was fought mostly in a standup style and he was excellent standing up. I couldn't get any of my good throws in for what seemed like an eternity. He just blocked me almost effortlessly. Finally, as time was running out, I caught him with a throw and he just went up and came down flat but the officials didn't call anything. I got into a pin but I didn't think. I went in too deep and he just rolled me right over and casually got to his feet. They didn't go into overtime automatically in that tournament, so we had to wait for a decision from the officials to see if an overtime period was even going to happen.

I didn't know how that decision was going to go and it seemed to take forever for it to be delivered. I knew that I had a throw so I thought that it was possible for me to win that decision and only fight a ten-minute match with Osako. I looked across the way and the Japanese judge put up a red flag, which meant that he voted for Osako. The judge on the other side voted for me and the referee declared a five-minute overtime period.

I felt that I was lucky to go into overtime with Osako you know. Nobody else had even lasted two minutes with the man. We went around with some tickles and tackles, and ups and downs. I tripped him and followed him to the mat and attacked him with an osae komi,

which is a hold down scarf hold. A side pin where you held you opponent down for 30 seconds won you the match. After about 15 seconds
he tapped out and gave up. I thought that maybe he had just run out of
gas but when I analyzed it many years later after watching a tape of the
match, I realized that I had a neck lock on him. It was an illegal move,
but this is the only time that I ever mentioned that to anybody. Osako
never knew why it hurt so much. He just told people that I was very
strong. I cranked the head forward and left his shoulders pinned to the
mat. Cranking his neck slowed down his breathing and cut part of the
blood supply off to his head. It hurt him so he gave up. That was his
only loss.

It's interesting to think about because the wrestling and the finishing holds that I had learned from the pros at the LA Athletic Club
helped me with the pin. I believe that if you're going to go into a competition like judo, or wrestling or these get-tough contests, you should
put a little pain on your opponent and why not? That isn't just my the-
ory - that's the way that a lot of the old time wrestlers like Lou Thesz,
Karl Gotch, and Vic Christy did things. The idea was that when you
pinned your opponent, you should always crank his neck or his back or
his arm or his shoulder. Not necessarily enough to really make them
give up in many cases but just enough to make them squeak so they
think that you are just really strong. In reality, it's not so much that
you're strong, it's that you're pinching a nerve somewhere along the
line that transmits pain. That's how I beat Osako that day. It was maybe
a little bit of that old dark side of the moon. 100 years from now, my
name will still be in the record books as champ – not how I won but
that I did win.

All of the other matches that Osako had were quick and good and
I still believe he was better than me that year. In matches that we had
with the same people, he beat them very quickly without breaking a
sweat, while I struggled to beat them. I still won, but Osako did it so
much more easily than I did.

I won my weight division, but the judo nationals were far from
over for me. Back then, the champions from the four different weight
divisions competed in a round robin contest to determine the overall

champion. They did this for a little over the first ten years of the nationals and I always liked it because the contest for the overall champion determined who was the best in the United States. Later on it was the sanctioning body's perception that too many of the heavyweights were winning, which was true in most cases but not all of them. In the 1960s, Hayward Nishioka, a student of mine and others, won the 160 pound class and went on to win the overall competition. A good big man does have an advantage over a good small man, which is the case nine times out of ten, but the lightweight would always be a lot faster. It was, after all, Jigoro Kano's original concept of kodokan judo that skill was everything and your height and weight weren't as much of a factor. In more traditional judo tournaments, we competed by belt ranking and not by weight divisions. For me to truly be the national judo champion in 1954, I had to win the overall competition, and winning the overall contest would at least give me a claim to being the best in the United States.

In my first match of the overall competition, I had to go against the 180-pound champion. Remember that Larry Coughran convinced me to enter the nationals as a heavyweight because he thought that the 180 and under division was too tough, and here I had to face the best man in the toughest weight class to move onto the final round of the tournament. The 180-pound champion was Vince Tamura and he sliced through his division like a hot knife through butter and threw everyone very fast. Tamura was an amazing judo man and I figured that he would give me as much or maybe even more trouble than Johnny Osako did. I was in for the fight of my life, but Tamura went into our match almost too casually. He attempted a right uchi mata which was an inside thigh sweep. As he came in, I stopped his throw and he came out a little too casually. I was able to counter his move with an utsuri goshi, which is a switching hip throw. I lifted him up a little bit and got him off of the mat, and then once he was off balance, I stepped in front of him threw him to the mat. My match against Tamura wasn't that long, but it should have been. I scored a clean throw and won. Although I beat Johnny Osako and Vince Tamura that year, in my mind I was still only the third best man in that tournament. If I went against the same men ten times, they probably would have beat me eight out of the ten.

Another great judo man named Kenji Yamada won the other semi-final round of the overall competition. He was the 150-pound champion and he beat the 130-pound winner. There were a lot of Japanese there, and they were all cheering for Yamada while almost no one (except for Larry) was cheering for me. He was very tough but I won that match too and became the overall judo champion. On paper and in the record books anyway, I was the best judoka in the United States.

That was April 17, 1954 and I had become the AAU National Overall Judo Champion. A couple of years later, I found a small piece of paper with the words "April 1954" handwritten on it. It was the date that California Governor Goodwin Knight had predicted that my life would be changed forever. April 17, 1954 was the first time that I won the judo nationals and then it pyramided into many incredible careers. I became a professional wrestler because of judo. I became a stuntman because of professional wrestling, and from there it lead to many acting roles so it did change my life. I then was a sports commentator for wrestling for 15 years in Los Angeles and everything sprang from what I accomplished back in April of 1954 so that was undoubtedly the date that my life had changed forever. The governor was right, you know.

To add a little bit more to the thoughts of synchronicity, one of my best black belt students and closest friends was born on April 17, 1954. He later became a great professional wrestler and a fantastic movie star. You might have heard of him: his name is Roddy Piper.

However back in 1954, a lot of people said that my win was pure luck. I got a bad reputation in certain judo circles that year even though I was the only person in the nationals to go to overtime with Osako let alone beat him. No matter what anybody said, I was the champion on April 17, 1954 and nobody could take that away from me. Still I knew that I had to enter the nationals in 1955, and probably go up against Osako again to prove that Gene LeBell wasn't a fluke. I have always believed that you have to aim for the future because a guy that doesn't think of the future doesn't have one.

CHAPTER 5

TURNING PRO

While I was training for the state and national judo tournaments in 1954, I was also learning every finishing hold that I could from some of the greatest professional wrestlers ever to lace up their boots. I wanted to train with bigger and tougher guys than I would be matched up against in the amateurs so my mother suggested that I go down to the Hollywood Legion Stadium where some of the pros worked out in the daytime. When I first showed up there, this very good wrestler named Vic Christy was showing amateur wrestlers and ex football players the ropes of professional wrestling. Vic helped a matchmaker named Lou Nichols size up the new talent and determine who had what it took to make in the pros. Christy had a shorter brother named Ted and they both claimed to be full blooded American Indians but they never came into the ring with headdresses on or anything like that. Both of them were talented wrestlers and they were great at hooking and sub-mission holds and they were main eventers wherever they wrestled.

The great submission master and world champion Lou Thesz was also a regular at the Hollywood Legion when he was wrestling on the Los Angeles circuit. I learned a lot of submissions and takedowns from Thesz and Christy. These guys were all from the old-time shooter and hooker tradition and each and every one of them could really wrestle, and by wrestling I mean grappling. A few years later at the Olympic, Karl Istaz Gotch also showed me some very effective holds. A lot of the moves that I learned from the pros at the Hollywood Legion were pretty much the same as the moves in judo but I was learning varia-tions. There's a lot different ways to do a hip lock for example, and the pros showed me a lot of ways of applying moves that my judo oppo-nents weren't ready for.

The professional wrestlers helped me with the judo because what is called an uchi mata in judo is called a whizzer in wrestling. An osoto gari is a schoolboy trip. A kata gurama is a fireman's carry. A kanset-suwaza is an arm bar. All of these Japanese techniques that were said to be invented by Jigoro Kano in 1882 were used centuries before that in pro wrestling only with different names and no gis (workout clothes). When I tell this to the judo guys, they get very mad. They say, " Gomenesai sensei, Jigoro Kano in 1882 took the best features of jiu-jitsu and made it into a sport, and called kodokan judo." After that, I get accused of shaming judo with all of my talk of professional wrestlers, although today in Japan, professional wrestlers freely compete against judo and jiu-jitsu champions in get-tough contests like Pride as if to prove my point.

But the moves that Kano instilled into sport judo were utilized in the carnival challenge matches and wrestling meets in America and Europe long before 1882. Shooters like Thesz were keeping an ages-old tradition alive and I was learning everything that I could from them as well as studying with the Japanese. A lot of the maneuvers that the wrestlers taught me were perfectly legal in judo competition and a lot of them weren't, but it is easier to beat an opponent with what they don't know. By training with so many different teachers in so many different schools, I had a slight edge in whatever competition that I went into, whether it was wrestling with the pros, amateur judo, or working out with amateur wrestlers.

One of the arts that is very good today is Brazilian Jiu-Jitsu. They have a name for a lot of these same holds and at this time their art has been around for about 75 years. They call one of these holds the trian-gle and it is a leg scissors chokehold that you can convert into an arm bar using your legs in the figure four position. To some of them, the move comes from Brazil, but I have a picture that hangs on the wall of the Cauliflower Alley Club in Las Vegas (of which I am a member) of Ed "Strangler" Lewis putting that move on somebody in 1916, which is long before Brazilian Jiu-Jitsu was in effect. Now the Gracies and the Machados and the other Brazilians are all excellent wrestlers and they have done a lot for the cause of grappling over the last 10 or 15 years. I even refer people to the Machado brothers all of the time because Rigan, Carlos, John and Jean Jacques are some of the best grappling instructors out there. When Royce Gracie, who is very good, beat a incredibly tough and skilled wrestler named Dan Severn with the triangle choke in the Ultimate Fighting Championships in the mid-1990s that was the first time that a lot of people had seen that hold or anything like it. Severn was beaten because he wasn't familiar with a lot of finishing holds, but he has since added those moves to his repertoire. But the fact of the matter is that the Brazilians didn't invent the move. Give credit where credit is due. I give credit to all of my teachers, and I've had a hundred teachers in all of the different martial arts. Now we can call these moves by their Japanese judo names or their Brazilian jiu-jitsu names, but to me, they are all just professional wrestling finishing holds.

Still, some of the moves that I learned from the pros were not allowed in the judo dojos. Pro wrestlers used to finish a lot of guys off with heel hooks and other leg locks, but these moves were forbidden in the dojos and the senseis were very adamant about it. They would tell me that leg locks weren't part of kodokan judo. When I would openly use these moves, Sensei Frank Kukuchi used to laugh at me with his hand in front of his mouth and he often said, "Jigoro Kano would turn over in his grave if he saw that hakujin Gene was doing all of these illegal things on the mat in a kodokan dojo."

The guy that I've learned almost 80 per cent of my finishing holds from was Lou Thesz. Lou Thesz was the best ever. There was nobody who could beat him and he could do anything. He could insult you and what were you going to do about it? Get in the ring with him? I don't think so unless you really liked to feel pain. I myself have a very good physician today named Dr. Jack Ditlove and believe me; you would need to pay him a visit if you ever got the idea of tangling with Lou Thesz.

When Thesz entered the ring, nobody would say anything to him because he would hurt you and he would hurt you big time. I'll tell you how good he was: you could take the best five jiu-jitsu/judo fighters or get tough guys in the world today and he would have lined them up and wrestled them one after the other and he would have beaten them all. Lou would have just played with them. Now that's not a knock against the grapplers of today -- that's just telling you how awesome Lou Thesz really was.

Lou Thesz is the greatest wrestler that I have ever seen or known because he had charisma as a professional wrestler and he also could hook, which means that he could beat most anybody. He had an arsenal of moves like no other and he possessed amazing reflexes. You could attempt to put a hold on him and he could turn around or reverse you in less time than it took for the blink of an eye. He wrote a book called "Hooker" that was really good but he knocked a few people in it. He knocked people but he was so tough that if he said something you had to believe it and that was that.

Lou never changed expressions so you wouldn't know if he was happy or mad, and he didn't like guys that he thought were clowns. Mr. Moto was a Japanese wrestler that had the misfortune of getting on Lou's bad side in the ring. Moto was a good sumo guy and a pretty fair wrestler but he used to put a little showmanship into his ring entrance and he threw salts to the four winds to purify the air. That didn't ring too well with Lou so Lou would just put the poor guy in a series of excruciating finishing holds just to have fun with him. "I hate to wrestle this guy," Charlie Moto often complained, "He hurts me every time I do, but I make so much money because it's a sellout every time we wrestle." I recall Moto saying that it took him over two weeks just to recover from the bumps and bruises that he incurred during one match with Thesz.

Lou didn't like people that strutted around the ring. To him, you looked straight at your opponent when you entered the squared circle. You didn't count the house while you were wrestling. He was a very serious man and he liked wrestlers that were just as serious as he was about his sport such as Verne Gagne, Karl Gotch, Christy and too many others to mention. Those guys could really hook and had great amateur backgrounds and Lou respected them for it. Wrestling was his life yet the guys on top now are making 10 or 20 times as much as he made and he made more than anybody during his time.

I'll tell you a little story about Lou and this is jumping forward but a bit but we're on the subject. I was in Omaha, Nebraska and all of these guys from the university were working out. Thesz was back there wrestling professionally. He called me up and said, "You've got to come in and roll with these guys." I went there and they had the city champion, state champion and their heavyweight was a national champion. So I got on the mat with the heavyweight. I was a lot lighter in those years and I weighed about 185 pounds. We went about 8 or 9 minutes before I could beat him. This guy was unbelievably strong and the only way that I was able to take him was with a leg lock that was illegal in amateur wrestling. If I had to fight him under his rules, he would have had me for lunch for sure. Then Lou went and worked with the city champion and state champion, and he just played with them like you would a baby.

When he got to the heavyweight and I warned him. "This guy is good," I said, "especially good at takedowns."

The national heavyweight champion went for a double leg takedown on Thesz. As Lou went down he put a foot over the back of his head like you do in a triangle. After that, I thought that Lou was going to break the guy's arm and the match lasted less than a minute. That's how long it took Lou to beat the guy and that guy was world class - a national champion.

One of the other pros that also came down to work out that day said, "He's lucky Lou wasn't mad."

Now when I was taking time in the mornings to wrestle with the pros at the Hollywood Legion Stadium, my stepfather Cal Eaton ran the wrestling booking office in Los Angeles and Southern California. I always went by my last name of LeBell, so none of the wrestlers there ever suspected that I was related to their boss. I never told them. I just went there and wrestled and when you wrestle a guy who's 230, 250, or 300 pounds, it can be a pretty good workout you know – especially since I only came in at about 170. Eventually, Vic Christy and some of the other wrestlers asked me why I kept coming back to work out of with them.

"I want to learn as much as I can and maybe someday I could become a pro," was my answer and that was exactly what those guys wanted to hear. There was one major problem however: my step dad Cal Eaton never seemed to like me. He was always putting me down although later in life I realized that most of it was just a tease.

"If I ever hear of you talking to any of the wrestlers, I'll kick you in the butt," was his answer when I asked him about breaking into professional wrestling. He was only about 5'6", so I wasn't really deterred by this threat, but it did make things difficult. Cal thought that everybody should be a white-collar man who wore suits and was good at pushing pencils and I must have been a kind of disappointment to him because I was just a jock. Even after I had won state and national championships, he never understood me or saw any worth in what I was striving to accomplish.

To discourage my professional wrestling ambitions, Cal Eaton went so far as to arrange a fight between me and one of his wrestlers named Louie Miller. Miller was a former circus strongman with big cauliflower ears and he sometimes wrestled with a mask on. He possessed tremendous strength and he could drive a nail straight through a solid board bare handed. Cal bet me one hundred dollars that Miller could beat me five times in five minutes and he arranged the bout for the following Wednesday at the Olympic Auditorium. Now I wasn't really swimming in cash back then so it would have really been nasty for me if I had lost, but what Cal didn't know was that Louie Miller was one of my coaches. When I first started wrestling Miller, he could easily beat me, but after a few years, a few more pounds, a couple of extra inches, and a lot of judo and wrestling training, I could hold my own with him pretty well. I used to get a kick out of beating Miller with the same holds that he had taught me.

Wednesday rolled around and I ran into Cal at the Olympic and asked, "When is this guy coming down? Is he afraid of me?"

Eaton got really hot and he said, "I'll talk to you tomorrow," and then he stormed out of his office.

So when I saw him the next morning, I asked, "Where's this superman who's going to beat me five times in five minutes?"

"Shut up and get out of the house!" Cal yelled.

"You talked to Mr. Miller," I said with a devilish grin knowing then that Eaton had discussed me with Miller. "Wow! Good!"

Like most of the wrestlers, Louie Miller didn't know that I was related to my step dad and I found out later that he said all sorts of nice things about me when Cal mentioned my name. "Hell, he'd beat any of these guys around here," he informed my stepfather much to Cal's chagrin. Louie later became a promoter in Northern California.

But the pressure to go pro was still on from Vic Christy, his brother Ted and some of the other wrestlers. "If you want to get into wrestling," Vic told me on a few occasions not knowing the situation, "you have to talk to Cal Eaton." I couldn't talk to Cal about becoming a wrestler because I knew what the answer would be and I also wasn't the kind of guy back then that could just come out and tell Vic Christy what was really going on. I was only 21 then, and I was really trying to be the strong silent type for lack of a better way of putting it.

Then one afternoon I was going through my regular routine of training with the wrestlers at the Hollywood Legion and in walked Cal Eaton and this 400 ex-wrestler and booker named Jules Strongbow that put together the matches at the Olympic Auditorium. They both went down to the Hollywood Legion every so often to see if there was anyone with potential to hire, so it was really only a matter of time before my stepfather caught me there. Eaton and Strongbow stayed way in the back so I didn't notice them while I was in the ring working out. From the rear of the auditorium they saw me take down guys and beat them. Vic Christy, who was at the ring apron watching me and my opponent spar, spotted Eaton and Strongbow after they had already been in there for a while. "Now you want to be a wrestler," he said to me, "here are the guys you have to meet."

I looked up and I saw Cal Eaton and Jules Strongbow. I quickly leapt out of the ring, headed for the dressing room, and got the heck out of there. I knew that Cal was going to chew me up one leg and down the other for training with the wrestlers. He didn't want me working out with the pro wrestlers or with the boxers at the Main Street Gym but that was my life. I was like a gambling addict and that's what I wanted to be.

During the time that they saw me wrestle in the ring, however, they saw that I could hook a lot of guys and they liked guys who could really wrestle. Also Vic Christy put in the good word for me and told my stepfather and Strongbow that I had the most potential to go pro out of any of the new guys that he was training at that time. By sticking up for me with my step dad like that, Vic became one of the guys who changed my life forever that day. He really did.

The chill that Cal Eaton had towards my professional wrestling career began to thaw that the day. "You want to be a wrestler," he said the next time that he saw me, "okay, we'll start you off." It must have been really difficult for a hard man like Cal Eaton to reverse himself like that.

"Okay," I answered trying to contain myself, and then I paused for a moment. I couldn't make the jump to pro right then because I had to go into the 1955 AAU judo nationals and to do this I couldn't jeopardize my amateur standing.

"I have to do the nationals in April and if win that I get to represent the United States in Japan," I told him. Going to Japan and wrestling at the Kodokan was the chance of a lifetime, but I also had to prove that all of the nonbelievers who said that my win in 1954 was a fluke were wrong. Competing in 1955 was very important to me for a whole host of reasons.

He told me that it would be no problem but then he asked me where the nationals were being held that year.

Now Cal seldom went to work and my mother handled most of the business at the Olympic Auditorium. One of the events that she had then recently booked at the Olympic was the 1955 Judo Nationals. I told Cal that I would be competing in the judo nationals at the Olympic, which was his wrestling stronghold and he went through the roof.

"LA!" he screamed blowing his stack. "Not only that but at my Olympic Auditorium no less! I'll have to talk to your mother about that."

"If they see the results in the papers," Cal continued, "and you come in second you know it's no good! We can build you up as a judo champion but not if you're #2. If you want to wrestle, you can't go into this tournament."

"You don't understand," I explained, "This is my life. I have to win this thing! I beat a couple of guys in 1954 and a lot of people said that it was luck. I need to be able to prove that it wasn't luck by winning two years in a row plus I'm a lot better this year."

Cal shook his head at me and relented. "Unless you win," he scowled, "you will never be a pro wrestler!"

At that moment, both my past reputation and my future career were both hanging on the outcome of the 1955 Judo Nationals. If I lost, not only would I have somehow proved all of my doubters right from the year before, but I would also never make it as a pro wrestler. This tournament was going to be in my backyard, and the newspapers would report on whatever I did. Cal was right about one thing: I couldn't make a splash in pro wrestling if I had lost. To go into the pros as a reigning national champion would mean something, but to come in as an also ran would mean less than nothing. If I came in second place or didn't place at all, I don't think that I could have entered pro wrestling as even an under-card curtain raiser. One pin or one throw that went against me would have the power to erase everything that I had worked for my entire life up to that point.

The competition was a lot stronger in 1955 than it was the previous year. Osako was back, but he went into the 180 pounds and under division while I entered the heavyweights once again. This meant that we wouldn't be facing each other unless we both made it into the overall competition, which meant taking our respective weight classes. There was also a very good African American judo player named George Harris who represented the Air Force. He was definitely one of the guys to beat at the Olympic Auditorium that weekend, but the reputation of the Amateur Athletic Union Nationals were spreading and there were even formidable judo men that trained in Japan and all over the world coming to Los Angeles that Spring to participate.

To make matters worse, right before the weekend of the nationals, I came down with the worst case of adult tonsillitis that I think that anyone has ever had. On the first day of the tournament, I was running a fever of 104 degrees Fahrenheit. Today, you can win four or five matches and become a champion, but back then it felt like I had to spend the whole weekend fighting probably because I did. I fought over ten different matches on the first day and I somehow got through it all, but the nationals had really just begun for me at that point.

On the second day, all of the competitors who weren't eliminated had to go in for another weigh-in and that even included the heavy-weights. Due to the fever, the cold sweats, zero appetite and fighting for my life, I had gone down from the 180-pound cutoff weight to 168 pounds. I was still allowed to finish out my competition despite dropping 12 pounds in 24 hours. God, I wish that I could do that today.

When I came to weigh in for the finals everyone who wasn't a judge or a janitor was banged up, bruised, and limping. Most of the guys who were left had a lot of mat burns on their legs, arms and faces. Everybody was soar and I was too. While I waited to step on the scale, one of the guys turned to me and said, "Jesus, I don't know if I can compete. I'm hurting so much." He shook his head and almost looked like he had lost already.

"I feel great!" I said. "I think I'll run ten miles before my first match just to loosen up." I was really just teasing but I didn't have to let him know that.

After I was weighed, I got up to leave and I heard that man say, "Boy that Gene LeBell is really good. He didn't get bruised up or tired from yesterday's matches. He's a winner."

As I heard him say this, I straightened up and made sure that I wasn't limping in the slightest. For that moment, I put everything that I had into not looking as soar and exhausted as I was just trying to live up to that hype.

Cal Eaton stopped by the Olympic. "The guys you went up against yesterday couldn't tie their shoes and they all jumped for you," he said shaking his head. Now there wasn't enough money in the world to make any of those judokas take a dive. Everybody in the nationals, especially those who made it to the second day, were world class and they weren't going to take a fall for anybody. Pride was on the line there and when you compete as an amateur, pride was everything.

At that moment, I almost hated Cal Eaton because he was always putting me down, but that remark gave me more determination than ever to win that day. I had to take it all and prove Cal Eaton wrong, but my strength was starting to wane. I had three or four matches left to go and my tonsillitis had killed my appetite so I wasn't eating. I was running on fumes and I really was forcing myself to continue. For some reason, one of the coaches from the Strategic Air Command team handed me an orange and somehow eating that piece of fruit revived me. I don't know if it was the citrus, the vitamin C or the sugar rush, but after eating that orange, I felt like a new man and I had renewed energy.

I won the heavyweight division, which put me into the overall competition. In my first match for the overall title, I threw Kenji Yamada who was the 150-pound champ. I had fought him in the final match of the nationals the year before and he was a two-time 150 lb. champion and an amazing judo man. Then came the match to crown the overall judo champion for 1955. It was the biggest match of my amateur career and it was against Johnny Osako.

Even with my tonsillitis, my technique had improved greatly from the year before, but I still wasn't the technical master that Osako was. All-Japan Champion Ishikawa refereed the match and it was a tough one from the opening bow. Osako was a much better judo man than me technique-wise, but I had only gotten better since our first meeting and he wasn't nearly as determined as I was. I believe that heart plays a really big part in any athletic event and looking back at it, I think that it made all of the difference on that April afternoon. When I finally did throw Osako, Ishikawa called "ippon" or "point" while Osako was still in the air so I won the match before my opponent had even hit the mat.

After I was declared the winner, I walked up the Ishikawa and said, "Gomenesai, Sensei, excuse me, he was in the air when you gave me the point."

"I know judo," he said and who was going to argue with him? He was the two-time All-Japan Champion which pretty much made him the world champion. He was the best in the world in judo at that moment and it was an honor for him to referee that match.

To win both the overall and heavyweight divisions in the 1955 nationals, I had beaten two of the best judo men that I had ever seen in George Harris and Johnny Osako. They were probably better than me but somehow I had beaten them both. To let you know how good they were, Osako won the nationals in 1956 and retired. Following that, Harris won it two out of the next three years. Harris is a ninth degree black belt today. Both of these judo greats went to Japan with me as part of the US judo team later that year.

1955 was my last hurrah in the AAU Judo Nationals and I retired from amateur judo competition at the ripe old age of 22. Everybody loses and there is always somebody who can beat you, so I wanted to quit while I was on top to be like Rocky Marciano. I couldn't risk damaging my marketability as a pro by taking any more chances on amateur competition. I had won the Judo Nationals twice in a row and there was really nothing more for me to prove there. Also, you didn't make a living in the amateurs. You can't eat glory and I've won hundreds of trophies and if you put them all together they still don't even equal one house payment.

To make a living at what I loved to do (which was grappling), I had to go pro, but this caused an enormous flap in the Japanese judo community. Sensei Kenneth Kuniyuki, who ran the Seinan Dojo, was the president of the Southern California Judo Association (Nanka Yudansha Kai) and he was strongly opposed to any judo man turning pro. While I was competing as an amateur, Sensei Kuniyuki and I had always gotten along fine most of the time. When any judo players from Japan would visit his school, he called me up on the phone to come and work out to make his dojo look a little stronger and to make it seem like he had some real tough guys under his wing. He would even slip a five-dollar bill in my pocket just for showing up and five dollars was a lot of money when gas was only 22 cents a gallon. When I turned pro, however, he said that I shamed judo. But what is a guy supposed to do? The amateur tennis players want to be pros. The goal of a college football player is to make it into the NFL. The Olympic boxer wants to be professional so he can make money. Muhammad Ali, Joe Frazier and Oscar De La Hoya are just a few of the Olympic champs that went on to become professional champs as well as multi-millionaires. Muhammad Ali, when he was heavyweight champion, was the most recognized person in the world. I was no different than any other athlete from any other sport and the only way that I could earn a paycheck with my

grappling skills was to put on the tights and get into the world of professional wrestling.

But to the people who ran the Southern California Black Belt Judo
Association, Judo was strictly for amateurs, but the schools were not
free. They charged for the schools and I paid.

They weren't against me turning pro just because of some of the
more theatrical aspects of professional wrestling; they didn't like any
of their people turning to professional sports. If you opened up a judo
school and you had a neon sign in front of it that was a no-no back then.
When you went into Seinan Dojo, you wouldn't even know that it was
a martial arts school. It was next to a church and it was hard to tell the
difference. Hollywood Dojo, where I worked out for years, was the
same and so were the other Japanese schools. None of them had a sign
to let anyone know that it was a judo school. I opened up my own judo
school and a sign in front with "Judo" in big letters. After word of my
school got around, some of the other judo men would say, "Do you see
what Gene is doing? Turning professional -- shame." It was a different
way of thinking, not to say that they were wrong and I was right. Since
I love to eat, and I like a roof over my head and I don't steal, the only
thing left for me was to get a job. My turning professional was my job.
If you don't change with the times, I have found out that they have a
nasty way of passing you by.

Before my first pro match and while I was still an amateur, I traveled to Japan with the US Judo team. We had a pretty imposing team
that year. With Johnny Osako, George Harris, Kenji Yamada and
myself, our group had four US national champs in it. There were a few
other good contenders on that team as well.

Also on the team was Hal Sharp who was a real class act. Hal
learned judo in Japan when he served in the army there as part of the
US occupying forces right after World War II. He was the "Foreigner
Judo Champion" of Japan in 1954 and he wrote an instructional book
on judo for kids, which I highly recommend called "Boy's Judo." Hal
must have sold a ton of copies of that over the years. On the tour, Hal
was always racked with injuries but that didn't stop him from competing. He entered every tournament and more often than not, he was

hauled away to the hospital after competing only to go back and do it all over again the next day. Hal wasn't quite the judo man that Osako and Harris were but he was a real warrior and a great competitor.

We traveled all over Japan and fought in tournaments everyday and we did pretty well. It was a kind of a good will tour and it showed that the martial arts were really becoming an international phenomenon in the days before judo was an Olympic sport. We went to the Kodokan, which was the Mecca of judo and we also went to the Japanese Police Academy and Meiji University, which was a top judo college at the time. I absolutely loved working out and fighting in Japan because everybody was so good in the dojos over there. In the United States back then, every dojo had one or two really good judo players, but in Japan you could work out hard with everybody. It was expected of you there, and if anybody you were training with got tired, there was always another guy ready to fight you. In the US, I had to constantly travel around to different schools to find the one good judo man to work out with, but the big schools in Japan had at least fifty or more built-in opponents.

Our coach on that tour was Mel Bruno of the U.S. Air Force judo team. The Air Force team used to be flown to Japan all of the time to train there and that's definitely a major reason as to why George Harris was so good. When the US Judo Team went to Japan we were all flown there by the USAF Strategic Air Command and that was how I got to meet two of the most powerful military men in United States history – General Curtis LeMay and his then chief assistant General Thomas S. Power. LeMay may not be as well known as US generals such as Patton or McArthur but he was just as important a military leader as any of them. He spearheaded the daylight precision bombing that helped the US and Britain beat back the Germans in World War II and after that, he was behind the development of our nuclear bomber defense 1950s as well as this country's ballistic missile systems. When I met General LeMay, he was the head of the Strategic Air Command and Power was his chief assistant. A few years later, when LeMay was named vice chief of staff of the entire Air Force, Power became the head of the Strategic Air Command. Both of these men made the

American nuclear deterrent what it is today and at one time the only man who held more power in the USA than Gen. LeMay was maybe the president.

LeMay was a four star general and Power was well on his way to attaining that rank when I met them and I must say that there is really nobody in this world like a four star general. When I was first introduced to Lemay and Power it was at the Kodokan and I was actually overcome with a sense of hero worship. Now I never really liked my military service in the Coast Guard, but if there was an air force recruiting office around after I met these two men, I might have signed up for another four years. LeMay and Power had honorary black belts from the Kodokan because of who they were and I took falls for them just like I did when I met James Cagney. I made it all look convincing and I begged for mercy. After I took a fall for one of the generals and I hit the ground I said, "That's why you're a four star General and I'm not!" They knew that I was the national champion and I had beaten some of the Japanese champs on that tour, but I still thought that it was a smart idea to make them look good when I worked with them. Man it was the only way to go. I bragged about how good I was like a pro would do and then I let them throw me all over the place. It is always a good idea to let the four star general win because he might call an airstrike on your house, and those two guys could do it too.

I was flown all over the world to places like Russia, Alaska, Canada, Europe, Japan, and Hong Kong on Strategic Air Command transport planes. I've said it before, and I am probably going to say it again before this book is over: sometimes you can get a lot more from losing to a guy than you can from beating him especially if he's a general.

LeMay and Power were both really nice to me. One time I was talking to Power and a bird colonel came up and wanted to talk to the General. Power turned around and said, "Don't bother me. I'm talking to Mr. LeBell." At that instant, I was afraid to look down because I thought that I might have wet my pants. You know I was kind of impressed. That man had whole B-52 bomber squadrons with hydrogen bombs patrolling the world at his command, and there he was making time to talk to somebody who had only made it to boatswain's mate in the coast guard. The colonel asked to be excused and immediately departed.

Besides hobnobbing with four-star generals, the US Judo team was traveling around Japan and competing in so many tournaments that I can't honestly remember them all. In Japan when you competed in a tournament, they had women who would wash your gis. I believe that they were hand washed but somehow before one competition, my gi came back in a pinkish color. I mean it was obviously pink and I didn't have a backup outfit so I had to go out there and compete in this very pink gi. The next day the sports pages of Mainichi newspapers read, "Daikon Wins." A daikon is a white or pink radish. I thought that they were referring my red hair but they were talking about my gi. I got a lot of teasing and I wasn't too good at comebacks back then. Some of my buddies said, "Oh there's the guy with the pink gi," and I'd pick them up and bodyslam them because I didn't know how else to respond. Later, as a joke, I started wearing the pink gi as much as I could and it has become my trademark. I recently bestowed a pink gi upon Bob Wall of "Enter the Dragon" fame, who is unfortunately a very good friend of mine, but I don't think that he has the guts to ever wear it.

Near the end of our tour some officials from the Kodokan told us that they would promote us up a degree in our black belts. To get this promotion, however, we had to learn all of these forms or katas. There was a whole host of them too. There was nage no kata, ju no kata, kime no kata, and some others, and they were basically a series of pre-arranged movements designed to simulate judo moves and self defense forms. Now katas have never been my strong suit. I have always done things that work on the street or work on the mats. I have a more hands-on approach and would rather spar or work on moves with people. I like to feel the pain, but I like the guys who I am working with to feel it even more. How can you know if a move or a throw even works unless you practice it on a real, live body? Today, I insist that all of my students feel the move applied to them so that know how it is supposed to work. We take the slack out of a hold because there's no reason for anyone to get hurt unless he has an attitude problem – then we give him an attitude adjustment.

So four of us went down to the Kodokan to learn these katas and be tested on them. Johnny Osako didn't have to go because he was 33 at the time and was considered beyond testing age. Learning all of these katas took some time (about eight hours_ and only two of us stuck it out for the full time to learn all of these forms and we both had them nailed. When it was time to be tested, this elderly, Japanese teacher with a big head and even bigger cauliflower ears entered the room. The Air Force guys all called him "Stink" Sato because he never washed his gi for some reason, but he was the kind of judo man that I had nothing but respect for. We both stood ready for our tests to begin and then the teacher said, "Katas bullshit." That nearly knocked me down as well as any judo throw could have. I didn't even know that he could speak English, but I sure understood what he meant by the word bullshit.

"For show only," he continued after that shocking revelation and then he told us to shiai which meant to get into a contest. That eight hours spent learning all of those katas felt like time that I could never get back and I was soar and tired from it on top of all of that. Then Sato Sensei motioned and four fourth degree black belts entered the room. To get moved up from third to fourth degree black belt, I had to fight these four well-trained judo experts after I had spent the whole day drilling on katas like I was a ballerina or something. But my determination to win was still there and I beat the four guys and was ready for my promotion.

On the last day of the tour, on the airstrip before we boarded the plane we were supposed to all be handed certificates noting that we had been promoted. Osako was jumped up two whole degrees from fourth to sixth, which was unprecedented but that is how great he was. Everybody else was given their promotions as they made their way to the plane but I didn't get anything. Sensei Kuniyuki, who had many contacts in Japan, had called and informed the officials there that I was disgracing judo by turning pro. So there I was holding out my hand in front of my team expecting to get this tube with a certificate in it, but they didn't have one for me. Sensei Kuniyuki was a great judo man, but he had his opinions and I had mine. I had the best showing of anybody on our team that year, but because of politics the degree that I had earned was withheld from me.

Years later on a professional wrestling tour of Japan, I brought my son David with me. We went to the Kodokan to work out and met Professor Kotani, 9th degree teacher. He gave me a big promotion but years later degrees didn't mean that much to me anymore probably because of the politics.

When I returned home and went to work out at the Hollywood Dojo, I found that I wasn't welcomed there anymore. I had been expelled from Nanka Udansha Kai, but Sensei Kukuchi didn't have the guts to tell me that I wasn't welcomed at his school or any other schools in the Southern California Judo Association anymore so he had Frank and Art Emi do it. They were some of the younger black belts and they were second generation Japanese Americans. I had my gi and I was ready to suit up and roll but the Emis came up to me and said, "I'm sorry. You can't work out here anymore. You're a professional wrestler." They were talking for their teacher and it was as if they were talking for their parents. No matter what their opinions were, they stood behind their dojo, which was like their family.

I gathered up my gear and started to walk out. Shig Tashima, my big sparring partner was walking in and he said, "You're going to work out aren't you?"

"No, I've been kicked out," I told him. "I am a professional wrestler and I'm not welcomed here anymore."

He looked at the older teacher and had some cross words in Japanese that I didn't understand. He then turned to me and shrugged his shoulders to tell me that there was nothing that he could do. He had a lot of respect for his Sensei too and for him what Frank Kukuchi said was the law whether he agreed with it or not. He started to walk into the dressing room as I headed for the front door but he turned around and looked at me twice, but that was it. My time training with the Japanese at the Hollywood Dojo had come to an end.

Eight years later, Art Emi invited me back to the Hollywood Dojo. He said, "Bring your students to work out, but they have to wear white belts." I brought two of my best, Igor the Russian Bear and Dave Pagenkopf. They put on white belts, although they were very good and they played with everybody there and toyed with the black belts. After that, I could do no wrong. It takes a big man to forget and forgive. They did, I'm just not sure that I'm quite there yet.

Later on, I was on location and I went into this dojo that I found in the phonebook because I had the night off. It was an old Japanese school and I looked on the wall and there was a newspaper clipping that Shig Tashima, who ended up being the president of Nanka had passed away. It hit me -- you know what I mean. I never had the chance to tell him that he was one of the good guys. Much of my ability I got from him through hard sparring. He only did two techniques, but he was very good. One of his specialties was a leg stop, not a sweep, and I used it in tournaments and I still use it and teach it today.

CHAPTER 6

SWERVES

When I turned pro as a wrestler, I had to report to the Southern California booking office every Monday to get my bookings. The office was run by Jules Strongbow and his assistant Sandor Szabo, who was a Hungarian champion and a very hard man. Both of them sent wrestlers out all over the Southern California territory. As a wrestler, you worked almost every day of the week and traveled all over the territory to places like Long Beach, Santa Monica, San Diego, Santa Barbara, San Bernadino, Southgate, and Visalia. You also picked up some spot shows or once a month shows in the small, out of the way towns that dotted the desert and coastlines of the southern half of the Golden State.. Making your matches could have you driving hundreds of miles across the interstate highways of California. Of course, Strongbow and Szabo also put together cards for the Olympic Auditorium but you didn't always get to wrestle there. The Olympic was the jewel in the crown and wrestling there meant earning the big money.

On Wednesday and Saturday, we did TV tapings where wrestlers were interviewed to build up main event and semi-main event matches that wouldn't be televised so you could draw a big house filled with paying customers at the Olympic. On the TV show you might wrestle and then again you might not. If you did wrestle, it was always against somebody that you knew you could beat to show the TV fans how good you were. This was so the fans would want to pay to see you wrestle somebody good as good as you were at the big shows and thereby drawing some big crowds. The real big attractions and great wrestlers such as Lou Thesz, Mil Mascaras or Andre the Giant usually wrestled in handicapped matches on the TV shows where they took on multiple opponents all at once or one after the other to really get the fans going.

To kill the boredom of being on the road all of the time, the wrestlers played swerves on each other. A swerve was a joke or tease and some wrestlers played them on each other for fun and others just did it out of sheer meanness. The wrestlers that wouldn't play the jokes were the ones that were the biggest recipients of them in and out of the ring. A common swerve was to put itching powder in a wrestler's trunks before he went on so he'd be adjusting his trunks and, oh hell just say it, scratching his testicles while he was in the ring in front of a full house. It was extra points if the guy fell out of the ring on purpose while scratching himself to get disqualified. Nothing was better than swerving a guy into dropping his own match.

An example of purposely disqualifying yourself came when I was wrestling a very young and very green Rowdy Roddy Piper in the 1970s. Roddy talks about this in his book "In the Pit with Piper." I was wrestling him in one of these small towns and for some reason Roddy hit the backstage dinner buffet pretty hard before our match. They had a full Thanksgiving meal backstage at this arena and Roddy ate a whole turkey leg and then chased it down with an entire blueberry pie. I don't know what Piper was thinking but he was still a growing boy so he must have been hungry. It turns out that Piper thought that he would have time to digest but the preliminary matches were shorter than he had anticipated.

We both stepped in the ring and the bell rang and I started throwing Roddy from pillar to post. I was really tossing him around and, to quote his book, he was "earning his frequent flyer miles" wrestling me. I was getting the best of him and here's how quickly the tides can turn. As I grabbed him and squeezed him in a bear hug, he suddenly threw up purple liquid with chunks of pie in it right in my face. I was grossed out and almost lost my lunch myself. There was only one thing left for me to do to save my dignity: I had to sacrifice the match and run as quickly as I could to the dressing room to hit the showers to clean the puke off of me. The referee actually disqualified me for not returning to the ring, but the real culprit was Roddy Piper! I think that the ref should have disqualified Roddy for upchucking in my face. That should have gotten him an automatic DQ in my book. Roddy got his hand raised while I was scrubbing his barf out of my chest hairs. Today, Piper says that his claim to fame was that he beat me. Now that wasn't really a swerve but it couldn't have been a better one if you had planned it.

I later ran into Roddy and challenged him to a death match in my judo school. Usually guys find a way not to show up when you throw down the gauntlet, but Roddy not only came in to sacrifice his body, but he stayed there and studied with me for years and went from a green, enthusiastic young man to a champion grappler and was awarded a black belt in judo. Many years later, I'm proud to say he's not only a great wrestler but also one of my friends.

Back when I was a young man, I wasn't the good humored, effervescent Gene LeBell that everybody knows today. I was a very serious young man and all I thought about was putting a championship belt around my waist. More than anything, I wanted to be like my idol Lou Thesz. I wanted to be able to beat anybody just like him and I emulated his stern demeanor as best as I could. While the other wrestlers would be out drinking, partying and chasing women, I was back in my motel room doing push-ups and sit-ups. When the rest of the boys were hitting the nightspots, I was working out in the dojos. Of course my serious attitude made me a magnet for swerves. I had more swerves played on me that you can shake a stick at so much so that I wrote a script about all of them later in life called "The 12 Second Champ." Now "The 12 Second Champ" has yet to be made into a feature film, but the one thing that I can say about it is that everything in it is absolutely true.

My idea in writing the "12 Second Champ" was not to talk about the wrestling but to talk about the swerves that we did and there were a lot of them. It made it interesting. It took up the boredom. Today professional wrestling is more business like. A guy may have a booking in Chicago one day, and Florida the next day, and New York the next, and they have to catch the planes. If they're a big a star like in the WWE, the promotion will pay for their transportation but if they're not a main eventer they will have to get there anyway that they can. With those schedules, I'm not sure how much time the wrestlers have for the good old swerve today, but in my time as a pro, I was on the receiving end of so many swerves that I can fill the rest of the book with them. The undisputed master of most of my grief in those days was none other than my professional wrestling coach and benefactor Vic Christy.

Vic Christy was the biggest practical joker of all times. He burned a lot of bridges and had a lot of fun. He even got stabbed a couple of times for teasing people, but everything was very, very casual to him. If a crisis came, he would pass it off. He did anything to make you laugh and he got me in more trouble. He ended up changing my way of acting towards society, not only because he helped launch my professional wrestling career, but also because it was through him that I realized that nothing is more important than enjoying life because you are a long time dead.

My first professional match was at the Olympic Auditorium and I was booked against Vic's brother Ted. Vic was always out to play practical jokes on any of us wrestlers, but he really loved nothing more than pulling a swerve on his brother. Ted was shorter and wider than Vic, and he had a big head and a very menacing look. He was a real sparkplug. Before our match, I was very nervous and I ran into Ted in the dressing room. Just as he passed me, he took a lunge at me like he was going to hit me or something. Ted had me backed against the wall and he growled at me like he was a werewolf. He made a noise at me that went something like "Raaaaaarrrhhhhh" as he made his way out of the dressing room and I was really shaken up by it. Shaken up, hell, I had to sit down when I went to the bathroom.

Vic was there and he was coaching me on what do. I was really nervous and I didn't know what was happening there.

"I think that they might have booked you too tough with my brother," Vic told me. Now I always thought that Ted was crazy anyway, because every time that I saw the man he did something really out there. "Oh he's crazy," Vic said making me even more nervous. "You've got to watch him. He can't help himself. Even our mother was afraid of him."

While I was waiting in the wings for my match with Ted to start, Vic turned to me and gave me some advice on how to handle his brother. "What you've got to do," Vic said, "is you have to hit him in the groin as hard as you can and then the match will belong to you."

"I can't do that, that's not fair," I said.

"He'll beat you up," Vic told me. "He'll bite you on the neck and rip your throat out. You've got to have confidence in me. Look, I've got you this far. I know how to handle my brother."

I thought about it and what Vic was telling me seemed to make sense at the time. After all, Vic did grow up with Ted, so he should know how to handle the guy. At that moment, Vic had me convinced that the only thing to do was to hit Ted as hard as I could right in the Christy family jewels.

It was time for me to make my way into the ring for my pro wrestling debut. It was a sellout crowd with Lou Thesz on the top and my match was a special added semi main attraction. Because I had just gotten out of the service, they had the Marine Corps color guard there and they played the "Star Spangled Banner." Why they had the Marines there I will never understand because I was in the Coast Guard. The audience was throwing confetti and the match was hyped as a real big deal. Vic accompanied me as I made my way through the crowd. As I was about to enter the ring, Vic said, "Don't forget: hit him in the balls as hard as you can and then the match will belong to you okay. I'm the coach – do what I say or you'll lose."

So I climbed through the ropes and Ted lunged at me again like he was going to bite me and tear me apart. I said, "Oh my God!" He had a crazed look in his eyes.

The referee pushed Ted back and said, "Wait until the bell sounds."

Right before the bell sounded Vic said, "Have confidence and hit him as hard as you can." I was a good listener so that's exactly what I did.

The bell rang and Ted came in for a tie up and I hit him as hard as I could in the crotch. Ted dropped to his knees and held his groin in severe pain. He looked right at me and he shouted, "That fucking Vic!" I looked up and saw Vic running up the aisle and Ted was watching him. I knew that they had swerved me good and Vic had done it to hurt his brother as a joke on the both of us. That was his sense of humor. I gave Ted time to get his breath up and we had a good match after that, but Ted said, "That was a great joke but I'm gonna' get my brother good for this! It's my turn now." It was a never-ending cycle for those two guys.

Another time, both Vic and I were booked in San Diego. I was one of the preliminaries and Vic was booked at the top of the card. Christy rode down with assistant booker Sandor Szabo who couldn't take a swerve but he liked to play them. Szabo spoke with a heavy Hungarian accent and he always said, "I am the booker. If you don't like something, I will cross your name off the booking sheet and you will never vork again – you will never never vork again!" You didn't mess with Sandor Szabo because he would cut your bookings. I drove down with these two identical twins that weighed 400 pounds apiece. They were big guys and they both had their front teeth knocked out except for their canines. They were very good as a novelty hillbilly tag-team but they probably never took first place in any spelling bees if you know what I mean. Back then you got paid in cash after your match was over. When I was done wrestling, I approached Szabo and asked if he could pay me so I could leave.

"No, you vait until everything is over," Szabo told me. "Just stay in the dressing vroom until I come out."

So I waited in the dressing room with nobody to talk to but the two twins. Now the reason that I had to drive them to San Diego was because neither one of them could pass the written part of the their driver's test. I sat down there and waited and waited. It was humid as hell in there and the conversation had long since dried up. Finally, at 11 O'clock, I opened the door and the arena was empty. I found some janitors sweeping up the arena and I asked them if they had seen Sandor Szabo or Vic Christy.

"They both went out laughing about 45 minutes ago," the maintenance crew informed me.

We got in my car and headed for this all night delicatessen in Newport Beach where Christy and Szabo always stopped to get sandwiches after a show. We spotted Vic's car parked on the street in front of the place just as I had predicted. It was a sharp, brand new, red Oldsmobile 88 convertible. It was really a beautiful car. Now to get them back, I wanted to move their car about ten feet forward just so they would know that somebody had messed with them. I used a slim jim to open the locked car door and got into the driver's seat. I put it in neutral while the giant twins gave me a push. The twins weighed at least 800 pounds between them and they got that car moving at a good clip down the street. I made a left turn, which took me down a steep hill. I went clear down to the bottom of the hill with the car and I pulled into a driveway in the nick of time. I pulled Vic's car right next to a car that was already parked there so it couldn't be seen from the top of the hill. I had no idea who lived in that house but whoever it was, they must have thought that they had won a brand new convertible when they looked out their window the next morning.

I ran back up the hill and found the twins there waiting for me. "Can we go in and eat now?" One of them asked.

"No," I said, "We're getting the hell out of here," and we got back in my car and took off.

I went into the booking office the next day to see where I would be wrestling and Vic and Szabo were there trying to figure out who had stolen the Oldsmobile. It turned out that after Szabo and Vic were through with their late night snack, they got out of the deli and found that Vic's car was missing. They called the police, but when the cops arrived, Vic couldn't resist playing a joke even when he thought that somebody had made off with his new car. He got on one of the officer's bullhorns, faked a Hungarian accent, and said, "Now hear this! Somebody stole Szabo's car, Hungarian Champion, and he'll never vork again in this territory." Vic teased Szabo the whole way home on the bus and Sandor got so mad at Vic that he killed his bookings for three months right then and there.

When I came into the booking office, Vic asked me if I knew who had moved his car.

"You mean pushed your car?" I said, "It wasn't me."

"What do you mean it wasn't you?" he asked

"I'm not strong enough to move that car," I said.

I thought that I was going to worm my way out of that one, but then the twins came in and said, "Yeah, he didn't move the car. He just sat at the wheel and steered it."

The twins possessed tremendous strength but they had room temperature IQs so nothing happened to them even though they had implicated themselves in the prank. I mean if intelligence were measured in Cadillacs, those two guys would be on roller-skates. Szabo came to the conclusion that Vic and I were in cahoots so we both had our bookings cut for three months in the Southern California territory so we had to make our own bookings elsewhere. Vic wasn't soar at me either. In fact he thought that it was the best thing since 7-Up. I ended up wrestling in Arizona for a while and then Vic and I both went to Texas.

I wasn't able to escape the swerve in any state. Anywhere you have pro wrestlers, you have swerves and I even had one played on me in my very first bout in Texas. I was wrestling in a tag-team match and my opponent, who was a big weightlifter named Art Nelson, whitewashed me. A whitewash in professional wrestling is when your opponent slaps your face really hard. This guy just hit me with all of his might and we were wrestling. I was ready for a collar-and-elbow tie up – not a smack in the mouth. After smarting from the shot, I went to tag in my partner so he could get in the action (which is what you are supposed to do in tag-team matches) but he wouldn't tag in so I had to go back and wrestle my opponent some more. I went to the middle of the ring and my opponent delivered an open handed slap to my face once again. I could taste the blood in my mouth as he laughed with his partner and they went back and forth talking to each other. I went to my partner to tag him in again and he just leaned back out of the way avoiding my tag. My opponent then tagged his partner and when the fresh man entered the ring, I hit him as hard I could. He went down and crawled to the corner and tagged Nelson back in. Once Art came back in the ring, I just went from head to toe doing every finishing hold that I could on him. I let him go right before he had a chance to give up just to put another hold on him so he could feel it. I cranked his neck. I cranked his arms and his chest. I beat the tar out of him.

Nelson was playing a swerve on me to see what I would do – to see what my reaction would be. I really laid some hurt on him in the process. After the match, I went to the dressing room to give him some more in there. Art looked at me and said, "Great match Gene," and he never talked about the match again. I knew that I had been through some kind of a test.

After that, I went to my partner and slapped him so hard in the face that his mother could feel it as payback for not tagging in. "It's a swerve! It's a swerve!" he said with my handprint right across his cheek.

"Some day you are going to get booked against me," I said and then I laughed like I had one up on him. Nothing more was said about that match after that. To the wrestlers, I was okay -- I was one of the guys.

But even in the Lone Star State, Vic Christy was not to be outdone at playing swerves on me and getting me into heaps of trouble. We traveled to all of these different Texas towns to wrestle in, and as you know everything is big over there so the travel time got to be a bit extreme. On top of that, we weren't making good money for what we were doing back then. You got 40 or 50 dollars for a match in a small town and the cost of a nice hotel room was three or four dollars a night. You had to buy food and gas out of the rest of your earnings. All expenses weren't paid in pro wrestling back in the 1950s and they still aren't today for the most part. There was this one town where all of the wrestlers stayed in the cheapest, fleabag hotel that we could find. I think that it was only a dollar and a half a night. You had to go down the hall to use the common shower and bathroom. I wasn't the champ, but I wanted to look like one, so I was always doing pushups and exercising in my room. I was obsessed with following in the footsteps of Lou Thesz.

We wrestled at the local venue and after the matches I went to this hotel. I didn't leave my room. I even brought my food back with me. I had some store bought sandwiches and some fruit and I ate in my room and then went to sleep.

I woke up in the morning and got my bags, which were already packed and ready to go from the night before, and went downstairs. I saw a couple of wrestlers there with some real redneck sheriffs. The sheriffs wore big brown cowboy hats and carried the biggest side arms that you had ever seen. When I walked up to the reception desk to check out, they looked at me and said, "Is this the guy?"

Vic Christy was on his knees and he was crying. "He can't help himself," Vic explained to the Texas lawmen. "He's a kleptomaniac."

I was completely confused and I didn't even know what a kleptomaniac was. The sheriff then turned to me and asked me what I had in my suitcases.

I was a little dumbfounded. Hadn't this guy ever seen me wrestle on television? I couldn't conceive that he didn't know who I was.

"This suitcase has my wrestling gear," I said. "I'm a professional wrestler. This other suitcase has my street clothes in it and now I'm going to San Angelo, Texas to wrestle if you will excuse me."

I then started to leave but the sheriff put his big hand on my chest and stopped me. "You're not going anywhere," he said, "open up your suitcase."

I was happy to open my suitcase. After all, I didn't even drink or smoke – let alone steal. I had never stolen anything in my life so if the sheriff wanted to look at some wrestling trunks and some boots he was welcomed to it. So I opened up my suitcase but it didn't have any wrestling gear in it. To my shock, the sheriff found some sheets and towels. I was confused. It was my suitcase. I didn't know what had happened or how those things could have gotten in there.

"Did you steal this?" the sheriff asked holding up a bed sheet.

"No this is my wrestling gear," I answered.

"Do you wrestle with a sheet on?" he said with a chip on his shoulder. "What are you? A member of the Ku Klux Klan!?!" Hell, that sheriff was probably more of a member of the Klan than I ever was. This was back in the days when they had different water fountains and bathrooms for the white and colored people in states like Texas.

I had no idea how those sheets could have gotten into my bags because I didn't think that I had left my room, but it turned out that I had. After I had eaten and exercised, I went down the hall and showered and went to the bathroom. I couldn't have been gone for more than 10 minutes and I locked the door behind me but that hotel used old skeleton keys for the door locks and unbeknownst to me, every room had the same lock and key. They had one key that fit all of the doors.

The sheriff then told me to open the other suitcase while I was trying to explain to him that somebody had swerved me but he wasn't having any of it. He made me open my other suitcase and in there was a roll of toilet paper, a pillow, pillowcase, and even a Gideon's Bible. It looked like I had made off with everything in the room that wasn't bolted down.

I reached into my pocket and I discovered that my wallet was gone too. "Hey," I said, "somebody is playing a joke on me here and they stole my wallet too! I really have to get to San Angelo and get to the bottom of this."

The sheriff stopped me once again and said, "Your first stop is jail buddy."

They made me get into their police car and I tried to explain what had happened to me. "They're doing a swerve on me," I said.

"What's a swerve?" the sheriff asked me.

"They're jokes," I explained, "wrestlers are always playing jokes like this on each other. I have to get to San Angelo to wrestle. They stole everything from me."

Finally, they started to believe my story and after they held me for an hour and half they let me go. As I left, the sheriff said, "I don't want to ever see you in this town again."

I tried to borrow ten dollars from the sheriff but he said, "Do you want to make this jail your home?" I then left quickly.

So I got to San Angelo with two empty suitcases and no wallet because the sheriffs dumped the stolen goods out before they returned them to me. I didn't know what I was going to do when I got to the arena because I didn't have my gear. I almost wished that I had those sheets because I might have had to wrestle in them after all. When I got to the arena, I looked at the marquee and saw that I was wrestling "The Baron" Vic Christy. Boy, I was going to have some fun with him, but I still didn't have any wrestling clothes.

I went to the dressing room right away to plead my case with the promoter. Maybe they had some gear that they could loan me or maybe they had some for sale. I didn't know. When I got into the dressing room, there was a paper bag mysteriously sitting on one of the benches with my gear and my wallet in it. There was no note or anything. It was the gear that Vic had stolen.

When I was a young man, I wasn't any good at coming up with ingenious ways of getting back at people who had swerved me so my only recourse was slam them and slam them hard. That night, when I got into the ring with Vic Christy, all thoughts of good sportsmanship or putting on a good show for the fans were out the window. I was there to punish Vic 100 times over for everything that he had put me through that day. The bell rang and Vic came in like he was going to do a headlock from the side that he would maybe work into a hip throw. He came in and I got behind him. I picked him up backwards and suplexed him as high as I could and I landed him right on the back of his head and he was out cold. I really cold cocked him there. I then pinned him for the one, two, three and it was a short match of a minute or two.

I was really teed off so I went straight to the dressing room and a couple of the wrestlers and ring crew turned around and jumped into the ring to help him because he was still unconscious. I hopped in my car and I headed back to Amarillo, which was where I lived when I wrestled on the Texas circuit. Now that I think about it, I never did find my clothes – just my wrestling gear. I have no idea where the hell they ended up.

On my way back to Amarillo, it started to rain really hard. It was one of those hard Texas downpours that was like a biblical deluge. There was a diner on the way in an out of the way town where all of the wrestlers used to stop and eat. They served really good home cooked meals there. They used to make biscuits there the size of your fist that were just warm from the oven and they made big, thick hamburger steaks that came with a baked potato. I stopped there to eat hoping that the storm would pass. When I walked in, there were two wrestlers there sitting in a booth but I went up to the counter because I was by myself. I nodded at them, but I didn't say hello because people would recognize us from television where they regularly saw all of us fighting each other. You never wanted people to think that you knew the other wrestlers that you worked with. Of course, you had to know them. There was only one locker room in most arenas after all but the fans didn't know that. The promoters thought that it wasn't good for business for the wrestlers to be seen in public going out to dinner and socializing with their worst enemies. In pro wrestling you were either a fan favorite or a despised villain. In wrestling parlance, you were either a baby face (good guy) or a heel (bad guy), and if you were a heel, you couldn't be seen palling around town with the baby faces. In reality, however, we often knew and liked our opponents.

The place was cold and I was kind of wet although I only ran from my car to the inside of the restaurant. Pictures of Jesus and signs with sayings from the gospel adorned the walls. It was a very religious place. The waitress there was also very religious. She always said, "God bless you," or "Jesus loves you" when she took your money. She often looked at her customers and said, "I can see that you're a God fearing man." Of course, all of the baby faces were God fearing and all of the heels were atheists.

I was still looking over the menu and all of sudden the door swung wide open. Behind a gust of wind and a stream of water came Vic Christy and he was dragging his leg as if he was crippled. He was in a suit but it was all muddy like he had been rolling around in the dirt parking lot. He must have tripped because of his bad leg. I took a long look at him and thought that I must have given him a brain injury during our match. He didn't look at me and he just dragged his foot and he was drooling. He slowly sat down two stools away from me.

I was sick to my stomach. I thought that because I had lost my temper and dropped him on of his head that he had a brain injury. He was the man who had taught me so much and had helped me get started with my career and now he was almost a vegetable and it was all my fault.

The waitress went up to Vic and she asked if she could help him. He stuttered and stammered and after five minutes he finally told her that he wanted soup. She never blinked an eye through all of his convulsions. They used to make a vegetable soup there with big chunks of meat in it but the soup that they offered that night was split pea. She brought him a bowl of split pea soup and it came with these oversized soupspoons. He picked up the spoon and his hand was shaking so badly that he was spilling the soup all over himself. He got it everywhere but his mouth. He got mad and he was hitting the spoon down on the table and he grunted at the steaming bowl. "I know that you are a good Christian," the waitress said comforting him. "God will give you strength."

It then dawned on me that maybe Vic was swerving me again. Nobody was that good of an actor but Christy was laying it on a bit thick so I started to laugh. The waitress pinched me on the forearm hard and said, "There but for the grace of God goes you."

Believing her, I said, "Yes m'am," and turned around in my seat.

If Vic was really messed up from taking that hard fall, I started to think that maybe God would heal him. The waitress started to feed him and some of it went down his mouth and the rest of it went all over. Finally after quite a long time, she finished feeding him. He spent another couple of minutes holding her hand with both of his hands so she couldn't get away. The other two wrestlers were just staring at him in disbelief wondering how bad he was really hurt.

He started to stutter and was choking on his words again. "H-H-H-How m-m-m-much?" he asked. It was 25 cents for the soup, which was a lot but it was a big bowl of soup. Then he started looking all over for money and he couldn't find it. He had a double-breasted suit with a little pocket on the right side like a watch pocket. Finally he reached in there and he was shaking. I was reaching in my own pocket because I was going to give him the 25 cents because I felt so bad. At that time the Lord should have struck me down instead of what had happened to Vic. Vic then pulled out a quarter and his hand was trembling but then he flipped the coin high in the air and he caught it and slammed it down on the counter. He stood up like nothing was ever wrong and said, "Lady, that's the best damned service that I've ever had."

I was so shocked that I fell off of the stool backwards and hit my head. I had a knot on the back of my head the size of an egg for a week. That night as Vic walked out the door, he left the door open and the wind and the rain was coming through. I got up off of the floor rubbing my head and the waitress's mouth was wide open. He played a swerve on me and everybody else in that diner. At that point I said, "Any time he does something on me, I'm going to lay some hurt on him." My biggest ambition in life at that time was to be known as one of the great wrestlers but word of that swerve that Vic Christy had played on me got out all over the territory. Vic was a big hero for it while the great wrestler that was Gene LeBell was nothing more than the butt of another one of Christy's jokes.

Let's get down to business

Youthful me after winning the judo nationals. Was I good looking or what!

Look out, I'm coming at ya!

With my good friend George 'Superman' Reeves on my birthday

I've never feared nobody – I refuse to be beaten

Freddie Blassie and me

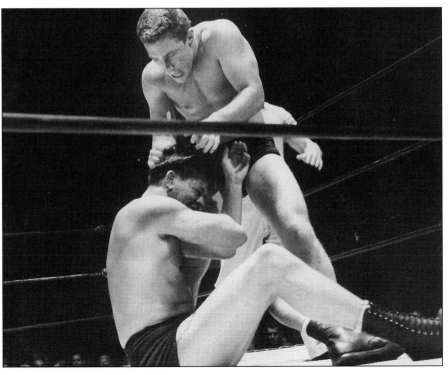

In the ring

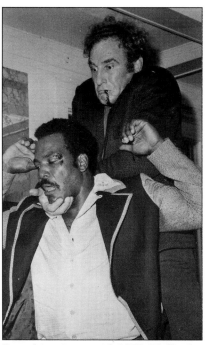

Roughing it up with NFL Hall of Fame turned Hollywood tough guy Jim Brown

My mother with the 'Greatest'. Muhammad Ali

On the set of 'Killer Elite' withJames Caan

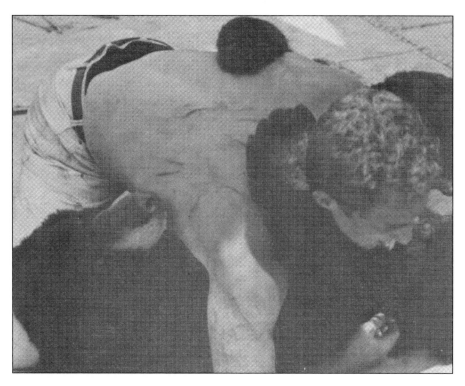

I wrestled and beat 800lb bears on many occasions

Choking out my son David to teach him proper manners in front of the ladies

Streetfighting is all about fighting dirty

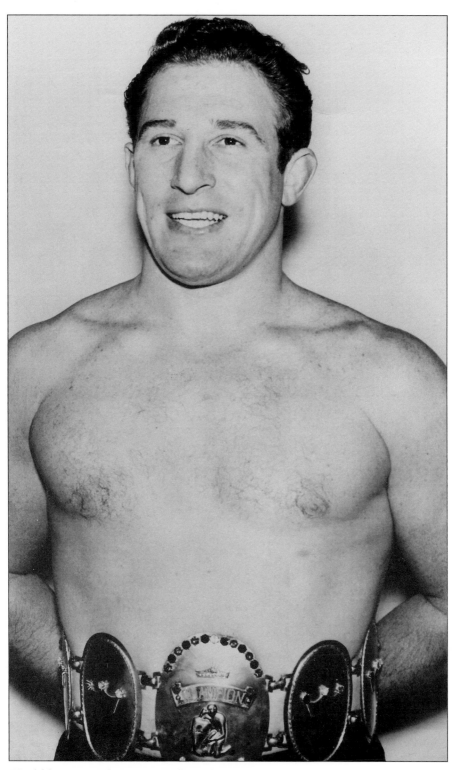

World heavyweight pro-wrestling champion

A night of champions. Left to right: Archie Moore, Larry Holmes, me, TV star Lee Majors, Sugar Ray Robinson and Bobby Chacon, on the set of the boxing episode of 'The Fall Guy'

Don't try this at home kids

CHAPTER 7

SWERVED AGAIN

When I wrestled in Texas, I regularly drove from Amarillo, where I made my home, to the arena in San Angelo. Another wrestler named Jesse James also lived in Amarillo and one night we were both booked on the same card so I went over to his house to pick him up. I had never met his family before so I didn't really know what to expect. He met me at the door and I asked if he was ready to go.

"I'm ready to go but you don't understand," he told me, "I've got a babysitter here and I've got my baby and I love my baby." He then took the baby and he kissed him and he said, "Oh this is my whole life. I work. I take beatings wrestling just to feed my baby. I love my baby. My baby's my whole life."

And he went on and on and he was acting more than just a little touched. "Let's go. We don't want to be late. It's a three hundred mile trip," I said already looking for any excuse to get out of there.

But he wasn't fazed by my presence at all. He still went on and on about the baby. Then he grabbed this gal who was the babysitter who was a good looking young lady. Jesse then said, "This is my babysitter and this is my baby."

She said, "I know," looking at the child. "He looks just like you."

"I want you to change him," he said, "I want you to feed him. I don't want him to cry. He doesn't like to cry. He's a happy child." Then he grabbed this babysitter and he kissed her first on the hand and then the neck with his mouth and then kissed her right on the lips for an extended period of time. I couldn't believe what I was witness to and I wanted to crawl into a hole and hide. This was too much. Now I had heard about Texans and Southerners but this was ridiculous. After that, he gently nudged her down on the couch and got on top of her. He started to gyrate his pelvis on her like they were having sex and he said, "You will take good care of my baby. I love my baby. He's my whole life."

She was half trying to get away and I didn't know if I should intervene. I backed up against the wall and I didn't know if I should call the booker or the police. I thought that he had gone crazy. "I know he's your baby," she said. "Don't worry! The baby won't be wet! I'll change him. I swear! I'll change him!" After she had said all of that, she worked herself into a fit of tears. Both of them started sobbing.

"Will you change him? Do you swear?" he pleaded for what seemed like the hundredth time.

Now I was almost in tears myself I felt so bad. I finally thought that we were about to get out of there, but he stopped me as we were almost out the door and said, "I've got to touch my baby once more. It's my baby! I love him!"

He finally left his baby and his babysitter, but I was kind of creeped out that point because I had to ride with him in the car all the way to San Angelo. We then drove to San Angelo for our matches and the next day we drove to Abilene to wrestle other opponents. Then we drove back to Amarillo and I dropped him off at his house but there was no way that I was going to go back inside again.

Two weeks later, we were on the same card again and I saw him and his babysitter. I didn't look at her in the face because I was embarrassed and ashamed, but she saw me. She came right over to me and she grabbed me, gave me a kiss, and said, "Hi Gene."

I looked at her like I didn't know who she was.

She looked at me quizzically and said, "Don't you remember? I'm Jesse's babysitter." Then she held her hand up so I could see her wedding ring on her finger. It turned out that the babysitter was his wife and she was also a champion lady wrestler! I wanted to beat the living tar out of him.

I turned beet red and said, "He is bad people and you are too." I was so mad because they really got me and I even told them both that I hated them. Now you might not believe this but later on we all became the best of friends.

That was a harmless swerve, but some of the swerves were just plain mean and were no laughing matter to the person that was on the receiving end of them. Some swerves went horribly wrong. Jay York was a wrestler who had to use these inhalers for his asthma. After he was done with a match he ran down to the dressing room and breathed in his medicine so he could catch his breath again.

One time York was wrestling Buddy Rogers. Buddy Rogers was one of the greatest in ring performers ever in this business but he is one of the guys that Lou Thesz knocked a lot in his book because Lou thought that Rogers' mouth was bigger than his grappling ability. York got through with his match and he couldn't catch his breath as usual. He went to the dressing room to grab his inhaler, but Buddy Rogers had put lighter fluid in it as a joke because he knew what would happen. Instead of breathing in his medicine, York took a big whiff of lighter fluid. It knocked him out colder than a mackerel and it could have killed him. Jay York dropped down to the floor and hit his head on the concrete. When he woke up, Rogers was just laughing at him. York stormed out of the dressing room and went to his car and got his sawed off double barrel shotgun.

Buddy Rogers was a very successful wrestler and inside his very expensive, handmade leather suitcase he carried a diamond ring, custom-made leather shoes and his interstate championship belt. Rogers' bag was all packed up and he was ready to leave. Jay York returned to the dressing room and was ready to shoot him. Rogers caught one glimpse of York and his double-barreled shotgun coming at him and dropped his suitcase and hightailed it out of the auditorium. York spotted that fancy piece of luggage and put both barrels right into the suitcase and blew it apart with everything inside of it. The championship belt was blown to pieces and they never did find that diamond ring. Luckily for Rogers, York only had the two shells, so Jay just had to settle for chasing Buddy down the street while trying to hit him with the butt end of his gun.

One of the small towns that I wrestled in while I was based out of Amarillo was Littlefield, Texas. Littlefield was a small town that was almost on the border of Texas and New Mexico and it can't even be found on most maps. The arena there wasn't an actual building but was a big Quonset hut that they converted into a kind of a multipurpose exhibition hall. When I arrived there, the place was filled to capacity with rowdy Mexicans who were brandishing bottles of tequila and getting drunker as the night went on. I had been warned about the fans in Littlefield and I had heard that one wrestler had gotten acid poured on him, but I was not smart enough to fear for my well being. I had to wrestle this guy named Enrique Romero who was such a fan favorite there that he was a local hero. Romero wasn't the best grappler in the world but he was a crafty guy with some tricks up his sleeve plus the fans there would not tolerate him losing.

Now when I wrestled back then, I wanted to show the fans that I was a good wrestler. I wanted them to see my scientific mat skills in action and I wanted my opponent to feel their effects. As my match with Romero went on, everything was going well for me and I put him in a lot of holds. Romero's fans didn't like the one-sided bout and they got mad and started throwing bottles at me. People out of the audience started getting into the ring and there were no security guards in that Quonset hut to stop them. I tossed them out of the ring with some judo throws, but I realized that my life was in danger the longer that the match went on. Because one guy couldn't beat 100 crazed, drunken Mexicans, I had to figure out how to get the hell out of there – and fast.

I didn't want to let Romero pin me because once I was down, I would have had my shoulders to the mat and I would be at the mercy of his loyal followers. So I told Romero that I was going to throw him over the top rope. If you tossed your opponent over the top rope it was an automatic disqualification back then. Romero would get his win, and I could escape out of the other side of the ring with my life while the fans were distracted.

"I'm going to throw you over the top rope," I whispered in Romero's ear.

He then dropped to his knees to counter me and had a grin on his face and laughed at me. He seemed to be telling me, "Not tonight baby!" There was nothing else that I could do so I grabbed him by his balls and body slammed him over the top rope to get that disqualification. Romero fell to the floor and was clutching his groin in pain because I grabbed him pretty hard. The crowd went over to see if their hero was alive or dead and I got out of the ring and attempted to make it back to the dressing room as quickly as I could.

As I made my way through the crowd, somebody in the crowd hooked me in the arm with a banana knife and blood squirted all over the place. I grabbed a chair and started swinging it around and hitting anybody who got in my way. I fought my way to that dressing room.

I got into the dressing room and people started pounding on the door trying to get in. I grabbed a chair and shoved it under the door-knob to keep them outside. Now I had a hot date back in Amarillo. The gal that I was dating had a bunch of sportswriters over at her house and they were having a party and I really wanted to get over there. Little-field was a 120 miles away from Amarillo so I could get back to Amarillo in about an hour and 15 minutes in that 1951 Ford that I had. I honestly believed that the crowd would give up on me sooner or later so I took the time to shower up and put on my Sunday-go-to-meetings suit so that I was all dressed up for that party. The problem was, was that those devout fans still hadn't given up on me.

Then, looking out of in a crack in the window of the dressing room, I could see a flickering light and noticed that it was raining quite hard. I saw about 50 or 60 people outside in the muddy parking lot and they were building a massive bonfire only about 20 feet away from my Ford! These people were actually pulling chairs and benches out of that Quonset hut and lighting them up. All the while they were screaming in Spanish for me to come outside. Now I kept a gun in the trunk of my car back then, but it wasn't doing me any good in that dressing room. A lot of wrestlers carried guns in Texas in those days in case of holdups or situations like the one that I was in. I thought that if I could just get to that gun, I could fire it up in the air and maybe scatter them, or I could just get in my car and get my hindquarters out of Dodge.

There was no way that I was going to leave out the front door and get jumped by 60 tequila drinking Mexicans so I turned off the lights in the dressing room and climbed out of the window leaving my wrestling gear behind. I saw people looking in my direction while I was climbing out, but they must have been so drunk that they didn't notice me. I hit the ground and got on all fours. The parking lot was a mud pit. I then crawled on my stomach commando style to my car. I reached the driver's side of the car but for some reason the door wouldn't open.

Maybe somebody had damaged the lock while trying to jimmy it or my keys may have just been covered in dirt. I turned the key in the lock, but the door just wouldn't open. I had to crawl on the ground again to the other side of the car in the hopes that I would have better luck opening the passenger side door. The violent mob was only 20 feet away from me and if that door didn't open and I got caught, I would have been a dead man.

I crawled under the car filling my good Sunday-go-to-meetings-suit with mud to try to get the other side door of the car. The mud went down my shirt and down into my underpants and having wet mud in your skivvies is not a good feeling to say the least. When I got to the other side of the car, I somehow knew that that door wasn't going to open, but to my surprise it did. The law of averages was actually with me. The light inside the car came on and I quickly reached to the button in the door and pressed it to turn it back off before anybody noticed me getting into the car. I scooted my mud-covered body across the bench seat, getting mud everywhere, which really had me mad because I used to baby that car. There I was trashing my best suit and my front seat just trying to escape from that place.

I wiped the key off and I shoved it into the ignition. I heard the sound of the engine turning over and I felt good. I rolled down the window and I screamed out a bunch of swear words using my limited Spanish vocabulary. I put the car in neutral and shoved it into gear expecting to take off and started to smile but I was stuck in the mud. The wheels just turned and the mob rushed up behind me. The fans grabbed flaming boards from the bonfire and started hitting the back of my windshield and the side of my car with them.

I had to get out of there before they put me on the bar-b-q. I shifted the car from drive to reverse, moving it forwards and backwards attempting to get traction on the back tires to get out of there. The crowd kept on hitting my car with those broken up pieces of flaming furniture. Although they put some cracks in my windows, they weren't able to shove anything through them. When I started to take off, I heard a thud. I don't know if I hit a couple of guys on the way out but the noise that I heard didn't sound like the sound of one of those boards hitting my car. They weren't taking any prisoners and neither was I. I slowly started to roll out and I gassed it when I got to the hard part of the street. Luckily, it was a standard practice among wrestlers to fill up the gas tank in any town you went to before you left so if you had to get out of a town in a hurry you didn't need to stop for gas. I took off towards Amarillo and I saw car lights behind me for miles and miles. It looked like some of the fans had taken off after me, but I just put the floored that thing until they just disappeared. To this day, I don't know what happened to anybody in that parking lot, but when I went back to that town a couple of weeks later, nothing was said about it so I assume that no one was hurt too badly.

When I finally got to my girlfriend's house I knocked on the door and she answered it. She was in a yellow dress and her hair all done up in ringlets. That was the style at the time and she was very gorgeous. My suit was covered in mud and she said, "What happened to you?"

A couple of the newspaper guys were there who used to cover the wrestling and they started to tease me for being covered in mud and she went along with it. I grabbed her and took her into the shower and left the door open in case anybody wanted to watch. I hosed us both off and the hairstyle that she must have worked on all day started to fall out and her hair became straight and stringy. When I got out of the shower, I was still in my suit like a crazy man and I was dripping all over her house. I looked at the news guys and said, "Who's next? Who wants to take a shower with 'Judo' Gene?" Nobody volunteered and we spent the rest of the evening having a party and I was in a sopping wet and muddy suit.

Another territory that I worked in was Hawaii and it was Vic Christy who first got me booked there. Looking back at it I think that Vic brought me over there just to play more jokes on me. One day, Vic called me up and said, "I'm very close to the promoter out here. I'll get you booked in Hawaii. You'll be a big star there because judo's very popular." Vic then told me that he was going to pick me up at the airport but that was very unusual because promoters usually didn't want the wrestlers to be seen together in public because you never could tell who your next opponent was going to be.

I went there with a girl that I really dug. I was a young man and I was head over heels in love with this gal. I wanted to marry her and the whole bit. But what did I know? How smart can you be when you're only 23 years old? But now that I'm older and shooting for 100 I can't really say that I've gotten any smarter with age – maybe only better looking. I have always believed (even back then) that you have to go away with a person to get to know their real personality. Before I went with her she smoked and drank but she quit smoking and drinking because I didn't like cigarettes and I didn't like booze. When we arrived, Vic met us at the airport wearing a huge Mexican sombrero and a garish Hawaiian shirt.

"Won't the promoter get mad if he finds out that we were seen together in public?" I asked.

"Nobody will notice me in this outfit," he promised. After we got out of the airport, he said, "I'm going to take you to the movies tonight."

We got to the theatre a little bit early and we were waiting in line. "Can't you just walk into the movie?" I asked. I wasn't exactly the most patient guy in the world when I was a young man.

"No you have to wait until the movie is over and we'll all walk in together after the ushers have finished cleaning the place up," Vic told me. The line went halfway around the block we were right at the front of the line.

"You're my guests here so I will buy." Vic told my girl and I. He then went and bought the tickets while we held our place in line.

"I wouldn't wait in line," I said making small talk with my date while we waited for Vic to come back with the tickets. "No movie is that interesting to me." Vic came back and the line finally started to move but when it did, Vic put his arm around my girlfriend. He reached out and he only gave two tickets to the usher. I started to walk in the usher asked me for my ticket.

"That man over there had my ticket," I said pointing to Vic.

The usher then asked Vic if he had my ticket and Vic said, "I've never seen this guy before in my life. This haole." Haole is the Hawaiian word for Caucasians or mainland Americans and it isn't usually given as a compliment.

The usher made me go to the end of that long line to buy a ticket while Vic walked right in with my girlfriend. I was hot under the collar. He really got me! He was all dressed up with his Rolex watch and everything and she was going along with him. I bought a ticket and then went to the end of the line. I had to wait and wait until I finally got in. The theatre was packed and I don't even remember what movie it was because I was so mad. I found a seat a couple of rows behind them. He put his arm around my girlfriend and then he turned around and waved to me.

"Hi Gene," he said "It's good to see you here. Great movie, huh?" He then turned back around and started kissing my date on the ear and on the neck. I was hot and jealous and I didn't know what to do.

The movie finally ended and we all started to file out through the exits. The theatre was this beautiful Hawaiian styled movie palace in Waikiki. There was a garden courtyard at the theatre as you walked out and it had a big pond with these big gold koi fish imported from Japan swimming around in it. The pond was about three feet deep.

Vic stopped me on my way out and asked me how I enjoyed the movie.

"Vic," I said, "it was great."

Vic then dug a coin out of his pocket and asked my date if she wanted to make a wish. He stood over that pond for a second like he was thinking of something. Then he turned to me, offered me a coin and said, "Excuse me Gene, did you want to make a wish too?"

"Not a wish," I answered, "but a hope."

"What's a hope?" Vic asked.

"A hope is," I said as I stepped in closer to him, "I hope you can swim!"

I picked Vic up and slammed him into the pond where all of the koi were. All of the moviegoers were walking out at the same time and there was a big splash when Vic hit the water and just about everyone got wet.

Vic started to get up out of the pond while people were still filing out of the theatre. Everyone had stopped and they were watching us to see what would happen next.

"Don't get mad at me," Vic said in an effeminate voice while spitting water out of his mouth. "I love you. I'll never go out with another man. You're the one I love. You're the mahu that I love."

I had no idea what a mahu was, but I found later that it was the Hawaiian word for homosexual. Vic was giving me a real Hawaiian lesson that day.

An old woman passed us by and said, "Oh, he's one of them…"

"I love you Gene!" Vic yelled. "Gene LeBell! You're the best lover I've ever had! I will never look at another man as long as I live!"

People made their way out of the theatre with disgusted looks on their faces and they were just trying to get away from us. I couldn't take it anymore and I was trying to duck down and get out of the place. "I've got to get out of here!" I told my girlfriend. "Don't you see what he's doing?" She did but she was too busy laughing her butt off. She thought that this was funnier than a pig in slop.

I took her hand and started to run down the street with a sopping wet Vic Christy chasing us and dripping all the way. "I love you Gene!" he screamed over and over again so that everybody could hear. "Please don't get mad at me!" I couldn't get away from him fast enough. Since I prided myself on being a straight young man, I had never been so embarrassed before or since, but embarrassing me seemed to be Vic's life's work.

Vic had eight wives before he was 40 years of age, but he never even had a chance to pay any of them alimony because he played such big practical jokes on them that they just wanted to get away from him as fast as possible. They never left a forwarding address even for the checks.

Now Vic's brother Ted, as we already know, was a similar practical joker and he also had a lot of wives. He had suspected that one of his wives was cheating on him for a while so he followed her to this guy's house and she stayed there all night. He must have been hiding across the street from the house or something because he saw her walk out of the house the next morning and kiss the other man good-bye. She then headed back for her and Ted's home and Ted took off and got there really fast to beat her there. When Ted got home he got into bed and made it look like he had been there all along. When she walked into the bedroom she gave him some kind of funny story that she had had trouble with this and trouble with that. "You must be tired," he told her, "Why don't you just go to bed." She took Ted's advice and when she was sound asleep, Ted pulled back the covers, squatted down over her and defecated right on her face. You know, I think that might be one of the reasons that they got divorced.

The thing about both Vic and Ted was that nothing would embarrass them no matter what they did or what was done to them. They never gave a second thought to the consequences of their actions.

When I wrestled in Hawaii, I stayed at the Honolulu Biltmore, which was right on the beach. It was a class hotel and the manager was a wrestling fan so Vic was able to get us rooms for four dollars a day, which was so cheap for that place that it was like stealing. About four days into this wrestling tour of the islands, Vic got into the elevator wearing nothing but a jockstrap. His butt was hanging out for everyone to see and he kept on telling people that he was Gene LeBell. When the elevator doors opened, he struck this Charles Atlas pose and said, "I'm Gene LeBell the professional wrestler as seen on TV!" All the while other hotel guests got on and off of the elevator. He said that over and over again while practically naked in these absurd muscle man poses until almost everyone in that hotel had seen him. Before you knew it, people started saying, "What's with this Gene LeBell?" Vic had everybody in Hawaii thinking that I was some kind of crazed exhibitionist before too long.

One of the wrestlers that Vic had a lot of trouble with was Crippler Karl Davis. Karl Davis had a mean temper and a foul manner in and out of the ring and he wouldn't think twice about turning over a table in a restaurant if he thought that his steak was overcooked. Turning over tables and busting up furniture was his way of telling the waiter to take back the food back. One time on the road, Vic was in The Crippler's car and he kept on needling him. Vic kept on calling Crippler his chauffer. "Turn to the right. Turn to the left. Go Faster! Slow Down," Vic commanded.

Karl told Vic to shut up or else he would stab him to shut him up, but Vic was never one to heed warnings. Vic kept at it and Karl turned around and jammed a knife about three inches into Vic's thigh. The Crippler pulled the blade out and blood sprayed all over the inside of his car. Vic looked down at his bloody leg and said, "Does this mean that you don't love me anymore?"

For a while, some of the wrestlers were living in a hotel with a swimming pool. Karl Davis was at the pool and Vic came out of his room into the pool area wearing a real nice suit. Now Vic usually wore Hawaiian shirts so it was unusual to see him all decked out like that especially just to take a stroll by the pool. He walked by the Crippler and they both started to get into it. They were both pretty big guys. Vic was 6'5" and so was Karl Davis. Things got kind of heated and Karl said, "I'm going to beat the hell out of you and drown you in the pool!"

"You wouldn't touch me because I'm wearing such a beautiful suit," Vic said, but Davis just picked him up and dumped him right in the drink. Vic didn't put up any resistance and just let Crippler Karl Davis toss him in the pool.

Vic got out of the pool and was soaked to the bone and looked right at Karl and said, "You shouldn't have done it."

"Why not? You deserved it and I'd do it again!!!" Davis replied.

"Because I'm wearing your suit," Vic answered.

The last time that I worked on the same card with Vic Christy, somebody plugged up the drain in the dressing room as a joke and turned on all of the water faucets and the showers so that the locker rooms were completely flooded. We had to get dressed with the floors covered in six to eight inches of water. Vic stood on a bench and took his pants off. Of course I naturally assumed that Vic had done it. While he was wrestling his match, I tied one of his pant legs in a knot. When he came back, he went to put his pants on and he slipped and fell in the water and got all wet. Now Vic had thought that this other wrestler, Joe Blanchard (Tully Blanchard's father) had done it so they both started to slug it out in eight inches of water. A couple of the other guys there knew that I had tied up Vic's pant leg, but I don't think that anybody there told him that it was me because they liked to see swerves as much as anybody. Vic played so many jokes on so many people that I doubt that he could have ever figured out who had pulled a particular swerve on him. Just about every wrestler that he worked with owed him payback ten times over because you could get one over on Vic, but you could never get one up on him. You might tag him with a snowball every now and then, but he would come back and hit you with a boulder.

Now all of Vic and Ted's ribbing and practical jokes loosened me up and taught me how to enjoy life for what it is. When I started in wrestling, I thought only of championship gold and being the next Lou Thesz, but after Vic had gotten through with me, I started to enjoy myself a bit after the wrestling cards were over.

Although wrestling was my life and my love, some of my wives were definitely in the top ten. I am on good terms with all of my ex-wives, but either I outgrew them or they outgrew me. I would say that mostly they outgrew me. I have had some good times with my wives and some good times with some of my girlfriends. I have been to Mecca and played with the Gods and a few wild women. When you don't drink or smoke you've got to have some bad habits.

My first wife was Olga and it was a very short-lived marriage as we were both very young at the time that we tied the knot. Although that marriage didn't last long, Olga did give me my son David in the short time that we were together. Today David is a skilled stuntman and a pretty good actor. David is blessed with a photographic memory and he can just glance at a page of a script once and then recite it like he has gone over his lines all day. I wish that I had that ability.

My second wife was Joyce. The first time that I introduced Joyce to my mother it was at my mom's office and my mother was scaling the house for a big fight at Wrigley Field in Los Angeles. Now this wasn't the place that the Cubs play at in Chicago, but they used to have a big outdoor coliseum in LA called Wrigley Field as well. Scaling the house meant adding more seats to the venue to up the profit margins while not breaking any building or fire codes. What my mother didn't know was that Joyce worked for the state as a drafting consultant and she had over 200 people working under her. Joyce possessed an amazing talent for drawing up plans and she was also an incredible artist and cartoonist. Joyce kept on looking over my mother's shoulder at the plans while my mother was on the phone with this 250-dollar a day professional drafts-man. Joyce then asked my mom if she could look at the plans for a second and my mother looked very unhappy about it like she thought that Joyce might have been overstepping her bounds and trying to work her way into the fight game or something. Joyce looked over the floor plans while my mother sighed impatiently. After Joyce was done, we went back to her place where she had a drafting table and all of the right tools for the job. Joyce then spent a couple of hours scaling the house. She worked really fast and put the new floor plan into this machine that converted writing paper into blueprints.

She then rolled up the new plans and put them into a tube and we went back to my mom's house. I handed my mom the blueprints and said, "Why don't you take a look and see if this is anything near what you had in mind for the seating at Wrigley Field." My mother pulled out the plans and them across a big table and put ashtrays on each corner to hold them down. At first my mother was just trying to be polite to us and you could tell that she didn't think that the plans that Joyce had drawn up would amount to much.

My mother ran her finger along the blueprints and said, "Hey these perfect." She then tried to cut Joyce a 250-dollar check for the job but Joyce wouldn't hear of it. Joyce was a wonderful lady and after that my mother really warmed up to her. My mother liked people that were workaholics and respected people with vocations that took a bit of brainwork. Joyce and I were very much in love at that time and she even took a break from her important job and risked her safety to accompany me on a wrestling tour of Texas where the fans literally wanted me dead.

As for Vic Christy, he became afflicted with cancer in his later years. He used to live about one mile away from me and he would call me in the middle of the night to help him back up when he had fallen out of bed. His leg was black from his knee on down and it was so sad to see such a strong man and great wrestler unable to pick himself back up off of the floor. Throughout his whole life, Vic made a joke out of everything and his illness was no different. The Screen Actor's Guild has a nursing home and I did everything that I could to get Vic in there but it wasn't easy. It helped that Vic had a couple of movie credits to his name so I had something to work with. After a bunch of phone calls and trips to the doctor's office, I finally helped get him in and it made me feel really good like I had done something right. Vic wanted some pins and a picture of my wife Midge and I so he could hang it up in his hospital room and show it to everybody. We never did get it to him because he passed away the next day on October 25, 1995. Vic Christy played a lot of jokes on me and got me in more than my fair share of trouble but he did a lot of nice things for me too and I wouldn't be where I am today without him.

CHAPTER 8

THE POLICEMAN

There used to be a position in the old days of professional wrestling called the policeman, but it wasn't a job where you carried a badge. Sometimes blowhards in the audience started shouting that wrestling was fake and phony, predetermined and scripted and it was the job of the policeman to show them otherwise. The policeman was wrestling's enforcer and it was a job that always went to somebody who could really wrestle or hook like Lou Thesz or Karl Gotch. When those guys in the audience got a little too cute or loud with their running commentary, somebody like Thesz or Gotch would challenge them to get into the ring so that they could feel how phony professional wrestling really was. When these wannabe tough guys entered the ring with the policeman, professional wrestling became all too real for them – sometimes real enough to land them in the hospital. Thesz and Gotch were two of the men who taught me how to use the tools of their brutal trade and those tools were heel hooks, leg locks, chokeholds and neck cranks. I could never be quite the policeman that those two giants of pro wrestling were, but from time to time I was called upon to fill that unique position.

To say the very least, the job of the policeman wasn't an easy one. There was a really good wrestler named Tim Woods who wrestled under a mask using the name of Mr. Wrestling. One time, Woods was taking on challengers out of the audience and actually got his finger bitten off during a fight with a particularly vicious brawler. Woods was an NCAA national collegiate wrestling champion and he could handle just about anybody on the mat. The problem was that his coaches never taught him how to cheat in the sport of amateur wrestling. Lou Thesz taught me that if you didn't cheat, then you weren't trying hard enough. "If you draw your sword," Thesz instructed, "then you had better put it back with the other guy's blood on it."

Because of Lou's tutelage, I only played with a guy if I knew that he was a complete jabroni (somebody who couldn't tie his own shoes).

If I even suspected that a guy was going to give me the slightest bit of competition, then I was going to hurt him and hurt him good. If somebody challenged Lou Thesz, he made sure that he ended up with a dislocated hip or shoulder for his trouble. Lou wanted me to protect wrestling and to make sure that any challengers that I faced walked out of a fight with me with a Tasmanian twitch. "If you don't hurt him and you just beat him," Thesz said, "he'll tell the story a year or two later and he will make it sound like it was an even match. You have to leave some hurt on him so that he remembers what really happened."

The policeman wasn't only there to handle amateurs out of the audience – he was also there to keep the boys in the backrooms in check. Sometimes, certain professional wrestlers went into business for themselves and tried to edge their way up higher on the card despite the wishes of the bookers and the promoters. When this happened, the policeman also came into play.

An example of this occurred when my good friend Freddie Blassie, who was the Pacific Coast Champion at the time, was scheduled to go up against this wrestler named Bearcat Wright. Wright was a 6'6" African American man and he weighed in at 300 pounds. He was very strong and was a big drawing card with the African American fans but he had a reputation behind the scenes for being completely crazy. A week before Freddie's big match with Bearcat Wright, Blassie came down with appendicitis and had to have his appendix taken out. Just about anybody else would have canceled their match right then and there, and nobody would have held it against them, but Freddie was (and is) a class act and didn't want to hurt the arena or the promotion. "I have to wrestle," he told me in his dressing room before the match, "it's a big house."

"You're crazy," I replied," Bearcat has a reputation for being nuts. He's going to hit you right where you just had your appendix out. He's that way. He'll hurt you."

Freddie wasn't swayed by any of this. He was a professional in every sense of the word and he wasn't going to let the fans down whether they were paying their money to boo him or to cheer him on. Freddie drew pretty well when he was a fan favorite, but he was even more popular when he was a villain and he insulted the audience. Knowing that Freddie couldn't be persuaded against going on with the match, I gave him a kneepad to put over the spot in his abdomen where the surgeons had just removed his appendix. The stitches were still there and it wasn't going to take very much to bust them wide open.

After Blassie and Bearcat stepped into the ring and the bell rang, the first thing that Bearcat did was punch Freddie right there in the appendix. Blassie went down throwing up blood and he had to be taken to the hospital. Freddie was one of our biggest draws and he was laid up over a month because of what Bearcat did. This caused a lot of problems with the booking office to say the least and attendance suffered throughout the territory while Blassie was on the disabled list.

A few days later, Cal Eaton and Jules Strongbow booked Bearcat Wright with this German wrestler named Fritz Von Goering at Valley Gardens (which was in Southern California but it isn't there anymore). The promotion put out some publicity that Bearcat hurt Freddie on purpose and that he said was the world's toughest wrestler and that he could hurt anybody. Goering got in the ring with Bearcat, but he jumped out right after the bell rang and I got in instead to see how good Wright really was and hopefully dish out a little bit of payback for what the man had done to Freddie. Wright wasn't supposed to be afraid of anything, but he knew who I was and what I was there for so he got out of the ring and took off running. I only weighed about 190 pounds back then so you would have thought that Bearcat should have been able to just beat me up, but he ran anyway. Jules Strongbow and my stepfather had told me what to do but they never bothered to tell any of the police or security what was going to happen. When I took off after that big wrestler, fourteen police officers pulled me off and held me back while Bearcat ran to his car. I shook loose of the police and I ran out to the parking lot as Wright was getting into his car. Bearcat stopped and pulled out the biggest switchblade knife that I had ever seen in all of my life – it must have been a foot long.

"Gene," He said holding up his blade, "I don't have a beef with you."

"You hurt Freddie," I said, "If you think you can wrestle come on up and take your shot."

Bearcat shook his head and said, "I'm on my way to Texas." He disappeared and that was it. He left town and turned up wrestling in Texas, which made both Blassie and the booking office very happy.

It was only a couple of years later however when my brother Mike was running the booking office with Jules Strongbow that he decided to bring back Bearcat Wright without even a second thought about what he had done to Freddie. Mike told me that Bearcat was a big draw with the African American fans and that was the reason that they were bringing him back. It wasn't like Blassie was just somebody that we had worked with either. Freddie was practically family to all of us. I should have known right then and there that the only thing that my brother was ever concerned with was a cheap buck. Mike could have found some other black wrestler to build into a draw, but that might have taken a little bit of work. Mike didn't even take into account all of the potential gates that Wright had ruined by putting Freddie back in the hospital either. Nothing could stand in the way of Mike and business – even if it was bad business. Sure, Bearcat Wright might have brought in a few fans here and there, but it was only a matter of time before he did something stupid to drive them away again.

Back in the late 1950s, not too long after I had turned pro, I was wrestling in Portland, Oregon and I got this call from this promoter out in Texas named Doc Sarpolis. His promotion was having a lot of trouble with the local chapter of the Air Force judo team. This group of judo men had been showing up at Sarpolis' shows and saying that wrestling was fake and that they could take any of the wrestlers. Since I was a two-time national judo champion as well as a professional wrestler, Doc Sarpolis tracked me down to see if I could help him out with that judo team.

I told him that I could and I agreed to take on the job and fly out to Texas. They gave me a double guarantee for a week. It was arranged that I was going to wrestle the Air Force judo team's champion, but when he entered the ring on the night of our match I grabbed the ring microphone and said, "I don't want to wrestle him. I want to wrestle the whole team one at a time so get the hell out of the ring." I made a big deal out of it and strutted to and fro the way that a villain would. For whatever reason, the crowd's sympathies were with the local servicemen out of the audience so I was booed pretty heavily. Those Texans were already starting to hate me, which was a good thing. In professional wrestling, you want the fans to either love you or hate you. You have to decide whether you are going to be an Indian or a chief and I definitely wanted to be the latter.

Somebody on the Air Force judo team, whether it was a coach or one of the players, had to know me by reputation at that point, but they had all believed that I had gone crazy, which worked to my advantage. There was a pretty big crowd there to see me take on the judo team's champ, but when word got out that I was going to take on the entire judo team the very next week, it was a sold out house. Before the contest began, I got on the microphone again and said that I was going to annihilate, mutilate and assassinate every last member of that judo team and that packed house really booed me then.

I had all twenty guys on that judo team line up and I took them on one at a time. It was actually a common practice in judo for a good black belt to take on a whole class one at a time in that manner and they called it a slaughter line. This was nothing that I hadn't experienced with a group of judo players before, but the difference was that to me, the wrestling ring was my house. Now you could divide in the ring into four parts with one corner being the living room, the other being the bedroom, the third corner being the kitchen (where it can get pretty hot). This meant that the fourth corner had to be the bathroom, but we really shouldn't get into that here. The long and the short of it was that I had home field advantage in that squared circle and that judo team was going to fight me on my home turf under my rules.

When the contest began, I threw them around, played around with them and arm barred some of them, and choked some of them out. I made use of a lot of knee locks, neck cranks and other moves that weren't legal in kodokan judo but were perfectly fine in professional wrestling. Any thought of AAU or kodokan rules went out the window when they stepped through those ring ropes. I was on top of my game that night and I was a lot heavier then when I went into the nationals so it was easy pickings for me and I dispatched of the members of that team one by one.

After the whole affair was over, I got on the microphone again while the audience was still focusing their full attention on me. "Do you know why it was so easy to beat these clowns?" I said throwing the question out to the crowd. "I beat them because I'm from California and they're from Texas and anyone knows that any one Californian can beat any 10 Texans!"

That audience went nuts and just about everyone there wanted to get into that wrestling ring to get a piece of me. I then got down on my knees and I said, "I'll challenge anybody and I'll give them 100 dollars if they can beat me and they're from Texas and 50 dollars if they're not from Texas."

I insulted the crowd and said, "The reason that you people are so stupid is because they get the school teachers in Texas from the Norwalk Crazy School in California!"

The crowd was incensed over what I was saying about the Lone Star State. In pro wrestling they call getting that kind of reaction getting heat and I was sure getting it whatever you wanted to call it.

"The reason that you can see so far on a clear day when you're walking down the street in Texas," I continued, "is because all of the women are so bow legged that you can see a mile right through their legs!"

There must have been a line of big Texas cowboys lining up for the chance to earn that 100 dollars for beating the tar out of me. Things were going so well as far as paid attendance was concerned that Doc Sarpolis decided to continue to have me take challengers out of the audience after I had already beaten the Air Force judo team. The next week, Sarpolis had a folding table and two chairs set up in the middle of the ring with a pen in a penholder and two contracts on top for somebody from the crowd and me to sign. Three or four guys crowded into the ring ready to sign that contract to fight me. "No, no, no," I said on the microphone. "I only take on one challenger a week because I don't want to hurt too many people the same night! If I wrestled a thousand of you Texans a day, pretty soon there would be nothing but desert here!" The audience hated my arrogance, but the real reason that I only wanted to take on one opponent a night was so that I wouldn't run out of challengers too quickly and we could make this gimmick last for weeks. Doc Sarpolis was a promoter who was nuts for gimmicks so we had a good thing going there.

After only one guy was left in the ring, we sat down to sign the contracts, but then I looked at him and stood up and tore up the contract and threw the pieces of it right in his face. "This guy isn't from Texas!" I said grabbing the ring microphone. "I can tell that he's from Chicago! His driver's license is a phony! It has a woman's picture on it!"

The audience at the arena booed me even harder than they ever had before at that point. The guy from the audience, with his big cowboy hat and cowboy boots on and obviously from Texas, then got up and chased me around the ring a little. I just jumped out through the ropes and stalled for time to garner even more of a negative reaction. It wasn't a match at that point. It was just a teaser to build up the gate even more the next week.

"Now I will fight you right now for fifty bucks," I said on the microphone, "but there's no way that I'm giving you 100 because you're not from Texas!"

Of course the guy was from Texas so he wanted that hundred bucks. "To fight me for hundred bucks you have to bring in ten witnesses that can prove that you are from Texas," I told him. Of course the next week, the guy came and brought twenty of his pals and they all paid admission. Soon it just pyramided as his friends told their friends and more and more people started showing up in the hopes that they would get to see their buddy beat me up.

I was never worried about taking on unknown challengers out of the audience because I knew everybody who was really good in the United States at that time. I knew all of the great wrestlers who could hook you and I trained under a lot of them and I knew all of the martial artists who could have given me a run for my money. There is no way that even the toughest Texan could beat a trained wrestler who was skilled in submission holds.

When the payoff match finally took place, the arena was filled to capacity. I got in the ring with this big cowboy and he tore of his hat and shirt and then flexed his muscles at me and chased me around the ring. I let him chase me for a while because I didn't want to end things too quickly. I still wanted more fans to get out that audience thinking that they could beat me because this was turning out to be a real drawing card. It was hot and I wanted to keep it going.

Finally after I had let my unschooled opponent chase me around the ring to build up anticipation, I turned around and grabbed him and threw him down on the mat. I rode him for a bit and let him back up to make the match last a little longer, and then I choked him out. Once he was fast asleep, I sat on the man's chest and blew kisses to the audience to make them mad. Then I started to go through the guy's pants and found his wallet and I pulled out some dollar bills and put them into my trunks. I then took out his pictures and said; "Now here's a picture of my wife and my girlfriend!" I tried to get a laugh out the crowd at that point but nobody in that arena was laughing because they just hated me so much. Finally, after I had played with him enough, I revived him and he started to leave the ring while the crowd was screaming at him that I still had his money.

At that point, one of the wrestlers from the back room that Sarpolis was building up named Dory Funk, Sr. came out and grabbed me, pulled down my trunks and took the money away from me and give it back to the guy from the audience that I had just fought.

"No, it's mine, it's mine, it's mine!" I said but then Funk body slammed me and I took a fall for him to make him a super star good guy and make another match between me and the good guy we had just built up that would draw a big crowd the next week. Every sport is a form of entertainment, and there is always some showmanship involved in it even when a match is a contest. We kept on building this up with challengers out of the audience and then we would continue it by having me fight one of the pro wrestlers at the end of it all.

To further cement my reputation as a top drawing pro wrestling bad guy, I found out that I could get even more heat by drinking from the colored drinking fountains at the arenas that I wrestled in. Texas was heavily segregated in the 1950s and they still had the white drinking fountains and the colored drinking fountains. During a card in Amarillo, I was doing an interview on the ring mic and I stopped in mid sentence and went and took a drink from the colored drinking fountain. The audience had followed me and they were shocked by what I had just done. I then ran back into the ring and got back on the microphone and said, "I'm going to win because I drank water from the chosen peoples' fountain of youth!" The African Americans all had to sit in the upper deck and I went up there and hugged the black women, which was completely unheard of. I was a main eventer by that point but my matches had to go on early because the crowds that I drew were one third black and they had to get back to their side of town before their curfew. Black people had to be back on their side of town by 9pm or else some of the local white, good ol' boys would beat them up or maybe even kill them.

Now I have never had a prejudiced bone in my body and it was strange to me that all of the whites in the audience thought that I was the antichrist and showed up to the matches to hate me and see me get beaten while the blacks came to cheer me on. I was a villain to the majority of the fans there, but maybe I was on the right side of history with that little piece of wrestling shtick.

"They either have to love you or hate you and here they hate you," Doc Sarpolis said looking down his glasses at me. "I even hate you because I'm a prejudiced son of a bitch. I hate those niggers, but you know the only thing better than hating those niggers is having a sellout."

By that time, I had married Joyce and she had taken time off from her job as a planner and accompanied me to Texas. She wanted to come to the wrestling matches to be with me. This would have been okay if I was good guy, but I wasn't. I may have been the most hated wrestler in that territory at that time and those fans got pretty violent. "Fans" (well they were fans of somebody I guess but they weren't fans of mine) kept attempting to stab me during my wrestling matches. There was one bout with Dory Funk, Sr. where we were fighting outside of the ring. He was really trying to hit me and I was really trying to hit him. All of a sudden he said, "Duck!" As I ducked some guy had tried to stab me with a knife and Dory knocked the guy out. I turned around and the guy was out cold and with his other hand, Dory punched me. He saved my butt from having knife holes in it, but Dory wasn't always there to take the heat for me and I got cut about five or six times with different knives. I had to have few stitches here and there and bled pretty good some of those times, but that is what comes with the territory.

Joyce was gorgeous and she always dressed up in gloves and gowns to go out so people paid attention to her. If anyone sitting at ringside found out that she was my wife, then they would have gone after her to get to me. The fans were different back then. I really cared about her and I didn't want her to get hurt. Sarpolis even tried to get me to use Joyce as a tag team partner because in Texas at the time they had a man and a woman form a tag team and go up against other male/female teams. Joyce told me that she liked the idea, but she wasn't a wrestler. That promoter didn't care whether she got hurt or not, and I did and I didn't want her coming to the wrestling matches any more.

I was also under more pressure than usual at that time because I had two weeks until I was going to wrestle Pat O'Connor for the National Wrestling Alliance World Heavyweight Championship. The NWA belt was the most prestigious wrestling championship in the United States and possibly the whole world. The belt that I was going to fight O'Connor for was the same one that was held by my idol Lou Thesz and more recently it has been around the waist of more contemporary greats such as Harley Race, Ric Flair, and Terry Funk. This was the chance that I had been working and waiting for since I had first laced up a pair of wrestling boots. Your whole life you want screen credits. You want to be recognized among your peers. I desired to be the heir apparent to Lou Thesz and to do that, I needed to win the NWA heavyweight title. Wrestling for that belt was like performing at Carnegie Hall for me. It meant prestige. It meant money. It was the top of the line for me and I couldn't be distracted by worrying about Joyce's safety. Joyce and I even stayed at different locations in the days leading up to my world title shot, which put a heavy strain on our marriage.

But the championship was on the line and I felt that I had to do it.

My match wasn't going to be easy because Pat O'Connor was a tough New Zealander and he was a very talented wrestler. You didn't win the NWA title if you didn't have those credentials. The National Wrestling Alliance wouldn't even let you into to the ring with their world champ unless you could apply finishing holds with the best of them. Only real grapplers and wrestlers earned title shots back then and my reputation as being somebody who could really wrestle coupled with the houses that I was drawing by taking challengers out of the audience was why I was honored by the booking committee with a title shot.

Our match was scheduled for San Angelo, Texas. Dick Hutton, who was a former world champion himself as well as a former NCAA amateur wrestling titlist, was the referee for the big match. The bout was a tough one from the opening bell. O'Connor liked to show people that he was a good wrestler so he attempted to put me in every finishing hold in his arsenal and there were a lot of them. I had to fight for my life in there and it took every bit of grappling skill that I had to ward off his attacks. Sometimes the audience doesn't realize what they are looking at or appreciate what they are seeing when they are watching a wrestling match and there was definitely a very serious story being told in the ring that night during our match. Pat O'Connor had some great moves and he was using them all but finally I had a chance to lock in my chokehold and worked it into a pin.

I had won. I won the National Wrestling Alliance World Heavyweight Championship! Dick Hutton handed me the belt. It was the same belt that I had seen around the waist of Lou Thesz. I held up that strap of world title gold and I got excited. I kicked O'Connor while he was down for good measure and security got in the ring along with the Texas State Athletic Commissioner. I was so elated with my victory that I started to swing the belt over my head like a crazy man. The belt was about 17 pounds and it had sharp edges and diamonds on it and I absent-mindedly tagged that commissioner right across the forehead with it. The commissioner fell out of the ring and onto the TV commentator. He had a big gash across his head and ended up having to have several stitches for it.

The commissioner then got on the microphone and said, "As athletic commissioner for this state, I am holding up the championship belt. I am suspending Gene LeBell!"

That was it. My world title reign had lasted all of 12 seconds. I was nothing more than a 12-second champ and I had to get out of that ring and get the hell out of Texas. There wasn't going to be a paycheck waiting for me in that state anytime soon and, for some unknown reason, I never got another shot at the NWA World Heavyweight Championship. I wonder why? Could it have been something that I had done? I wonder.

After my match and my short-lived title reign were over, I couldn't wait to get back and see my wife Joyce. It had been over two weeks since I had laid eyes upon her and I was worried that she might have packed up her bags and left me. She was mad at me because I wouldn't take her to the matches and business always comes first. I went to the house where we lived while we were in Texas. I got there and knocked on the door but there was no answer. I wanted to leave her a note so I turned the doorknob and let myself in. The house was really dark with only the light from the big Texas moon streaming in from the windows. I could see that she pictures of her with some guy around the living room and on the fireplace mantle but it was so dim that I couldn't tell who it was. Could she have found somebody else? I hesitated to go into the bedroom because I was afraid that I might go into the room that we had once shared and find her laying next to another man. I summoned up my courage and opened the bedroom door to find her on the bed, alone and crying.

I sat down on a corner of the bed and asked her if those pictures in the living room and on the fireplace were of her new boyfriend. She nodded a yes and wiped the tears away from her eyes. It turned out that those pictures that were making me so jealous were of me all along. I gave her a hug and a kiss and we got back together like nothing had ever been wrong between us.

We packed up our bags and quickly returned to California, but things quickly took a turn for the worst. We were only back a couple of days and Joyce came down with encephalitis meningitis and collapsed. She was rushed to the hospital but she died almost instantly. She didn't have time to deteriorate and she was gone almost as soon as she had gotten sick. She was very young and she traveled with me when I was wrestling. I had depended on her and she had depended on me. We had only been married a little over nine months but now she was gone. I had lost my love.

She was a devout catholic and the family had an open casket at her funeral. I have always hated funerals and I usually stand in the back of them because I want to remember somebody how they were when they were alive and not when they are dead. I wanted so badly for her to get up and tell me that everything was going to be okay. It was like a bad dream that I could never wake up from.

It was over a year before I look at another woman again. Every time that I saw a woman who fixed her hair the way that she did or walked like her or wore gloves like she did, I just stared at them. I didn't mean to be rude but I couldn't help myself. I gazed at them steadily hoping that it would be her – that she was still alive and everything had been nothing more than a nightmare after all. There was a young woman that came into my dojo and signed up for judo lessons. Something about her reminded me of Joyce and I just stared at her like I had done with all of the others. I didn't even know that I was doing it and I hoped that I didn't give her any wrong ideas. She understood everything once I explained it to her. We still exchange Christmas cards with each other to this day.

Despite the tragedy of losing Joyce, my life soon returned to normal because it had to. I had to move on. I started wrestling at the Olympic Auditorium again and at almost every show I saw this attractive woman in the front row with her one-year old son Danny. I always wondered why she was bringing such a young baby to the matches. I inevitably got to know her and I found that her name was Elinor. I couldn't remember her name. She was less than five feet tall so I called her Midget. Years later I dubbed her Midge and still years after that, Midgo.

CHAPTER 9

ENTER THE STUNTMAN

Ozzie Nelson was the producer, star and director of the hit family sitcom "The Adventures of Ozzie and Harriet" on ABC. He was producing a show that focused on his son Ricky Nelson who was rapidly becoming as big a star in his own right not only on television but also as a rock and roll singer. There was fight scene with Ricky Nelson in this particular show and Jack Alaina ran the stunts on it. Jack was a former UCLA All-American football player and he placed second in the amateur wrestling nationals one year. I knew him from professional wrestling where I showed him some hooks and finishing holds that they don't teach you in collegiate wrestling and he was greatly appreciative so he hired me for that fight scene in "Ozzie and Harriet."

In those early days of television the Ozzie and Harriet show was probably as big a deal as "Friends" is today. It was a big hit and everybody watched it so it gave me another hat to wear by launching my career in television and motion pictures. Ozzie Nelson was a very nice fellow. He even put a pad against the wall when Ricky Nelson had to shove my head against it. I told him that he didn't need to put that pad there and that I could take it, but he did anyway. Everyone on that show was very nice to me.

I earned my Screen Actors' Guild (SAG) "A Card" from doing that show which was a pretty big deal because you can't work on major studio motion picture or network television shows in the United States without being in SAG. You could work on independent films without being a member, but with those you don't earn retirement, are uninsured, and there is no guarantee that you will even be paid. As a member of SAG you earn retirement and have health insurance and after 1960 you earned residual payments on shows that you had worked on when they aired on television or were shown in theatres. Now if you worked on a non-union show while being a member of SAG, you could be thrown out of the union and your benefits and residuals could be jeopardized so as my friend and fellow Guild member Glenn Hiraoka always says: "It pays to work union."

Wrestling came first but pro wrestling has no retirement and if you got hurt in the ring you were out selling pencils on the street corner. In acting and stunts if you got hurt you had insurance and a lot of good benefits. Despite my usual ignorance, I was somehow smart enough to see the value in all of this and I juggled my various careers. I took the movie and stunt jobs when I was in town and turned them down if I was booked in a big match or was going to be out on the road wrestling.

I did a lot of unusual things back in those days, but the strangest was probably wrestling the bear. Tuffy Truesdell owned this 900-pound Canadian black bear named Victor and they (Tuffy and the bear) barn-stormed around the sportsman shows and wrestling cards. Victor even went against a professional wrestler in the under card of my champi-onship bout with Pat O'Connor in Texas. At those sportsman shows the bear took on all challengers. Tuffy offered a thousand bucks to anyone who could beat his bear and make him give up. Now that may sound like a lot of money and a pretty good offer to you but the catch was that you just didn't beat a 900-pound black bear unless he let you. The rea-son the owner never had to pay the money out is because the bear was great at wrestling and he couldn't speak English so he could never say, "I give up."

If Victor knew you, he just rolled with you. I used to train with the bear back when I was preparing for the judo nationals. When you have a 900-pound bear on you and you work your way out from underneath him, a 230-pound man becomes easy pickings by comparison. You just don't move a bear the way that you could an ordinary man. Bears have great balance. I used to wrestle with Victor with and without his muz-zle. At the sportsman shows, he wore a muzzle because he had a ten-dency to grab a guy with his teeth. When I wrestled Victor without the muzzle, there would be blood all over the place and every last ounce of it was mine, but I knew that deep down inside, Victor loved me.

Those bears were strong. When they grabbed you and pulled your hands in, you just couldn't stop them. On top of that, Victor was a very smart bear and he knew some cues. The tougher you were with the bear, the harder he was on you. When he wrestled kids, he just played with them and never hurt them, but if a man came and grabbed him hard, that was Victor's cue. When guys clamped a tight headlock on Victor, he just smashed them and smashed them hard. Tuffy always encouraged all of those would-be challengers to grab Victor really strong. "Get him in a headlock," Truesdell advised the crowds, "and he'll just fall right over." Of course, all of the pro wrestlers who earned a couple of extra bucks tussling with the bear on various kinds of shows knew better.

One time, I was wrestling the bear at a sportsman show and I had this buddy of mine named Bob with me who was a real egomaniac. He saw me wrestle Victor for a little while and of course, Victor liked me so he rolled around with me a bit. You could say that Victor was making me look good so that made my buddy think that bear wrestling was easy. "I saw you wrestle that bear," he told me, "and I know that I could throw him just like you did."

He was really arrogant about it so I said, "Be my guest, but remember to hold him really tight when you grab him around the head."

At the sportsman shows, they just had a cage and some mats over cement for the bear to wrestle in. When you hit the ground, you felt it. Bob grabbed Victor really hard just like I told him to, and that bear just picked him up several feet in the air and threw him so far that he missed the mat. Bob hit that cement with a thud and you could just hear his ribs crack. It was wonderful. I had this camera but I cried so hard from the laughter that the salt in my eyes blurred my vision and I couldn't focus the lens. I took about 20 shots and only two of them came out because I was laughing so hard. I was in hysterics as I was watching Victor crush that guy but Truesdell had had enough. "We've got to get the bear off of him," Tuffy said, "He's hurt!"

"So what," I said, "You listen to the tune and you pay the fiddler." That might sound a little bit sadistic but you don't go into another man's backyard, play by his rules and expect to win. Finally we coached Victor off of Bob with a bottle of Coke which was pretty hard for me to do because I was splitting a gut laughing so hard you know. Tuffy the trainer didn't laugh. He said, "Gene, you are a sadist."

"Well that doesn't make me a loser," I joked.

Not too long after I had worked on "The Adventures of Ozzie & Harriet" I got a call from Jules Strongbow in the wrestling booking office about working with George Reeves who played "Superman" on television and was a real superstar. TV stars made a good living back then, but they didn't make the millions of dollars per episode that they pull in today, so they often booked public appearance tours to earn some extra money when their shows weren't being filmed. They wanted a wrestler to play the evil villain "Mr. Kryptonite" (who came from the same planet as Superman and possessed the same powers as he did) on a string of public appearances with Reeves.

When I went down to the audition, there were a lot of people there trying for the chance to get tossed around by the man of steel. It turned out that George Reeves had taken some judo lessons, which worked to my advantage. He had a certain enthusiasm for the sport that I appreciated. He saw me at the audition and said, "I want to throw you." I was skinny, and a little bit of a tumbler, so I went six feet up in the air. I then bounced with a bit of comic timing. I bounced around three times and then I sprang to my knees and waved my hands and started begging for mercy. "Please sir!" I exclaimed. "No more! Mercy! I've got a wife and seven kids!"

Reeves took one look at me and he went outside the door and said, "Don't have anybody else come in. This guy's got the job."

Everybody that you meet in this world changes your life. If I talk to you for five minutes, I have taken five minutes off of your life that you'll never get back but it might improve it. The only thing that it costs you to talk to people is time and after walking this Earth maybe 104 years (nobody really knows for sure), I have found that in life all you have is time. Of course some people change your life for the better and some change it for the worse. I have been very fortunate in life to have met several people that have profoundly changed my life for the better. My judo teacher Larry Coughran was one of them and so were Babe McCoy in boxing, Vic Christy and Lou Thesz in professional wrestling and too many people to mention in acting and stunts (although I am going to try before this book is over). My mother had probably the greatest impact on my life out of all of them, but I can also say that George Reeves is another individual that changed me forever. After picking me to play Mr. Kryptonite, he became like a mentor to me and really showed me the ropes in Hollywood. He did a lot for my movie career and gave me a lot of confidence. Because I had lost my dad so early in life, George Reeves also became a father figure to me.

The one thing that Reeves didn't like about playing Superman was wearing that costume. The Superman suit was made by Western Costume and each one that George had cost 300 dollars a piece to make which was an astronomical amount at that time. His outfit had these big shoulder pads in it and portions of it were made out of rubber. Reeves really didn't like changing in and out of that suit.

The Mr. Kryptonite get-up wasn't too big. It was supposed to fit somebody that weighed 170 pounds and I weighed 190 so it was pretty tight on me but George told me to wear it anyway. It was a black outfit made out of itchy wool with a big "K" for Kryptonite on the chest that was in the same style as Superman's "S." When I tried on the costume for the first time and showed it to George he said, "Now do you see why I don't like wearing these things?"

George had an agent that booked his tour and we traveled from town to town in three or four cars and we played a different city every night. We put on a full stage show and George, Noelle Neal who played Louis Lane on the TV show and I did a Superman routine and then after that, Reeves performed a set with his three-piece band. Our act consisted of me in the Mr. Kryptonite costume grabbing Noelle and playing the part of the villain. Then, George came out in his full Superman suit with the cape and everything and beat me up in spectacular way and rescued Louis once again. I took some pretty big falls for him and we made audiences think that he really could bend steel with his bare hands and leap tall buildings with a single bound.

People reacted differently to movie and TV stars back then and I could swear that to a lot of those crowds actually believed that they were seeing the real Superman and not an actor who played that character on TV. At one of George's public appearances, some kid somehow brought his dad's gun along and tried to shoot George to see if the bullets would actually bounce off of his chest. He fired a shot into the air, but somebody got to him before he had a chance to actually put a bullet in George.

Reeves was treated like he was a superstar back then and he turned around and treated us very well. I was paid a lot of money to. go on those tours and part of the reason was that George loved for me to teach him judo and wrestling. Whether we were on the road or at his home in Beverly Hills, George had mats set up so I could show him some take-downs and holds. I made more money than I should have and it was a lot of fun. When I was on the mats with George, he was always fooling around and he wanted nothing more than to make me give up when we wrestled. He always asked me to show him a hold that you couldn't escape from, but I was a little leery of letting him get me in a hold like that. George Reeves was a very strong man and he could have easily hurt me because he hadn't learned much control in applying finishing holds at that time.

Finally, one time when we were on the road, I broke down and showed him one of those escape-proof holds. The move that I showed him was a counter to a leg-scissors from behind. What you do to counter this is an over-scissors where, if he has his left leg on top of his right leg, you put your right leg on top of his left leg and and your left leg on top of your right leg which makes you scissor his legs. Once that hold is clamped in and you arch back, there is practically no way of get-ting out of it and you can snap your opponent's ankles with it in two seconds by applying just a little bit of pressure.

I showed it to Reeves and put it on him lightly so I wouldn't shat-ter both of his ankles and cripple my boss. "That hurts," he said and then he asked if he could do it to me.

"Are you going to do it easy?" I asked and he assured me that he would.

I got behind him and I was telling him how to do the move and he started putting the pressure on. "Let go," I said as a sharp pain shot through my ankles.

"Now I've got you," he said and he started putting more pressure on. My ankles were about ready to snap so I cranked his neck and I choked him from behind really quick like. I didn't have time to put him in a nice chokehold and put him to sleep so I had to use a crude bar arm, which crushed his larynx. George always wanted to be an opera singer and half of his act was him singing and playing guitar with his band. We had several dates left on that particular tour, but the musical portion of the show went out the window because there was no way that Superman was going to croon with a crushed larynx. The tour agent came in and George opened his mouth and nothing came out. George started laughing and tears were rolling down his cheeks, but his agent wasn't too amused. "You're ruining the whole show!" the agent shouted.

"I'm just having fun," George attempted to reply but his voice was all hoarse.

For a week he didn't have a voice and we were doing different towns every day. For the rest of that tour he couldn't sing anymore, but it didn't bother him. Nothing ever bothered George. If you saw him in "Gone With the Wind," he had a straight nose back then. After he had been in that movie, he was riding his motorcycle and smashed it into a dump truck and it busted his nose. If you notice his nose on the "Superman" show, it looks like he might have been a boxer, but that didn't bother him. Nothing bothered him. A crisis would come and he would say, "It comes and it goes." That's why I knew that when he was shot that he didn't kill himself although that's what's the official police reports said.

It was after 1am on June 16, 1959 when a buddy of mine called me and told me that he had heard on the radio that George had killed himself. George Reeves was the last man in the world that I thought would ever commit suicide. It just didn't add up so I drove over to his house as fast as I could. I knew that something was up when I saw that there were several police cars in his driveway. I ran through the big doors of his house and found a lot of policemen there. I made my way up past some of them and into the bedroom. I noticed a rug on the ground in a place that I had never seen it before and I said, "That rug doesn't belong there." I kicked it aside and there were five bullet holes in the floor, but the investigators didn't seem to care. I tried to talk to the police and they told me to get out of there or else they were going to throw me in jail.

To this day, I don't know why the police didn't really want to investigate the death of my friend George Reeves and why they were so quick to list it as a suicide. They never found powder burns on his hands, which should have been there if he had actually held the gun and shot himself with it. Whether or not the death of "Superman" George Reeves was due to suicide or foul play remains one of Hollywood's most enduring mysteries, but I have always had no doubt that he was murdered. Although I wasn't there at the time of his death, I have always had my suspicions as to who did it.

George had a live-in girlfriend named Lenore Lemmon and she used to drink quite heavily and she sometimes got violent. I was over at his place one time and we were working out in the front room on the mats and she stormed in and said, "George, quit working out. I want to talk to you." You could tell that she had had a few.

"No wait another half hour and I will be right with you," he said calmly.

"If you don't talk to me now I'm going to break this lamp!" she said while holding this antique lamp over her head that George had bought for her for $1,500. 1,500 dollars was all the money in the world back then and she was just going to throw a fit and toss that antique and watch it shatter into 1,500 pieces just to get her way.

George wanted me to continue with our lesson, but I was kind of nervous. "George, she's going to break that lamp," I said, but he didn't seem to care so I started to show him a hold. Lenore Lemmon slammed the lamp down with a crash and sure enough, it shattered into hundreds of little pieces. George didn't blink. He didn't even look up. He didn't do anything. She stomped off and we just kept working out.

"George, she broke the lamp, " I said.

He turned to me and said, "Yeah, so. If she wanted to do and it makes her happy, let her do it."

He would have given her 1500 dollars to burn with a match if it gave her pleasure. That wasn't what I would call common sense, but like I said, nothing bothered the man. "Why do you put up with that?" I asked him after one of her outbursts.

"Because I dig her," he said.

Lenore Lemmon was at George's house on the night that he died. She was the only person that the police had ever really questioned but they never followed up with her on anything and just seemed to take her word about what had happened at face value. A day or two after George's death, Lenore left California for Europe never to return again.

Over the years a lot of people have said that George was despondent over the cancellation of the "Superman" series, but that wasn't true. The show wasn't cancelled at all. George quit because he was sick of wearing that red and blue suit and there was even an option on doing another season of "Superman" being offered to him on top of that. At the time of his death, George was offered the lead in the TV western "Wagon Train," which ended up running forever and was a big hit. It was his big chance to shed the super hero image and he was going to take it. He also had a public appearance tour booked for Australia for the week after he died and we were all supposed to go and do our act. George may have hated putting on the cape and tights, but he loved doing those shows and performing in front of a live audience. George was going to start work on "Wagon Train" right after he returned from that tour but as it turned out, he never even made it to Australia.

George told me that I was going to play the cook on "Wagon Train" and become an actor instead of doing stunts. Now George had a good sense of humor. It was a little different and he was a little strange, but he meant what he said. If he gave you a promise, he kept it. When he told me that he was going to make me a TV star, he was probably right. Everything that he had done worked well for me.

Without George to guide my career and make me a TV sidekick on a popular western, I had to make my way in Hollywood as a stuntman, which is something that I have no complaints about. Sure, over the years I have thought about putting more into my acting career and giving up on stunts. You know a guy can get a little soar from crashing motorcycles. I knew a few directors and producers so I have thought that they might hire me as an actor and I wouldn't have to take falls but there has always been a reality check on my dramatic ambitions. I had a friend who was an actor and a good acting coach and he was telling me about a particularly good year that he had had. He told me that he had made "16."

I had to ask myself what he meant by "16." 16 million? No, this guy wasn't exactly Tom Cruise or anything. 16 hundred thousand? There's no such thing. It turned out that he had only made 16 thousand dollars in his "good year." At the time that he told me this, I had already pulled in 205 thousand dollars by being stuntman and the year wasn't even over yet. Now what the hell did I want to be an actor for? I'm a good stuntman and a lousy actor. I decided to stick with what I'm good at which I did. I didn't have the heart to tell my actor friend that I had made 205 thousand that year while he had only taken home "16."

When I first started doing stunts, four out of five of the jobs that I landed were just getting beaten up by some movie star, but as I met other stuntmen they taught me their specialties and I taught them mine. I would teach a guy a little bit of judo and wrestling and he would show me how to set myself on fire. I learned about fire gel and fire proof suits. I learned about nomax, which is a material that firemen use that looks like thermal underwear but it doesn't burn. People that know will teach you.

The more that you hang around the set, the more you will pick up the tricks of the trade. I learned high falls from Bob Yerkes who did a lot of the trapeze stunts in the old circus movies that they used to make. I got up on the trapeze and fell onto boxes and pads and everything else like that. You know you scratch each other's back and you learn everything that you can from everyone around you.

From the wrestling background I knew how to fall differently than many of the stunt guys who were mostly tumblers. Most of them were ten thousand times better than me as tumblers but they never got slammed down with authority the way that you would in pro wrestling or judo. In pro wrestling you really had to know how to distribute your weight. You don't come down like you're beautifying yourself. You are just trying to preserve your body you know what I mean? The wrestling helped me out a lot with the stunt work.

It also helped that when I was a kid I grew up riding motorcycles. I raced them. I did hill climbing with them. I was a little better than average, but I wasn't near what you would call really good. I was never good enough to be a professional. I was probably a little bit below that level, but from that I learned how to lay down a bike which really came in handy with the stunt work.

I spent a lot of time at motorcycle riding because riding bikes was a lot of fun, a challenge and a calculated risk but judo and wrestling were always my first love. Everybody has to have a crutch. Some people smoke cigarettes, some people drink and some people take dope. I get a high by getting my blood circulating and by putting a certain amount of either fear or energy into a situation. When I race a motorcycle around a track, if I don't stay focused, I will go off of the track and crash. That puts a certain amount of fear there, which enhances my coordination and makes it a challenge. I get a high when I go one-on-one against another man in martial arts, wrestling or boxing, but I also get high from racing bikes and doing stunts and wheelies on them. You can let other people have their drugs and booze or whatever kind of crutch that they need. I will take a good, fast Honda or Yamaha any day of the week.

In my own egomaniacal way, I thought that I was a good rider but then this kid named Gary Davis broke into the stunt business as a flat-packer doubling Evel Kneivel. He is arguably the best all-around motorcycle stuntman in all of Hollywood. He is phenomenal and made me look like an amateur at riding bikes. He's still a very good friend of mine and he taught me how to do wheelies standing on the seat and he taught me how to do slides and all sorts of hero stuff. I taught him some judo and the part that he liked the best was choking people unconscious and he liked to do that on the sets when he was running the stunts.

For over 40 years, I have been a member of the Stuntmen's Association of Motion Pictures, which is the largest stunt group in the United States. It was the first and the oldest stunt group but there's also a few outstanding stunt groups besides the Stunt Association such as Stunts Unlimited, Brand X, and ISA. There are also many great independent stunt people who are not in stunt groups who are also fantastic. We all exchange information, teach each other how to do things and help each other get jobs.

I remember the first time that I got tossed out of a car on a movie I asked one of the other stuntmen what he used for padding. The guy said, "Well you put on knee and elbow pads." They were soft. I put a wetsuit on and I went around a corner at 25 miles per hour and rolled out of this car and I didn't get hurt. The other guy looked like hamburger. The knee pads and elbow pads went up his arms and legs he got all cut up.

In stunts, I learned pretty quickly that you can't be casual. You've got to be cautious. Recently, one of the stunt guys took a look at me while I was suiting up to take a fall and said (and he was sort of teasing and knocking), "Hey when you go to the stunts you look like the Michelin Man." Now if I'm going to do a high fall, I'll put double padding on my knees and elbows. I might look 20 pounds heavier but I don't care. The guy that was making fun of me has been in and out of the hospital and has been carried away a lot of times but I've never have been carried away. I've had bruises and cracked ribs and a dislocated shoulder but nobody knew it when I left the set. I could walk away because I took the time to look like the Michelin Man when I went into the job. You don't tell people of your injuries in stunt work because nobody wants to hear about it. You don't want to put the idea in anyone's mind that you're hurt because then they might be passing you up for jobs for a long time to come.

While I was still mostly being tossed around by actors, I worked on a movie with Elvis Presley called "Blue Hawaii." In the movie, there's a barroom brawl scene where Elvis takes me down with a judo throw. When I was on the set working with Elvis, he was very respectful and almost subservient to all of the stuntmen. He treated me like I was rich and had a ten dollars in each pocket while we were going over that scene. Even though he was maybe the biggest superstar of all time, he was really just one of the guys. He didn't have any attitude. When we were done working on the fight scene, he gave all of the stuntmen crisp, 100-dollar bills. Nowadays when you do a stunt you come in on your basic pay and then you get extra for whatever stunt that you do like crashing a car, doing a fight scene, a high fall, fire, or repelling. Elvis gave everybody a hundred dollars and at that time our basic pay was only about a hundred dollars per day. Elvis was already getting into martial arts and taking kenpo karate from Ed Parker back then so he came into my school, but only once because he was very busy. He did some tumbling and worked out a bit and he was nothing but respectful.

Another guy that was really nice to work with was "Iron" Mike Mazurki. Mazurki was a famous pro wrestler and he turned to character acting and usually played big, lumbering henchmen in action thrillers. I mean he had the look and there was nobody better at what he did. He is probably best remembered for playing Moose Malloy in the Phillip Marlowe movie "Murder My Sweet" back in the 1940s. Mike also founded the Cauliflower Alley Club, which is a club for wrestlers that meets every year of which I am a member.

I first worked with Mike on a western called "4 for Texas" with Frank Sinatra and Dead Martin. Mike had to put his pro wrestling skills to work and bodyslam one of the bad guys during this one fight scene. He wanted to bodyslam me even though I was on his team so I had to change my wardrobe to be one of the bad guys. He bodyslammed me onto the ground, which I've done a million times so it didn't bother me a bit. After "Iron" Mike was done, the first assistant asked, "How did you like that Mike?"

"I didn't," he said, "Give this guy (me) an extra 300 dollars, and let's do it again."

Now I didn't think that there was anything wrong with that first bodyslam. I mean we were both pros and a bodyslam is a bodyslam, but they shot the thing again and he bodyslammed me for the second time.

The assistant asked him if he liked the second one and Mike told him that he didn't and he wanted to do it a third time. I was standing there scratching my head and I asked what was wrong with it and Mike barked, "Shut up kid!"

So he bodyslammed me for the third time and the first assistant came up to him and asked him how he liked that take.

"That was a lot better," Mike said, "Give the kid another $300."

"Mike, what didn't you like about the first two?" I asked.

He said, "Just don't worry about it and give me a box of those Havana cigars. Kid I've got to teach you how to make money in this business."

Another movie that I worked on with Mazurki was "7 Women" with Woody Strode. In the movie, they had planned this big fight scene using Mongolian wrestling. When one of the production people or the director or somebody asked about staging the scene, Mike Mazurki told them, "There's only one person in the world that knows Mongolian wrestling that speaks English and that's Gene LeBell."

So they called me up and made a big deal with me like I'm somebody important and asked if I knew Mongolian wrestling. I said, "I can do anything. I can wrestle with a broomstick and make it look good!" I thought that they were putting me on because Mike was a wrestler and liked to swerve you know. I got down to the soundstage and they had a special set with a wrestling ring in it. I had a whole week to train these guys on how to do Mongolian wrestling which wasn't going to be all that difficult because Mongolian wrestling is a lot like Greco-Roman wrestling. It's no big deal. I got on the set and said, "Well let's work out something."

Mike looked at me and said, "Wait a minute! Wait a minute! How long did they sign you up for?"

"One week," I answered.

"Okay, sit down," he told me. For the rest of that week, Mike sat in his bathrobe smoking those big, expensive cigars of his while Woody Strode was in the corner doing pushups. I tried to get them to work on the scene every morning that we reported to that set but Mike wasn't having it. Finally, about an hour or two before we went to shoot, I said, "Now?"

We worked out a routine that only took up about ten or fifteen seconds of screen time. It was nice, but it was quick. After we were done, Mike said, "Now kid remember Christmas."

"What about Christmas?" I asked.

"That's my birthday," he replied. "December 25th. I smoke Cuban cigars, but you knew that already." I never forgot that December 25th was his birthday and I got him yet another box of cigars.

"7 Women" bears the distinction of being the last film by director John Ford, and although I didn't really have much contact with the man, it is an honor to have worked with him. Woody Strode was a nice guy to work with. He told me about working with John Wayne and everything. He was an All-American football player at UCLA and he went into pro wrestling and didn't like it. He became an actor and did those spaghetti westerns in Europe and he did very well. John Wayne and John Ford both liked him and used him and Mike Mazurki in a lot of their movies along with people like Ward Bond.

Woody told me a story about working on "The Man Who Shot Liberty Valence" with Ford and Wayne. There is a scene at the end of the film where John Wayne dies and Woody was supposed to cry. Now he said, "I can't cry. I've spent my whole life being macho."

John Ford wasn't the kind of director that you said no to and he said, "You're going to cry before you leave the set." Sure enough, when those cameras started rolling, and Ford was sitting there in his director's chair staring at Woody, the big strongman started crying on cue.

I did a pro wrestling skit with Count Billy Varga on "The Jack Benny Show" back in 1960. Jack Benny was as popular a comedian as Billy Crystal or Jay Leno is today. As for Varga, I wrestled him more than my fair share of times over the years and he is a very good friend of mine. Varga is Hungarian and his father was the Greco-Roman World champ and he always wore his gold medal around his neck. They called him Count so he passed on countship to his son Billy.

"The Jack Benny Show" was filmed on a soundstage at Universal Studios and Benny played the referee. Varga and I were the wrestlers and we ended up throwing Benny out of the ring in that scene. In the next scene we're in the hospital with casts on and Benny looks over us and says, "I told you fellas, you shouldn't have gotten me mad."

Billy Varga's wife was the Countess Rosebud and she used to call me on the phone and we would talk all night. The Count told her to call me because he liked to go to bed at 9pm and he said, "Call Gene, he's always up late." I always had to interrupt our conversations to go downstairs to get something to drink so she bought me this little fridge for my office so that I wouldn't have to leave anymore. She made the Count come over and carry the fridge upstairs and I still have that fridge today.

One of the guys that beat me up a bunch of times was James Garner. He beat me up a lot on "The Rockford Files" but he started beating up way back on his first show "Maverick." You know I have a perfect record in movie fights: I'm 0-12,000. Sure, I have 12,000 losses but I have a perfect record. I have lost to just about every man in Hollywood and a lot of the women! But hey, that's my job as a stuntman. It's to make the movie star look good. I have made a lot more money in this business by losing fights than I ever could have by winning them.

The first time that I worked with Garner I wasn't really in a scene with him but I saw him. He was a superstar and I was a little bit intimidated. He was one of the most popular stars on television at the time. Now, I have never forced myself on anyone. I don't run up to people just because they are famous and say, "Hi I'm Joe Schlump the midget and you're James Garner and I love you." I don't go in for taking pictures with celebrities or getting their autographs and all that jazz.

A few weeks after I had first worked with Garner, I got a call for the same TV show. It was shot on the Warners lot and I saw Garner walking to the cafeteria and I was walking towards him. We're on the same road and you have to see each other so I was looking down. He must have noticed that I was trying to avoid making eye contact with him while I was walking past him so he snatched my arm and turned me around and he said, "Do you know who I am!?!"

"Y-Y-Y-Yes Mr. Garner," I said. I was startled to say the least.

He then stared at me hard for a minute and said, "No it's James!"

"Yes Mr. Garner, I mean James," I said as he turned around and walked away. It scared the heck out of me. I wanted to drop kick him into the nickel seats but I didn't dare. That would be a great of way to get drummed out of the movie business. Still, it left me scratching my head and I realized that he was a class guy.

Ever since then in the dojos, everybody calls you sensei or sifu or Mr. Lebell or master and I enjoy growling at them as I tell them, "It isn't Mr. LeBell, it isn't sensei, it's Gene! Can you remember that!?!" It's sort a way of letting people know that you're not playing God, and that you're an equal. People can feel free to talk to me. I'm a friend. I do a lot of teasing and I enjoy it. I think that also comes a lot from wrestlers because wrestlers put people on – on and off the mat. My best student Gokor the Armenian Assassin still calls me sensei but I really believe that's only because he can't remember my name.

CHAPTER 10

MUHAMMAD ALI
"I AM THE GREATEST"

When I was a young guy, I used to ride motorcycles. Actually, I still ride motorcycles and I know that I must have told you that I rode bikes at some point during this book already, but here I am telling you again. At my age that's one of the ways that you get sex. Anyway, the story that I was trying to get to is that I used to go by Bill Robinson's Honda in Hollywood. The grandfather who used to own the shop and died many years ago kind of liked me I guess because he was a wrestling fan. One time, he was telling me how a fella came in and bought a couple of motorcycles in a black suit and he wrote a check and took the bikes. They used to let you pay for motorcycles with a check back then. The checks bounced and Mr. Bill Robinson, Sr. called up the guy to complain about it and the guy with the rubber checks said, "The hell with you. I've got the motorcycles and possession's 90% of the law. You try to come over here and I'll blow your head off." The guy was acting like he was a real gangster or maybe he was.

I thought that I should do something for the Robinsons because they had always treated me nice at their dealership, but I couldn't figure out exactly what to do so I attained the counsel of none-other-than Freddie Blassie. In a situation like that there is really nobody better to call. I called up Freddie and asked him what to do. Freddie is one of the guys that changed my life and I got very close to him over the years – very close. Freddie gave me a little shtick to do so I went over to Bill Sr. and said, "Give me the address and let's see what I can do."

"I'll give you the address but they might shoot you," he told me.

"Well we'll see," I said, "but we'll be playing by my rules."

So I went over to this guy's house and I knocked on the door. I had a big box of wooden matches and I was lighting them and throwing them all over the place. He opened the door and I remember that he was a black haired guy and he said, "What do you want? What the hell do you think you're doing!?!"

I had these matches and I was lighting them and flinging them into the house. "I'm a pyromaniac," I said stuttering and stammering like I was a real halfwit. "Mr. Bill Robinson said I could burn your house down, but I want to go over by the curtains because the last house I burned down the curtains went up real quick like and had such wonderful colors."

"Get out of here!" he said as he tried to shut the door on me, but I had already stepped into the doorway.

I listened to him but I didn't pay attention. "You owe Mr. Robinson two thousand dollars and he wants it back," I said while lighting another match, "but you said bad things about him and he said I could burn your house down. I love Mr. Robinson and he gives me food when I'm hungry."

I was in his house and as I grabbed a hold of one of his curtains he said, "Get away from there."

"I'm going to start here and big flames will come up," I said continuing to pay no attention to him.

As I lit a match he screamed, "Don't! Don't!" He then went into the back room. He could have been going back there to get a gun for all I knew but I didn't have enough sense to quit while I was ahead and I was having big fun. He came out with a big wad of money that came to the $2,000 that he owed Bill Robinson Honda and he handed it to me. I put it in my pocket and cried out, "Does that mean I can't burn your house down? Mr. Robinson said that I could burn your house down!"

"Get the f—- out of here! You're crazy!" he said and slammed the door on me.

As I walked away I turned around and saw him looking through the window. I went back to Mr. Robinson and went into his office and told him, "Now you probably didn't say please when you asked that guy for the money that he owed you. I went there and said, 'Please give me two thousand dollars,' and he said, 'sure.'"

Of course this wasn't quite the story but I put this two thousand dollars down on Robinson's desk and I said, "here's your money."

He looked at the big roll of cash and said, "Anything you buy here is at cost forever. Absolute cost." That was years ago. I went downstairs a couple of days later and a new style of bike had come in. I only had a couple hundred dollars on me. I said, "Boy I would sure like this bike but it's too expensive. Maybe some day I'll be able to afford it."

Bill Robinson, Sr. asked me how much I had and I told him that I had about 200 bucks. He had a mallet in his hand sort of like the one that you would use for bodywork and he took it and hit the shiny new gas tank and put a dent in it. He then turned to one of the salesmen and said, "This bike is freight damaged. Sell it to this man 200 dollars."

I took the bike and one of the guys straightened out the gas tank and touched up the paint and in a couple of hours I had a brand new bike.

Since then, I have had a close relationship with all of the Robinsons who own Honda of Hollywood and Honda of North Hollywood. His son gave me the same deal that his father did and now the grandson does the same. I've bought hundreds of bikes from them and boats. One of my closest friends, Hugh Miller, manages North Hollywood Honda, which is their top grossing store. He comes to the dojo sometimes with his kids and I call it Miller Time. When I go in there I always tell him, "Miller Time, you're charging me too much."

"The grandfather is dead," he replies and then we both laugh.

This changed my life because I got all of these bikes for cost and I do a lot of public relations for the Robinsons (I always have) and I sell a lot of bikes to the movie studios and my friends.

In 1962, a young heavyweight boxer named Cassius Clay came to Los Angeles for a series of fights that were promoted by my mother Aileen Eaton. The first time that I saw Clay was in the 1960 Olympics in Rome where he won a gold medal. That made him a hero, but he was really no more famous than anyone else who wins at the Olympics. Of course we all know that Clay later changed his name to Muhammad Ali, caused a big uproar when he refused to be inducted into the service, and became, in my opinion, the greatest heavyweight champion of all time, but back then he was still a skinny kid with a little bit of charisma who needed some buildup. Now there was nobody better at building up a fighter than my mother Aileen Eaton and Clay's management must have known this when they brought their fighter to LA.

The first time that I met Ali, he was confident in his abilities as a boxer, but he was still very humble. He was one of the nicest, most polite kids that you could have met. Before his first fight at the Olympic Auditorium, my mother made him this big, clip on button that said, "I AM THE GREATEST." He was supposed to jog from the Olympic, which is on 18th St. to the Main St. Gym, which was on Third and my mother had made sure that there would be a lot of press there to cover it. It was about a two mile run. My mother handed him this button and he looked it over and said, "Mrs. Eaton, I'm sorry. I can't wear that. What will people say?"

"There's going to be a dozen guys taking pictures of you," my mother told him. "You're the Olympic Champion and we're going to get you a name so you draw something."

So he wore it because he was really too polite not too and he didn't want to upset his promoter. He just went along with what she wanted. After the response that he got from all of those sportswriters for wearing that button he started saying, "I'm the Greatest! I am the Greatest!" It became his tagline. It was what he was famous for and it was all from that big hero button that my mother had given him. She never gets credit for that but that's a true story. I was there.

Ali was also a big wrestling fan and he was a really big fan of Freddie Blassie but he always called Freddie Gorgeous George for some reason – I'll never understand why. I was the Celebrity Representative for the Olympic Auditorium back then, which was a big name for a simple gofer. Sometimes I had to drive fighters around and take runs to the State Athletic Commission or go to the printers and pick up posters and that sort of thing. Ali told me that he wanted to go see some professional wrestling so I took him to the studio where the wrestlers' interviews were being taped to see his hero Freddie Blassie. Ali just sat in the back and listened and he saw Freddie say, "I'll annihilate, mutilate, and assassinate that pencil necked geek!" When Clay saw the reaction from the fans when Freddie put everybody down, his eyes lit up. He told me that he wanted to be just like Freddie although he called him Gorgeous George.

I told him that he would have to be very good to be like Blassie because Freddie was such a good wrestler that he could insult anybody that he wanted to. Freddie got so much crowd-heat that the audience went out of their minds. Freddie was stabbed more times than he could remember his fans have even burned him with cigar butts and even acid.

Clay's first fight in Los Angeles was against George Logan at the Olympic and in the pre-fight interviews Ali started saying, "My opponent's a bore. I'm gonna' take him out in four!"

After hearing this, I said, "Cassius, you can't say something like that and knock the guy out in the first round. You've got to go four and then knock him out and I don't think that this guy can go four with you."

When Clay fought, I didn't know what he was going to do. Instead of blocking with his hands the conventional way, the young Cassius Clay just stepped out of the way. He didn't take a punch to land a punch like Rocky Marciano did. He was that fast. He was a different kind of heavyweight and he was more like a bantamweight or middleweight. During the fight, Ali played around and effortlessly moved around the ring. Logan took wild swings at him but never laid a glove on him. Ali threw a series of punches, but then backed off. You knew that he could finish Logan at anytime, but he didn't try to.

The fourth round came and bam, bam. Logan was down and 8, 9, 10 — he was out cold. After the fight, the TV interviewer asked Cassius about the fight and he said, "I told you the man's a bore, I couldn't stand him more than four!" A lot of people take credit for Ali's poetry, but he started making up all sorts of rhymes and predicting what round he was going to win the fight in here in Los Angles because of the influence of my mother and Freddie Blassie. You could tell that Clay/Ali had a little bit of show business in him, but it sure didn't hurt him to come to Hollywood to bring out that side of his personality.

Ali fought Billy Daniels and Alejandro Lovorante for my mother and she used those bouts to build him up as a draw in Los Angles before the big payoff match against Archie Moore. Archie Moore was a former light heavyweight champion of the world and one of the all-time greats. Archie was a powerhouse and he had big arms like a weightlifter. He blocked with his elbows in such a way that a lot of the fighters ended up hurting their hands trying to hit him. During sparring sessions at the Main St. Gym I saw him take good fighters and just knock them around the ring with the big gloves when he felt like it. Moore might have taken some punches when he fought, but he always caught up to his opponents and knocked them on their hindquarters with his heavy hands. Because of this, Moore was a ten to eight favorite to beat Ali.

I don't know if I should really say this but I bet a lot of money on Archie Moore on that fight. My mother would have skinned me alive if she knew that I was betting on fights at the Olympic because I worked there and it would look like the fights were fixed if the word got out that the promoter's son was gambling on boxing. But hey, I don't drink or smoke – a guy's got to have some vices. I heard Moore talk to the news media and he said that he was going to knock Clay's head off. I thought that I was going to get rich off of that fight and I placed the biggest bet that I ever had in my whole life. If I had lost that wager, I would have been working the next year for free. I had a lot of confidence in that fight.

About three days before the fight, Archie sat down to eat at this picnic table. There were a couple of people there at the table and I was sitting right across from him. I had a piece of meat and he had a piece of meat. Because he was training, he chewed his meat, swallowed the juice and then spit the meat out. I didn't say anything to him, but that made me lose my appetite. He told me that he swallowed the juice to get the nutrients without the bulk. While I was sitting with him, I really wanted to ask Archie about the fight with Ali because I had a bet on him, but I couldn't just come out and tell Moore that so I asked him what he thought of his opponent as a fighter. He looked at me and told me that Ali was going to be the champion of the world and that no one was going to beat him for years to come. I nearly fell out of my stool at that moment.

Now I couldn't place bets directly. I had to have somebody else do it for me because of my affiliation with the Olympic Auditorium. I couldn't cancel my previous bets either so I had to bet a lot of money the other way to try to balance out my original wager. I bet and I bet and I bet and I bet some more. I bet more money on Clay so if he won, I would come out ahead.

When the bell rang and the fight started, Ali moved around the ring the way that he always did, but Archie pressed the attack and won the first round. When the second round started, I thought that Archie could actually beat him, but then in the fourth round, Ali hit him with a blistering combination and knocked Moore down. Moore got up very slowly but he didn't make it time. The referee had counted him out. Ali was declared the winner and he jumped up and down as Archie made his way back to the showers.

Back in the locker room I asked Archie if he was all right. He looked at me and said, "You notice that I didn't get hurt."

Now I don't think that Archie Moore threw that fight or didn't try to win it. A guy like Archie Moore always tries to win almost out of instinct. Moore trained Ali early in his career and I think that Archie just believed that the young man named Clay was going to be one of the ones. Moore was 49 at the time that he fought Ali and he must have gotten the idea somewhere between the second and fourth rounds that he couldn't keep up with the 20 year old Clay.

Archie Moore's fight with Cassius Clay was to be his last, and the young Clay left Los Angeles well on his way to fighting Sonny Liston for the title. My path crossed with Ali's again later but that's another story.

But while I was watching one star on the rise in the early 1960s, I also had the displeasure of watching another one on the decline. I was wrestling in Oregon and Don Owens, the promoter out in Portland, asked who wanted to go up to Washington to wrestle Gorgeous George. I couldn't wait to get up there and wrestle George. I knew him back in the early days, but when I went up to wrestle him he looked old. His hair wasn't done up. He was well past his prime. It was the end of an era. I felt really bad because I remembered when I was in the coast guard and I had the opportunity to be his second and sprayed the perfume in the ring before he made his grand entrance. The audience was singing songs to him and he was a hero but it turned out that he was a mere mortal like the rest of us. Now everybody gets old, but when you dissipate the way that he did, it makes you appear older than your time.

When I was in college, he was the biggest exporter of broad-breasted bronze turkeys in the world. He had a big turkey ranch out in Chino, Calif. and he was quite successful, but as the years passed by and things went downhill, he ended up buying a bar on Sepulveda Blvd. in the San Fernando Valley. When I wrestled him in Washington, he told me that he had spent all of his money. He passed away a year after our match in 1963. He died completely broke and my mother ended up paying for his funeral.

Despite all of the distractions from movies and motorcycles and pro wrestling swerves, I was still very close to the world of judo in the 1960s. 1963 was the year that I defeated the boxer Milo Savage in the judo vs. boxing match and some of the martial arts magazines since then have said that that was "the day that Gene LeBell saved martial arts." Now that's a little too braggadocios for me. Believe me, martial arts would have kept on going whether I had beaten Savage or not. There were plenty of guys in the 1960s and into the 1970s like Ed Parker, Joe Lewis, "Superfoot" Bill Wallace, Bruce Lee, Chuck Norris, Jackie Chan and a few others that would have made martial arts continue to grow in popularity.

At the time that I fought Savage I was still expelled from Nanka Yudansha Kai (the Southern California Blackbelt Judo Association) because the group's president Kenneth Kuniyuki didn't like that I had become a professional wrestler. In his mind judo players remained amateurs and they didn't receive money for their matches. Now I've said it before, but that really hit me in the guts. It was like I was thrown out of my family. This meant that I wasn't welcomed at any of the Nanka schools. I wasn't allowed to train there but I was still a fanatic. I had my own school in Hollywood, but I still wanted to go to different dojos and exchange different techniques.

If you're in any sport, may it be judo or jiu-jitsu or tennis, there's always going to be politics. Almost every human interaction is somehow political. Everybody is jockeying for position. One judo man named Rene Zeelenberg ended up taking his AAU card that allows you to be in all of these tournaments and tore it up because of the politics of amateur judo. Zeelenberg was part of a five-man team from my judo school that I was the coach of. The elders of Nanka thought that our team was going to lose but they ended up beating everyone. It was obvious that our team would have won easily, but they disqualified citing some little technicality us to save face.

"I can't put up with all of these politics," Zeelenberg confided in me after that disqualification. He quit amateur judo because of all of the hurdles that were placed in front of him just to compete in a tournament. He then joined the Airforce and became the Airforce judo champ and did extremely well with the sport in the service. I saw him at a tournament recently, but I will always remember and respect him for doing what he thought was right.

Hal Sharp, who went to Japan with me as part of the American competition team in 1955, ran a Nanka school but invited me to come over to his dojo and work out anyway. "You could get your butt in a sling with Nanka," I said. "Are you sure you want to take the chance?"

"Nanka isn't making me any money," he replied. "I'll kick you out when they start paying my rent." Hal was and is a great judo man and an excellent teacher. He let me work out at his school because he is a class guy that is always in your corner. Hal told me to go and check out the Sun Valley Dojo to see if they would also allow me to train there.

I always carried a gi in my car and one day I passed by the Sun Valley Dojo and I had remembered what Hal had said. When I walked in all of the older Japanese teachers ignored me and it kind of made me want to leave but I stayed anyway. I can't really tell you why. I sat down as people were suiting up and getting ready to spar and this young Japanese kid came up to me and spoke to me in very broken English, "Gomenesai," he said, "are you going to randori? Are you going to get on the mat?" I thought that he must have been new there.

"My name is Gene LeBell and I'm blackballed from Nanka Udansha Kai," I said explaining the situation to him. I didn't want him to get into any trouble with his senseis for sparring with me.

"You mean you cannot get on the mat?" He asked clearly puzzled.

"I was in Japan with you and I worked out with you at the Kodokan and you showed me some nice moves." I didn't remember working out with him but at that moment I wished that I had. Then he pointed to a picture on the dojo wall and said, "See that picture on the wall? Who is it?"

I said, "Jigoro Kano," while looking at the portrait of the founder of kodokan judo that hung in every Japanese judo school in the world.

"Would Jigoro Kano ban you from getting on the mat?" the young Japanese judo player asked me. I got choked up when he said that. I was really touched. I told him that Jigoro Kano wouldn't ban me from getting on the mat and then he ordered me to quickly get changed, which I did.

Sun Valley Dojo was a big school and right then its students started to filter in. Many of the people who trained there came from San Fernando and the dojo in San Fernando was one of the schools that wouldn't let me work out there. I was pretty rough with a lot of the San Fernando students at Sun Valley but I was extremely nice to the little guy because he invited me onto the mat. I also wrestled some of the 10-year olds and took big falls for them to show everybody that I wasn't some kind of a bully.

Every week he had me come back to train. "You are my sensei," he said, "You are welcomed here any time. I need your help to train." He ended up winning the nationals in the 130-pound class. He was very good and I was very proud of him because he was one of the good guys. I invited everybody that I could from Sun Valley or any of the other Nanka schools to come to my school in Hollywood and train for free. It was very nice and I taught a lot of good students and met a lot of great friends that way.

Because of the politics, a number of the Japanese schools broke away from Nanka Udansha Kai and formed another group called the Reimei, which literally means splinter group. The Reimei was made up of high-ranking men who disagreed with Nanka's way of thinking. I think that there were ten schools that broke away from Nanka and joined the Reimei. At first, there were certain tournaments that we weren't allowed to enter because we were considered the bad guys.

Finally, after about eight years and a lot of public relations we had a six-man tournament team made up of competitors of various belt rankings and we were allowed to enter the nationals and I was their coach. But even after being allowed to compete in the AAU judo nationals, the people running the tournament refused to recognize our team's belt rankings. They made our brown belts and black belts wear white belts because we weren't sanctioned but our white belts did extremely well and ended up placing in the finals, which made their black and brown belts look really bad.

In the 1965 AAU Judo Nationals, there was one local Japanese-American man who trained at Kuniyuki's Seinan Dojo and he received his black belt in Japan, but he sneaked out to my school in Hollywood and trained with me every afternoon. His name is Hayward Nishioka and he is one of the best students that I have ever had. He won his weight division and the overall class in 1965 and after the tournament was over there was a big press conference there. In front of all of the newsmen, Kuniyuki said, "This is Hayward Nishioka and he's my student."

Hayward is what you would call a little bit of a rebel and he has a strong sense of fairness. "Yes, I do work out at his school," Hayward said, "but I work out five days a week with Gene LeBell in the afternoon and Gene is my teacher. I won because of Gene LeBell and nobody else."

After that Hayward continued to train at my school and he went on to win the nationals in 1966 and 1970 as well as the gold medal in judo in the Pan-Am Games. He became the captain of my judo team that never lost and he has coached the US Olympic Judo team as well. Today he is a physical education professor and judo instructor and Los Angeles City College and has written many best-selling sport judo books, which I highly recommend. In my book "Gene LeBell's Grappling World: The Encyclopedia of Finishing Holds" if you look up "Hayward Nishioka" in the glossary it says: "Excelling all others: the best you can be. (If you are called a Hayward Nishioka you are the best of the best and it's a compliment)." It is a little bit tongue and cheek but it is my way of thanking him for being in my corner all of those years ago. In the judo community a lot of people who have read my book tell each other, "oh you're a real Hayward Nishioka," which means that you are a good guy and someone to be admired.

CHAPTER 11

TICKLES AND TACKLES

I got a call from a stunt man named Benny Dobbins telling me that he needed me to take some falls on a half-hour superhero show that he was the stunt coordinator on called "The Green Hornet." The show was a spin-off from the "Batman" series with Adam West, which I had worked on a couple of times so I told him that I would do it. When I got to the set Dobbins told me about this guy named Bruce Lee who was playing the chauffeur and was very athletic and was stealing all of the fight scenes from the show's lead because he was doing every last bit of the fighting. Actually it turned out that Grant Williams, who played the Green Hornet didn't like to mix it up. After all, he was an actor and not a fighter and all Bruce was doing was taking advantage of the situation so he did all of the fighting because that was his thing. If you notice on that show, Bruce did all of the fights and he became the man that the audience was waiting to see because he would beat up two or three guys at a time and do all of those kung-fu moves. "You won't believe this guy," Benny told me, "he kicks like a jumping bean!" You have to remember that nobody had ever seen anything like Bruce Lee's fighting style in show business back then.

When I got to the set Benny pointed Bruce out and told me to go put him in a headlock or something. Well, I'm a good employee and I always listen to the boss, so I went over to grab Bruce and he started making all those crazy noises that he became famous for. He didn't expect me to pick him up, but I did as a joke. He weighed about 130 pounds and I weighed in at 190 so I put him on my shoulders in a fireman's carry and then I ran down the length of the set and back again. "Put me down or I'll kill you," he screamed at me.

"I can't put you down or you'll kill me," I said as I ran down the set again. I held him there for as long as I dared to and then I put him down and said, "Hey Bruce, don't kill me. Just kidding champ." The stunt guys all had a good laugh over it and went on to shoot our scenes.

Bruce called me for a few TV shows because he liked the way that

I took falls for him. Being a judo man made me pretty good at break-falls. We ended up becoming friends and worked out together and taught each other techniques. I liked working out with Bruce, but I kept getting sick from that incense that he burned in his gym because of my allergies. I told that him I wouldn't go there because his dojo smelled worse than a Chinese laundry house. Of course, I was only kidding with him, and once Bruce learned that my teasing was all in good fun he started to loosen up.

Bruce trained with me for about a year. He had a unique personality and he liked to work out alone. This is just the way that I read him. He didn't like anybody to know that he was learning anything. He wanted people to think that he was born being an encyclopedia of the martial arts, but whatever it was that he did, it must have worked for him. Bruce Lee is more popular today than he was when he was alive. If they could release "Enter the Dragon 2," it would be a smash hit and that would probably make Bob Wall, who played the villain in "Enter the Dragon" as happy as a pig in slop because he loves money.

Bruce loved to learn grappling. He really ate it up but he didn't believe that it would work in the movies. "You can't use any of those moves in movies," he said. "You know you get a guy down and get them in a hold that the audience can't see. They want to see everything standing up." He told me that they want to see fancy kicking, acrobatics and weapons.

"What happens when you get in a fight?" I countered. "Nine out of ten fights if it goes anywhere end up on the ground."

"Not in my movies they don't," he said. Bruce was a savvy show-man who knew how to give them exactly what they wanted, but he didn't believe that wrestling would sell in movies and on television. I wish he could be around today to see that WWE Professional Wrestling is one of the biggest things on TV and grappling is doing pretty well in the martial arts too. All that being said, if you look at his movies, he still finishes some of his fights with grappling moves. He ended his fight with Chuck Norris in "Return of the Dragon" with a standing guillotine choke and I seem to remember him using an armbar on Samo Hung in "Enter the Dragon." Bruce managed to slip a bit of grappling in here and there. As for Chuck, he's so gosh darned modest that you'll never hear it from him but he is a great grappler and I think that he could have beaten Bruce Lee without the help of his "Walker Texas Ranger" badge.

One time Bruce and I were training, Bruce kicked me really hard. I remember thinking that it was a good thing that he only wore a size 6 shoe instead of a 14 like me, otherwise that kick would have sent over the Great Wall of China. He was not only strong for his size but nobody was faster. I loved that man.

He used to take me to these authentic Chinese restaurants that had really weird looking food that I just couldn't bring myself to eat. I don't eat anything that doesn't have horns. He used to tease me about it - which was progress because he used to get offended at my ribbing when we first started hanging out (especially that Chinese laundry bit).

He had two students that I remain good friends with to this day, probably because they don't make me eat that weird food. Danny Inosanto, who is every bit as good as Bruce was if not better, and Richard Bustillo. Richard has carried on Bruce's philosophy of cross training and peak physical condition in order to become the best fighter that you can. Gokor Chivichyan and I still give grappling seminars at Richard Bustillo's dojo every year. The main reason that I do this for Bustillo is that he gives me free t-shirts with his name on it and I wear them with pride.

In the mid-1960s there was this show called "Honey West" which starred Anne Francis as a lady private eye who beat up the bad guys using judo and karate. Sharon Lucas doubled Anne Francis and in my opinion she was the best stunt gal of all time. Anne Francis was and still is one of the most beautiful women to walk the Earth and I was lucky enough to be picked to train her in all of the tickles and tackles and judo moves for the show. When I worked on "Honey West" she was all dressed up and everything and I didn't know her. I was very much of an introvert I guess and she came up to me and kissed me in front of everybody and I told her that I would never wash my face again. I washed my hands but not my face. Every man that met Anne Francis couldn't help but fall in love with her.

More recently Anne told me how she used some of the self-defense techniques that I had taught her for "Honey West" to protect herself when some creep was following her in a deserted parking garage. She turned around and got into a defensive position and her would-be attacker turned tail and ran back up the stairs to whatever hole he crawled out of.

Another show that I worked on around the time that I worked with Bruce and Anne was "The Wild Wild West." It starred Robert Conrad and Ross Martin as two secret agents who fought super villains back in the old west and the show was known for having a lot of fight scenes. It gave a lot of work to stunt guys.

That Ross fella was a good actor. He used to put on all of this makeup and played all of these different parts with different dialects. He did something that you remembered. He later had a heart attack and died when he wasn't all that old which was a shame because he was one of the nice guys.

I beat Ross Martin up in one of the "Wild, Wild West" shows and then Robert Conrad was supposed to toss me down a flight of stairs. As a stunt guy, you get extra money for each stunt that you do. You come in on basic pay then you get extra money for what they call gags. You know tickles and tackles where you take on extra calculated risks. So Conrad was about to save his buddy and throw me down the stairs but I played a deaf mute. A guy named Virgil Vogel was the director. He's one of those guys that always promised to make me a star. He was a good director but he never made me a star. We were about to film the scene and somebody from the tower came down, which meant some muckety-muck from the network or the studio or whatever, and said that you weren't allowed to beat up someone who had some kind of handicap or disorder on television. It was a standards and practices thing or it was against FCC regulations or something. They had already filmed scenes that established my character as being a deaf-mute so they wouldn't beat me up and I lost my bonus pay. Anybody who was handicapped had to be a good guy, but I had always played bad guys so that was kind of a stretch.

Robert Conrad was a little bit of a fanatic at boxing and he had a ring set up at the studios where they shot "Wild Wild West" where he used to spar with guys. He liked fighters and he had a lot of pugs (which is short for pugilist) working on his show. He wanted to have an amateur fight at the Olympic Auditorium. We were having amateur fighters for the first couple of fights back then and when it got on TV, they put the pros on for the top of the card. Conrad was a popular TV star then, so we would have put his amateur fight on the air and it probably would have drawn a pretty good rating too as well as a good crowd at the arena. Unfortunately he was too busy with his shows so that fight never came off.

One of the fighters that Conrad had working on his show was Tommy Huff. Tommy was a solid fighter. He wasn't destined to be a world champion or anything but he could box. One night when Tommy was fighting at the Olympic, I went to the dressing room to talk to the fighters and managers a bit. Doctor Bernard Schwartz was our staff physician. When he wasn't giving physicals to the boxers, he took care of all of the older minorities and fight people. He charged only five dollars cash for doctor visits but he never charged anyone who couldn't afford to pay. He saved many lives and he was a good guy.

That night, Huff was going up against this undefeated black fighter (I don't remember his name) that they were going to build up. Tommy Huff had ten wins and a draw, but he just wasn't up to his opponent's caliber. The other guy should have knocked Huff out easily because they were a different quality of fighter. I kind of liked Tommy but he was preparing to get his hindquarters beat. The matchmaker put him in tough.

I went into the dressing room and the guy that Huff was going to fight was throwing up and he had diarrhea and a 104 temperature. Doctor Schwartz told the boxer that he was too sick to box, but the fighter believed that he could beat Huff so he went on with the fight. I saw all of this so I decided to place a bet on Tommy. I mean his opponent could barely stand and it was going to be a six round fight. When I left the dressing room, Huff's opponent was a six to one favorite but nobody was even really laying odds on that fight so the best that I could get was three to one – three thousand of their dollars against one thousand of mine. Huff's opponent didn't get knocked out but Tommy won a one-sided decision and I took home a lot of money.

I ran into Tommy a week later on the set of "The Wild Wild West" and he told me that Bob Conrad had made him a movie stunt man. I told him that I had won three thousand dollars on him. He thought that I was kidding.

"Nobody bets that kind of money on preliminary fighters," he said.

"Yeah but I kind of like you," I told him. It was a couple of years later that I told Tommy the story and he believed me. That fight was Tommy Huff's last and he became a fulltime stuntman and he did quite well at it. He's still active today and he lives happily with his wife Robin.

I have a cabin up in Pine Mountain, California, which is about 75 miles from my home in Los Angeles. I have a lot of stunt guys and movie people over there and we ride motorcycles up the hills and mountains and generally have a lot of fun trying to kill each other. I have my stuntman buddy Gary Davis up there from time to time and he is as good a bike rider as you're ever going to see. Burt Reynolds and Roddy Piper have also both been up to the cabin to ride motorcycles. A lot of other stars have come up too but when they're at the cabin they're all just one of the guys.

Another friend of mine that went up to the cabin with me was the "Wheelie King" Doug Demokos. He went 68 miles one time doing a wheelie on a Harley and he would have made it farther but he had a flat tire. He taught me a hell of a lot about bike riding, but he died in a hang-gliding accident. Sometimes the good die young. He was a lot younger than I was, but his legacy of motorcycle riding lives on.

One time, I was at the cabin and Gary Davis and a few other guys were there and we were riding our bikes up the mountain. I had a big hill climber and I was riding up the hill with a guy named Randy Halls on the back of my bike. The bike was a 720cc Yamaha single and they don't go that big stock, but I had this special kit put in with special pistons and other parts and a special tire in the back. It could do a lot of stuff that hill climbers could do and it had a seat that you could ride double with. It was a very strong bike so I knew that I could make it go up that steep hill even riding double.

Now Gary Davis is as much a sadist as he is a great motorcycle rider. I blasted up the hill and all of a sudden, Gary was already at the top of the hill sitting on the top of his bike and watching me. As I was about to crest the top, Gary rode his bike in front of me and blocked my path. I immediately cut the throttle and Randy flew east and I flew west and my bike went north — straight up in the air. The good news is that anything that goes up must come down but the bad news was that the bike came down right on top of me and we both rolled down the hill together. I tumbled down to the bottom of the hill and blood was pouring out of my nose and my mouth. I slowly went and grabbed the bike and it started up. I asked Randy if he wanted to try it again and he agreed. It was a game of king of the hill and was going to aim at that son of gun Gary Davis and run his butt over. I put the powerful bike in gear and tweaked the throttle wide open and aimed for the top of the hill. Gary ran right in front of me only this time I didn't slow down. Just when I about to run Gary Davis over he moved his bike about four or five feet so naturally I missed him. He was that good and he started laughing at me. I was hurt pretty bad and I was getting pretty frustrated in my attempts to catch up to Davis and knock him down that hill. Everyone else was going to continue riding but I decided to call it a day. After all, sooner or later, I was going to catch Gary Davis without his bike on a show or at the grappling school so I knew that he was going to get his at some point.

I finally made it back to the cabin and hit the showers and headed on off to the doctor's office. I didn't want to let the other guys know that I was hurt. I guess the truth is that I was really on an ego trip.

I went to go see Doctor Bernard Schwartz at his office, which was in a beat up, old building in the low rent district. He told me to lie down and he was going to give me an x-ray. I was really in pain and I had a big bump on my back. I knew damn well that I had a couple of broken ribs where the foot peg on the bike jammed into me. I laid down on the x-ray table and I looked up at the ceiling and saw this big, fat spider. It was maybe the biggest spider that I had ever seen except for a tarantula. There were cobwebs all over the ceiling and it looked like a black widow with a red spot on it. I wasn't going to say anything. I just wanted to get that x-ray and get the Sam Hill out of there. Doctor Schwartz told me to hold my breath and then he turned the switch on the x-ray machine. Well the second that he turned that switch, there was big flash of light like an explosion and the place looked like it was on fire. I thought that whole building was going to burn down but the doctor didn't seem to notice like it happened all of the time. He told me that the machine was broken and he gave me some pain pills and told me to come back in a couple of days. When the smoke had cleared the cobwebs were gone and so was that big spider.

Today, I have my own physician and his name is Doctor Jack Ditlove. Being a stunt man, I've had physical problems and all that most of the other doctors have wanted was insurance money. They would get paid, but none of them seemed to be helping me out. In life, you meet a lot of people and being 104 years old as I am, I've met more than most. I've met a lot of people in the boxing world, the wrestling world, martial arts world, and the stunt world. I find that being naive that I've helped out a lot of people and then they disappear when they have a chance to return the favor. They say, "Well I'm busy now but call me back." Jack Ditlove never tells me to call him back. He takes care of me and has become one of my most trusted friends and he is a very good doctor. He calls me almost every day but maybe that is because he likes to see people who are ugly and in pain.

In 1966, my stepfather Cal Eaton, who ran the Los Angeles professional wrestling booking office, was stricken by cancer. Now I never really cared for the man because every time that I saw him, he insulted me to make himself feel good. A person who always has to put someone down to themselves feel good is not my kind of person.

Right before Cal Eaton died, he called me to his house, and he was the only one there. He was down to about 110 pounds at the most. He was a proud guy, but he was just a shell of his former self. Cal had never asked anything from me, but that day he asked me if I could help him upstairs. He couldn't stand. He was sitting in a throne-like chair in the front room and he just had a phone in his hand that he hadn't hung up. It must have been off the hook for 20 minutes. The front room was his castle and there were pictures of boxers, wrestlers and celebrities all over the walls. I had compassion for Cal at this time because he couldn't get out of his favorite chair. I picked him up and I couldn't believe how light he was. I carried him upstairs. I took his clothes off and I put him to bed and I asked him if there was anything else that I could do for him. I made a couple of phone calls for him — one to his doctor. I left when his doctor arrived. That was the last time that I remember seeing Cal Eaton alive. I felt sorry for him because when I went to carry him upstairs, I noticed that tears were running down his cheeks and he was always such a macho guy. He was dying and I felt so bad. I felt like a Christian forgiving him 70 times 70. Cal then realized that he wasn't the god that thought that he once was. He was a brilliant man, but he was just a mortal made of flesh and bone like the rest of us.

The death of Cal Eaton left my brother Mike in control of the Southern California wrestling booking office along with Jules Strongbow. Mike worshipped Cal Eaton and had even wanted to change his name from Mike LeBell to Mike Eaton at one time. He followed in Eaton's footsteps and picked up some of the more unsavory aspects of our stepfather's personality in the process. From that time on, when I wrestled in the Los Angeles area, Mike was my boss.

Dick Lane was the on-air commentator for the Southern California territory's pro wrestling TV show that aired on KTLA channel 5 and then later KCOP channel 13 in Los Angeles and was syndicated in several different markets nationwide. Lane was in a class all by himself and he was one of the greatest sportscasters ever to lend his talents to a calling professional wrestling match. In the old movie series "Boston Blackie" he played the police lieutenant that was always outsmarted by Boston Blackie. They offered him a lot of money to do those movie parts but he was happy doing the wrestling. I remember when he first started in the wrestling he got $100,000 a year from the company just to narrate. He invented the names for so many of the wrestling holds that are popular today because he didn't know wrestling when he started. He didn't know the first thing about it. He named a lot of the moves like the atomic drop and many other names that are still used in professional wrestling.

Dick Lane got three weeks off every year. One time, when he was about to leave, he told the producer to have me take over because I was what he called a "realie," which meant that I knew wrestling because I had done it. When I took over, I tried to mimic him the best that I could, but I quickly found out that I could study for 100 years and never be a Dick Lane.

I did the show for the first week and I got a check for five hundred dollars. I said, "Wow, they're paying me for the three weeks." The second week I got another five hundred, and the third week I got another. So I got $1,500 for three shows and at that time you could buy a nice new car for 2,000 dollars. Later on while we were on Channel 13, Dick Lane got sick and said, "Gene, I'm tired. How about taking over the show?" I guess that they didn't have anybody else around that knew pro wrestling holds so I took over and became an announcer. I did it for 15 years on channel 13 and then channel 34 and then channel 52, and I owed this all to Dick Lane who was not only an incredible talent, but was also one of the good guys.

I still wrestled professionally of course, and I also refereed from time-to-time as well as calling the blow-by-blow action from ringside for the TV audience. Narrating wrestling for an hour every week on LA television led some casting agents to believe that I was a smarter guy than I actually was and I started to get more speaking parts. I played a lot of referees and ring announcers in movies like "Raging Bull" and "Ed Wood," but my deeper involvement with the promotion led to more disagreements with my brother.

Freddie Blassie and I always had a lot in common mentally, which wasn't much. Blassie was the Mr. Money in Southern California. He was the top drawing card of all of the wrestlers. He wanted me to teach him how to ride a motorcycle before he was in the main event at this big show at the Olympic Auditorium that was going to be simulcast on closed circuit TV at the Orpheum Theater in Los Angeles.

I got him on a motorcycle that I had in the parking lot of the Olympic. He was riding it around and my brother came out and had a fit. He told Freddie to get his rear end off of my motorcycle. Freddie kept on circling that parking lot and screamed, "I only know how to make it go! I don't know how to make it stop!!!"

Mike turned to me and started yelling at me to get Freddie off of the bike and I told him that there was nothing that I could do about it. My brother wanted to kill both me and Freddie. At first Freddie motioned like he was reaching for the gold key on the merry-go-round at an amusement park as he circled us on that bike, but as Mike kept on screaming, Freddie started giving Mike the bird – you know, flipping him off. Freddie wouldn't take crap from anybody. Finally when Freddie got off of the bike there were some words said between my brother and I and Mike fired me. My brother fired me once a month. I guess that you can call that brotherly love.

When I was wrestling I always wanted to jump the ring on my motorcycle. I ran it past Mike and I told him that we could UP and AP publicity for the event. I could set up a ramp and a bale of hay and jump the bike over the ring into the bale of hay and then go up in flames adding my movie stunt work talents to the charisma of professional wrestling. It would have been big money, but if it wasn't Mike's idea, he didn't like it so it was nixed.

Anytime that there was a new wrestler in the territory that rode a motorcycle I would say, "Tell Mike that you want to ride the bike to the ring and he'll probably make you a main eventer." That probably got me in a lot of trouble because Mike heard it a lot of times and he wasn't really known for having a sense of humor. Some of the wrestlers actually believed that Mike would give them a title shot if they said that they were working out at my judo school to sharpen their tools and make themselves better wrestlers. Those poor guys probably got buried on the bottom of the card for letting Mike in on that one. The only wrestler who wasn't penalized for training with me (or riding motorcycles with me for that matter) was Roddy Piper because he was a top draw almost from the beginning.

I had a friend who had a hot air balloon and I wanted to have a loser leaves town match where we would have this balloon in the parking lot of the Olympic. After the match was over, we would put the loser into the balloon and send him up in the air while everybody watched him disappear into the sky. We could have charged a separate admission to people just to have them sit in some bleachers the parking lot and watch that balloon, but that was another idea that my brother didn't go for.

Andre the Giant was one of the biggest attractions that professional wrestling ever saw. He toured all over the country and all over the world and he was a main-eventer wherever he went. Andre was 7'4" and he weighed over 500 pounds and people just loved the guy. One time when Andre was wrestling in Los Angles, I was narrating wrestling for television and I had to interview Andre before he had a big match against Man Mountain Mike who weighed about 600 pounds. We had sixty seconds to do this commercial hyping the upcoming bout. I turned to Andre with the microphone and said, "You're wrestling Man Mountain Mike at the Olympic next Friday, so tell these people what you are going to do."

Andre picked me up and lifted me over his head. "Put me down Andre!" I said, "I said put me down now! I said tell not show!"

The Giant just stood there holding me up like I was nothing. The live audience was going nuts and I could see Mike in the control booth and he was just seething. Andre said, "Let me tell you people! This is what I am going to do to Man Mountan Mike!"

As Andre still had me suspended over his head I said, "Call for reservations: Richmond: 9Ö" I never got out the rest of the phone number before they cut us off and went to another commercial. I never had the chance to say 5171. After it was over, Andre put me down and the director and his assistants cut the tape and laughed. My brother was in the studio and he came down and screamed and hollered at me. "I couldn't help it," I explained, "Andre wouldn't put me down!" I mean, what are you going to do when Andre the Giant decides to hoist you up over his head?

"You're fired you dumb schmuck!" Mike yelled. "You didn't get the phone number in there!"

Now everybody who was watching knew that phone number. They knew that it was Richmond-9-5171. They didn't need me to tell that to them, but Mike fired me anyway. The next week, I wasn't on television and those fans that Mike thought didn't know the number kept on calling the Olympic and saying, "We want Gene. We want Gene!" The show where Andre fought Man Mountain Mike that was supposedly ruined by me not getting that number out, sold out in record time and they had to turn away over 2,000 people at the door. Mike had no real beef and I was back on TV the week after that.

I also went on a tour of Japan for All-Japan Pro Wrestling at the same time that Andre was there. It must have been in the late 1960s. Gene Kiniski was also on that tour along with this big, crazy 300 pounder named Lonnie Moondog Mayne and a 6'7" white South African cop turned pro wrestler named Tarzan Tyler. Tyler possessed an incredible physique and he liked to flex his muscles and pose a lot. When someone would ask him how he got such big arms, he would say, "Milk, milk, you must have milk!" It was pretty funny at the time and boy, he could have cleaned up with commercial endorsements if he was around today with that little bit of shtick.

Now in Japan, the wrestlers were treated like a million bucks and the promotion paid for our transportation. Back in America in those days, wrestlers had to pay for their own transportation, but in Japan we toured around the country in a big window bus.

So I was on the bus with Andre, who was just a giant kid if you know what I mean. He wasn't stupid or anything, but let's just say that he never got out of his first childhood so that he could get into his second one. One time Andre decided that it was a good idea to stick his enormous backside outside the bus windows. Of course at that moment, a bunch of nuns were passing by so Andre mooned the good sisters. The bus had the name All-Japan Pro Wrestling all over it so they knew who had done it. Later on, the tour manager came on the bus and asked who had mooned the nuns. Nobody would cop to it so I said, "Who in here has a butt that's two axe-handles wide?"

"Did Andre do that again?" the tour manager asked and everybody laughed.

I brought my son David with me on that tour when he was about 12. The Japanese knew that I was into motorcycles so they set me up so that I could go to the Honda factory and test-ride their bikes and cars at the Suzuki Fun Center. David smashed a few bikes but the Honda reps didn't seem to care.

My kid was always playing jokes on the wrestlers on that tour. He especially spent a lot of time trying to scare this Irish wrestler named Sean Reagan. There was a lot of trouble in Northern Ireland at that time, so Reagan was kind of jumpy. I told David to cut that out but he said, "Oh he can never catch me."

"He'll catch you and he'll stretch you too," I warned.

Finally, Reagan had had enough and he picked David up in a fireman's carry and took him on the high diving board above a swimming pool and tossed David as far as he could. David wanted me to do something about it but I told my son that if he listened to the tune, he had to pay that fiddler.

While all of the other wrestlers went to the different geisha houses for entertainment or whatever, I still went to the dojos to work out. I went to the Kodokan and I worked out in the daytime so I could do the pro wrestling at night. One day, I had been working out for a couple of hours, so I had had enough. I still had to wrestle that night. Since I had competed in judo in Japan as an amateur and judo was their sport, the Japanese press was always very kind to me and on that day they were covering my workout. Athletes were treated better than movie stars in Japan, which is just the opposite of the way it is here.

This 19 year old guy came into the Kodokan and he was throwing guys all over the mat. It turned out that he was the national college champion. I was through working out and I was talking to some of the reporters. While I was clearly busy with the press, the college champion came up to me and said, "We randori."

"No, I'm through for the day," I told him. I didn't want to go out and get thrown by a guy and look bad, while when I was fresh I was throwing people around and looking good. He then grabbed my gi and jerked me off the chair right to my knees about ten feet inside the mat area. I quickly took him down with a leg hook takedown. I cranked his leg. He tapped out and said, "matei," which means time and I let go of the hold. Leg locks are illegal in kodokan judo. Then, I cranked his neck, which is also a forbidden move. If you crank a guy's neck and you turn the head to the side, the man will not be able to move his legs from the waist down plus he'll have a tendency to pass out.

I put him to sleep and then I started playing with his body because the newspaper guys were looking and they were taking pictures. When he was coming to, I choked him out again before he was fully conscious. While he was again regaining consciousness, I grabbed his testicles and used them as a handle to help me lift him up over my head. Then I threw him really high so everybody could see it. Ten years later, nobody remembered how I beat the guy, just that I had beaten him. Sometimes when the competition gets really tough, you have to reach into the dark side of the moon (illegal holds) to enhance your repertoire.

You know it's a funny story but if I was honest to myself I had my doubts if I could have beaten that guy if I didn't cheat to win. The Japanese sportswriters that came to see me work out had seen leglocks in pro-wrestling, but they didn't really know judo that well so they didn't think that there was anything wrong with me using pro-wrestling finishing holds in the house that Jigoro Kano built.

Lonnie "Moondog" Mayne was a very tough wrestler but he had a room temperature IQ. To say the least, his demeanor was slightly different than the norm. In Japan, they eat a lot of sushi and raw fish and stuff while I don't eat anything without horns. All I want is a good hamburger steak with some potatoes. I finally got sick of eating all of that weird food so I decided to take my son David and Moondog out to dinner and I was buying.

We went out to this pretty fancy restaurant where the waiters all wore tuxedos and the walls were lined with these specially lit aquariums that were filled with all kinds of exotic live fishes. Moondog stared through the aquarium glass and asked David if he liked the fish.

Even after getting dumped into that pool by Sean Reagan, David was very mischievous throughout that whole tour. "Yeah, I like every fish in there but that one," David said pointing at a particular fish.

Moondog reached into the fishtank and got this one fish and swallowed it whole – no chewing — he just ate the whole thing all at once. David was then screaming and hollering, "No, not that one! The one with the big eye!" Now there was a fish in there that was only three inches long but half of his body was a big set of eyes. David pointed to that odd fish and said, "That one Uncle Moondog!" Then Moondog reached in and grabbed this big-eyed fish and gulped it down with one swallow and it was gone.

I was getting the dry heaves from this. All I wanted was nice, normal meal and there was Moondog Mayne scarfing down live fish. We got to our table and I ordered spaghetti. "It looks like worms," Moondog said trying to gross me out even further.

Moondog Lonnie was drinking pretty good and our waiter was dressed in a tux and he was only about four and a half feet tall. Moondog picked the guy up and started bouncing him up and down on his knee. The short waiter tried to escape to no avail. Moondog then started singing, "I've got a penguin here. I've got a penguin here," to the tune of "She'll Be Comin' Round the Mountain." He got David joining in with him too and they were both having a sing-along while Moondog was bouncing our waiter up and down.

I turned to Lonnie and I said, "Lonnie, People know that you're a pro wrestler. We're on tour in this country. The way that you're acting, we'll never be invited back here."

He looked at me and said, "Well I've got a penguin and you don't. Do you want to hold my penguin?"

I told him that I didn't but he finally got bored and let the waiter go and I asked for the check. The waiter brought me the check and it was astronomical. It came to 500 American dollars. I asked him how the bill got to be so high and he started speaking to me in Japanese about the fish. The one with the big eyes cost 300 dollars! David was laughing and hysterical. "300 fóing dollars!" I said, "You've got to be kidding!"

"Do you want me to eat another one?" Moondog said with a grin. Luckily he didn't but I was still stuck with the bill. I never had this trouble when I took young ladies out to dinner.

When the tour was all over, All-Japan Pro Wrestling put on a big party for us. I told the head guy there that I wanted hamburger. I wanted my meat to have horns. I didn't want it to bark or swim or have gills or anything like that so they got me this big steak and they ground it up and it must have been four pounds of meat. I mean it was really big.

All of the wrestlers were seated at this long table and there was plenty of booze and everyone was looking at me with that big hamburger steak and I was showboating a bit. They had these oversized salt shakers there and I picked one of them up and I turned it upside down to shake a little bit of salt on my steak. Someone had unscrewed the top of the salt shaker and it had come off pouring a mound of salt all over that beautiful steak. Andre the Giant and Kiniski and everybody were looking at me and laughing and I looked at Moondog and he was looking the other way. My own son was sitting across from me and he was also having a good laugh at my expense.

I was hot. I stepped up onto the table and I leapt about 10 feet over some wrestlers and across the dining hall and landed on Moondog. Down we went and we busted his chair. I double hooked him by double grapevining his legs. I don't know if he could have gotten up from that but he was laughing so hard that at that moment he couldn't move. One big wrestler teased me by showing me a saltshaker and I grabbed it away from him and poured salt all over Moondog. He had salt in his eyes, hair, mouth, ears and down his pants.

I went back to my seat and tried to get the salt off of my steak, but it still tasted salty. Moondog was still on the ground in hysterics and the other wrestlers were laughing too. When I looked back at them, they all turned their heads like they weren't laughing because they all thought that I was a loose cannon, which of course I wasn't.

On the plane ride back to the States, we all flew first class. The flight attendants were giving us free booze and I got them to give Moondog a lot of extra drinks. Finally, after he had passed out from drinking so much, they gave us our dinner. Now we were in first class so they gave us these nice, big T-bone steaks so I ate my steak and I noted that Moondog was still sleeping so I ate his steak too. After I was done, I woke him up. He looked down at his plate and there was nothing left but a big bone that had been picked clean.

A while after I had returned from Japan, I finally got to use one of those crazy ideas for a wrestling match that I had from time to time. I did a match with Roddy Piper where the loser got run over by a motorcycle. I won the match and then I rode over Roddy with my bike, which if you don't know how to do it right you could really hurt somebody. You have to lift the front end and bunnyhop the backend. I did that match in Bakersfield for wrestling promoter Ramona Strongbow who was Jules Strongbow's wife. Running over a wrestling villain in the ring with a motorcycle was a way of entertaining the fans and they liked it. With a movie, if your audience sees it once, you call that a success, but with boxing, wrestling, football or any other sport you want to keep them coming back day after day, week after week, month after month, year after year. You have to give the fans what they want in this world and keep them glued to their seats and coming back for more and that's show business.

CHAPTER 12

TAKING FALLS

I had to pick a friend up at the LA Airport and that's when you could still park on the streets there without the kinds of security issues that they have nowadays. Earlier in the day, I was working on my motorcycles and I was all greasy and dirty. I didn't have time to shower and clean up after working on my bikes so I just took off for the airport. I didn't want to run in and embarrass the people that I was picking up by showing up to their gate wearing a shirt freshly stained with motor oil and grease, so I took my shirt off and ran up to the front of the airport. A guy ran up to me and grabbed me and said, "When I saw a crazy shirtless guy running around the airport, I knew that it could only be you! Only Gene LeBell would use LAX as a honey wagon." (A honey wagon is what they call the dressing rooms on movie locations.)

It turned out to be Robert Wagner. You know he was married to Natalie Wood and was one of the stars of the long running TV-series "Hart to Hart," which I have worked on a couple of times. He also donned an eye patch to play Doctor Evil's sidekick Number Two in the "Austin Powers" movies. When he spotted me at the airport, I tried to humbly explain the situation him. "No, no," I said, "I only had a dirty shirt with me and I wanted to look presentable like you." Knowing my personality, he didn't buy it.

The following week, I was working on a movie with Bob Wagner and he teased me by telling everyone on the set how I ran around the airport without a shirt on. "I'm glad you're a stuntman and not a famous actor," he said, "otherwise people might recognize you and you would become an embarrassment to the industry."

I worked on a movie called "Walking Tall" with Joe Don Baker. He was playing a former pro wrestler turned tough guy sheriff who walked around with a two-by-four. I had to train him to do some pro wrestling moves. Joe Don is a real top of the line guy and a good friend of mine. He's mentioned my name three or four times, which ended up getting me some work in his movies.

"Walking Tall" was filmed on location in Tennessee. During a break in the shooting, I rode into town to go to the grocery store and I saw a bunch of guys running down the highway. They were all Caucasians. I stopped and it looked like somebody had gotten run over in the street. It was a black man and he was bleeding. I got him in my car and took him to the grocery store, which was about a half mile down the road. The guy was scared to death of me at first. He thought that I was going to hurt him. It had turned out that those other guys had cut his throat. I dragged him into the store and I told the store clerk to call an ambulance. She took a look at me and said, "He's only a nigger."

I slammed the cash register on her fingers, which I didn't mean to do but it got her attention and I said, "Call the police." I grabbed the phone that was there and she gingerly took it from me and made the call. The police came over and took the man to the hospital and they seemed genuinely concerned about his well being. I told a few of the locals that were working on the show and they seemed upset with me, but they didn't say anything negative. Joe Don called them rednecks but I didn't understand what that meant because I was raised in California. Sure we have racism out here but it isn't like that. It is more of a melting pot. I don't care what color you are, or where you are from, you can live right next door to me as long as you don't cause me any hassles. I don't want somebody who is going to hang their dirty underwear on the windowsill living next door to me but I don't want the Queen of England to move in there either.

I was doubling Ken Swofford (an actor that I have worked with for many years) on this Disney movie and I had to work with this 600-pound Bengal tiger. The trainer told me that I had to get to know the big cat because he had a tendency to bite and claw you if he didn't know you. I was on the set and there was nobody around so I started petting and playing with the tiger. The tiger and I were getting along fine while we waited and finally it was time to shoot our scene. The cameras were rolling and the villain came out of his cave and then the tiger came out and the cameras were only supposed to see the tiger's head as he was on a very thick chain. As a stunt double, my job was to fall down this hill as the ground gave out from under my feet. So when

I rolled down the hill on cue, the tiger broke his chain and leapt after me. I rolled down about 50 or 75 feet into this creek and the tiger jumped on me and started pawing at me. Everybody was panicking and they all thought that he was going to eat me. Finally the trainer got down there and pulled him away, but it turned out that the tiger liked me and he just wanted to make sure that I was okay. All he wanted to do was play with me. When they pulled the tiger off of me, I still had my eyes closed because I was supposed to be knocked out from the fall so everyone thought that the tiger had killed me. They ended up using the shot.

I was on "The Dating Game" once. I was single back then and I actually won and got to take a young lady to Paris, France. We were originally supposed to go to Morocco, but when we were at the Paris Airport to transfer over, some guy with a turban on his head gave them an envelope full of money and they told me to get off of the plane and give him my seat. I asked this French guy there who spoke English what had happened and he told me that this sort of thing happened all of the time and that they would put us on the next available flight. Now those Chuck Barris shows only sent you to these exotic faraway places for like three days so we decided to stay in France instead of waiting around for a flight to Morocco. I went to a French judo dojo a couple of times and my date and I went to the horse races where the horses run the other way. Since there was a chaperon with us, there wasn't much else to do.

I worked with O.J. Simpson in a movie during the 1970s called "Goldie and the Boxer." He was supposed to fight heavyweight contender Jerry Quarry and knock him out. Quarry was a big drawing card in boxing at the time and he had fought Muhammad Ali and Joe Frazier and he had beaten former heavyweight champion Floyd Patterson. Quarry was scheduled to be on the set for a 7 am call. At 10 o'clock he still wasn't there. I was already cast in the film as a gangster that drove all of the mob bosses around so the director asked me if I could get into the wardrobe for the fight scene in a boxing ring. I said that I could. They tried to get a hold of Quarry and they couldn't. They did get a hold of a couple of buddies of his and they said that he wasn't going to come down and take a fall for a football player. But it's a movie! Every star in Hollywood's beaten me up and so have half of the women!

So Quarry wasn't going to show up so I put the wardrobe on and I did the fight scene with Simpson and I've never worked with anybody that was a superstar that was any easier to work with. I gave O.J. a couple of suggestions and he was just a really, really nice guy. He had legal problems later on but I don't want to think about them because then I will make them my problems. My opinions on them don't matter a whole lot, but I've worked with him on a couple of shows and all I can say is that he was always friendly to me.

After I was done taking a fall for O.J., the production manager came up to me and asked me what I wanted to get paid. I was thinking of a stunt minimum. I don't remember what it was back then but it was probably in the vicinity of three hundred bucks. I thought it over and said, "Give me the same thing that Quarry was going to get." The production guy looked at me kind of strange. Now I believed that I was doing them a favor. I wasn't supposed to get an adjustment. I was coordinating the fight and that's why I was there. I was helping them out when Quarry didn't show because I was already on the payroll.

The production manager told me that it was okay but of course that's after I had done the scene already. Later on in the day they brought the contract and it was for 3400 dollars a day. Now $3,400 a day – that's more than the director was getting! That was a lot of money for doing a simple fight scene. When you're getting around three hundred dollars a day as a stuntman, that's a big jump. I kept my mouth shut and got two different checks for the same movie: one was for the driver (the stunt villain) and the other was for taking Jerry Quarry's place.

Besides touring with Andre the Giant in Japan, I also worked with him on a couple of shows. One day, somebody from Universal called up the Southern California pro wrestling booking office and wanted to hire Andre the Giant for a part in "The Six Million Dollar Man." "The Six Million Dollar Man" starred Lee Majors (who I later worked with on "The Fall Guy") as this guy who was called the bionic man. He had robot arms and legs and could run really fast and jump really high and they filmed a lot of the action scenes in slow motion with lots of sound effects to show this to you.

When they called up the wrestling booking office to hire Andre, I answered the phone. They wanted Andre to play some swamp giant. They said that it would be a week's worth of work. I told them that Andre had his bookings. "Well, we'll arrange it so can schedule around his bookings," they promised.

In the 1970s, Andre was a big superstar as far as wrestling goes. Back then, they paid the stuntmen maybe a thousand dollars for a week, which was big money then, but it wasn't anything compared to what Andre could pull in working the circuit. I mean he was a draw. I explained this to them and they upped their offer to 1,200 dollars a week.

I called Andre and told him about the job and the money and he said, "I'm making over $25,000 a week wrestling. What do I want to work for $1,200 for?"

I then called them back and told them that Andre wanted $25,000 a week. This was when the leads were only getting like $2,500 (check the zeros). Since I knew the casting director, I teased him a little over the phone and he said, "Gene, stop screwing around! This is business. If you ever want to work for us again, you'd better help us out!"

"Let's start out with $25,000," I said reiterating the original offer. He screamed and hollered and called me all kinds of names.

"We need him," he told me, "because the head producer is a big wrestling fan and Andre the Giant is 7'4" and he weighs over 500 pounds and he is going to play a swamp giant on the show."

Finally, they said okay and they were going to give him the 25 thousand. He did the show and they put an outfit on him and it was so heavy that he thought that he was going to drown. The next time that I ran into Andre I asked him how he liked working on the show. "I don't want to do it ever again," he told me. Andre liked to travel, wrestle, drink beer and live the good life. He couldn't stand waiting around a back lot all day in a big ape suit.

The producers of the show made sure that they didn't kill off the Bigfoot creature that Andre played. The show with Andre as the

Me and Muhammad Ali, refereeing the famous wrestler versus boxer fight against Inoki

Andre the Giant was one big dude

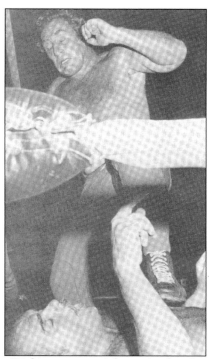

Dishing out punishmentin the ring

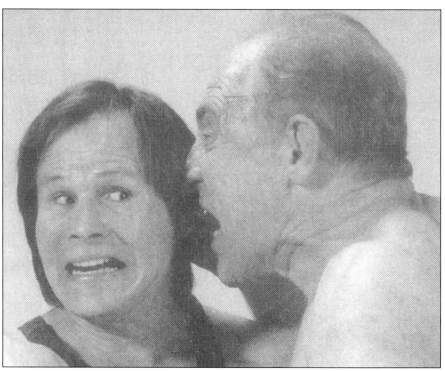

I've always told my good pal and student Benny Urquidez – the undefeated greatest kickboxer in history – that biting is perfectly legal in streetfighting

Look ma! No hands. Fighting has always been my first love, but motorcycles are a close second

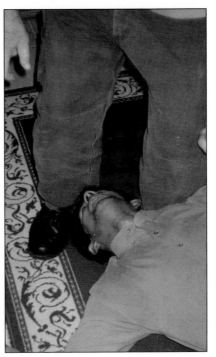

Just choking my publisher – he was out in three seconds

Who's afraid of Big Bad Gene? Feeding the local squirrels

Posing for the camera

A busy day in the office

With my daughter Monica

Showing Monica what I did to the legendary Bruce Lee

With our grandson James

What you looking at? Yes YOU!

My wife Midge and our good friend and Hollywood star Burt Reynolds getting all wrapped up

Gokor 'The Armenian Assassin' and me

Me and Sylvester Stallone in the movie 'Lock Up'

Chuch Norris and me. A great friend, student and film star

sasquatch was such a success that they wanted him to do it again. They asked me if he would work cheaper. I asked Andre and he said that he wouldn't do it for fifty thousand. I relayed Andre's message and they actually offered him fifty thousand but Andre was unmoved. "I won't do it," he said, "I just won't do it. I don't need the money and I don't like it."

They ended up getting another stuntman named Dick Durock who is only 6'6" and about 220 pounds to do the show. It didn't bother Durock to put on that suit, but they didn't get Andre. Vince Deadrick, Sr., who's a good friend of mine ran the stunts on that show — not that he had anything to do with the hiring. Vince is a really a good friend of mine. He's really a good guy.

Now Vince always liked to torture me on the shows that he ran – it was his way of showing affection. There was one show that Vince was running the stunts on and he knew that I didn't smoke so he told the director that he wanted me to have a cigarette in my mouth just because he knew that it would drive me nuts due to my allergies. Of course the director thought that it was a great idea and I spent the shoot trying to breathe in without inhaling any smoke from the lit cigarette which wasn't easy. Vince thought that it was pretty funny because I was somehow coughing without even breathing.

While I am talking about stunt coordinators and second unit directors, this book really wouldn't be complete without mentioning Terry Leonard. Terry did the famous stunt where crawled under the truck and was dragged behind it in "Raiders of the Lost Ark" and he is one of the most legendary stuntmen in the business. Every time that I call Terry on the phone I ask to speak to "the great Terry Leonard," and he always hands the phone over to his wife. I talked to his wife for six months before I found that they both had the same first name only he spells it "Terry" and she spells it "Teri."

Charlie Picerni, Sr. is another stunt coordinator who has hired me a lot. Charlie is not only a great stuntman but he is a fantastic movie director. Over the years, however, he has earned a reputation (maybe unfairly) for screaming at people to get his point over and a lot of people think that he has a really bad temper although he has never yelled at me. Another stuntman friend of mine named John Moio used to go motorcycle riding with me every Sunday. One Sunday he called me to tell me that he couldn't make it. "I can't go bike riding with you this weekend," he informed me. "Somebody on the set accused me of act-ing like Charlie Picerni and screaming at people to my point over so I have to go to church and beg for forgiveness." Now that is entirely understandable, but if John weren't so lazy, he would have gone to mass early so he could go motorcycle riding in the afternoon.

Another show that I worked on a lot back in the 1970s was "Kung Fu." It was a martial arts show and, being a martial artist, I got on it a few times. The show starred David Carradine who was a nice guy to work with. I've worked with him on quite a few shows and he beat me up on all of them. Because he beat me up so many times, it helped me buy a lot of my motorcycles. I made so much money on one of his shows that he beat me up in that I bought a brand new car and paid for it IN CASH!

In the mid-1970s martial arts in the movies was really exploding and a lot of that had to do with Bruce Lee getting really popular. Remember, that ten years earlier on "The Green Hornet" nobody really knew what to do with Bruce and all of those high kicks of his, but by 1975 nobody could get enough of them. There was this movie called "The Killer Elite," which was directed by Sam Peckinpah and was filmed up in San Francisco. For this movie, they had hired all of these different martial arts experts for the fight scenes. Whitey Hughes ran the stunts on that show and he called me up because he was having a lot of trouble with some of the martial artists that they cast in the show. They had gotten all of these guys together, and they were all very good martial artists, but some of them wanted to use what they felt were their best moves in the movie. Now what may work on the street or is effec-tive in the dojo might not look so hot on film. Whitey was about at the end of his rope so he called me because I had a background in martial arts and I had worked in movies, so he hoped that I could explain things to these guys. On a movie you have to do what the director or the stunt coordinator wants you to do. You might be a judo guy, but they might want you to do a kick or you might be a karate guy and they might want you to take a fall down a staircase. You never can tell so you should be ready to do anything.

James Caan was the star of "The Killer Elite," and while we were filming out by the mothball fleet in Vallejo, California, he hired this bi-plane to fly over the location with a sign trailing behind it with some disparaging remarks about Sam Peckinpah as a joke. I can't repeat exactly what it said, but I do remember thinking that Jimmy Caan must have been a pretty big guy or had a lot of clout to go and pull some-thing like that. James Caan is a talented athlete and does most of his own stunts. When the stunts get a little too risky, Jimmy Nickerson is standing by to double him.

In June of 1976, Muhammad Ali had signed to fight Antonio Inoki in Tokyo in a boxer vs. wrestler match. Ali had already won back the title from George Forman and had just fought Joe Frazier for the third time in the Philippines and the Japanese put up a lot of money to see him fight one of their wrestlers. I wanted to referee the fight and I told Ali that when he was at the Olympic Auditorium promoting the match. I grew up in the Main St. Gym, which was a boxing gym and I'm quite familiar with boxing and I also wrestled. They had 200 guys that wanted to be referees and I was the only one who did wrestling, mar-tial arts and boxing. I had known Ali for awhile and I even wrestled Inoki so both the competitors agreed on me. Ali brought Freddie Blassie with him to be in his corner but he still referred to Freddie as Gorgeous George because of his blond hair.

Going into it, I thought that it might be a business fight, you know, but it wasn't. It was a reputation fight. Ali got 6 million and Inoki got 2 million, which was big, big money back then and I got $5,000, which was big, big money to me. On the same live show but telecast from a different location, Andre the Giant went up against Joe Bugner who was also a rated heavyweight boxer and Andre thew Bugner out of the ring. Although Bugner was 6'6", he looked like a midget next to Andre. I thought that they might have had Ali take the match against Inoki to build up to an Ali-Andre fight. Now who wouldn't want to see "The Greatest" go up against Andre who was 7'4"? Now that would have done tremendous business.

Inoki fought a very cautious fight, but I wouldn't say that he was scared of Ali. Inoki was the Japanese pro wrestling champ at the time so he had a lot to lose, as did Ali. Leading up to that fight, Ali reviewed the films of different pro wrestlers to get ideas of what he could do to them, but some of that went out the window when the bell rung on that fight. Both fighters could have done something different and taken more risks but that's yesterday's mail. Since it ended up being such a defensive fight, I declared the fight a draw but the boxing judge voted for Inoki and the wrestling judge voted for Ali. I was the tiebreaker so the decision remained a draw.

The day after I got back from Tokyo I was working on a "The Rockford Files" with James Garner. He came up to me and he said, "I went to the Forum to see the Ali-Inoki fight on closed-circuit television and I saw was you in the ring so I paid 25 dollars to see you when I could see you here for free." That was Jimmy Garner's way of joking and he gave me a dirty look and then proceeded to beat me up once again for the cameras.

I played one of those comedy bikers for Clint Eastwood on that first Orangutan movie "Every Which Way But Loose," and all I can say is that it was fun. We shot in eight-hour days so there was no overtime. Working on a Clint Eastwood movie is very businesslike. He had a way of letting you know that he was the boss, but he didn't mind talking to the stunt guys and breaking bread with them. You could do a darned good fight scene with him, because he was a good athlete who trained for years in boxing. There's a scene in it where he hits me and breaks my motorcycle glasses. He also beat me up in a cafe in the San Fernando Valley with all of the other bikers before we went up to Denver, Colorado to shoot the rest of the movie. Clint's a real professional and the best catering that you will have is on a Clint Eastwood movie set.

I took a fall into a swimming pool in this Steve Martin movie called "The Jerk." In the scene, I was playing a henchman and Steve Martin was wearing all of these medallions and is doing all of these funny kung-fu moves on all of the bad guys. While we were shooting this scene, I got a call from a casting agent who wanted me for this movie. It was my last day on "The Jerk" and this agent was promising a week or two of work on another big show. I told him that I was work-ing on this Steve Martin movie and that I had to get thrown into a swimming pool, but he told me that I had to be in his casting office by 4:30 in the afternoon or I wouldn't get the job.

So it was almost 4:30 and Martin threw me in the pool and I was soaking wet. My car was parked about a mile away and there was no way that I could get to it in time. Luckily, there was a dog trainer on the set who was driving pretty close to where I needed to be and he said that he could drop me off at the casting office. He had a pickup truck that he kept the dogs in so he didn't care about me getting it all wet.

We went through every signal to get there on time and we got there in about 15 minutes. He dropped me off and I still had my wardrobe on from "The Jerk" and water was just dripping off of me as I ran up the stairs. I got into this casting guy's office that had called me for this part and I could tell that his office had just been remodeled. This was a very nice office with brand new carpeting and I was dripping water all over it. The guy took one look at me and asked, "Who the hell do you think you are?"

"Well you wanted me for this show and here I am," I said, "I'm Gene LeBell!"

"You ain't shit," he said, "Get the hell out of here! We don't need mermaids for this show!" He then opened the door and slammed it behind me as I walked out with my tail between my legs. Needless to say, I didn't get the job. I hailed a cab and paid the driver with a hand-ful of soggy dollar bills.

"The Jerk" was directed by Carl Reiner who is a beautiful, won-derful guy to work for. Reiner had the big part in this comedy in called "Americathon" where the United States goes into bankruptcy and the government tries to get out of it by putting on a telethon where people do many death defying stunts. I played a referee in that movie in a fight scene where Jay Leno from "The Tonight Show" fights his mother who was played by May Boss. It's kind of a funny scene in a sadistic sort of way where Leno gets hit in the privates and his gray haired mother is forced to fight dirty. Many years later, when Leno was host of "The Tonight Show," Mando Guerrero and I staged a comedy fight scene on his show. He broke a vase over my head and I took a fall for him just like I did for everybody else in Hollywood.

"The Big Brawl" was Jackie Chan's US movie debut. He had already been a star in Hong Kong for years and had even done stunts in Bruce Lee movies, so Jackie Chan and I have at least one thing in common. "The Big Brawl" was shot in Texas and a week before I flew out there, I was working on another show where I had to get tossed out of a bar and I hurt my shoulder. After the last night of filming, I went to the emergency hospital where they took some x-rays and said that there was nothing wrong with me.

So I went to Texas the next day to shoot "The Big Brawl" and my shoulder was still hurting me. It was a wrestling/martial arts movie and it had a lot of fight scenes where Jackie Chan goes up against all of these big, tough guys like Ox Baker, "Hardboiled" Haggerty and Jeep Swensen and beats them with his kung-fu moves. Jeep Swensen and I later had a scene together in "Batman and Robin," which starred Arnold Schwarzenegger and George Clooney. In the scene, I'm playing a night watchman and Swensen is playing this big, masked super villain and he pulls me through a wall.

In "Big Brawl" I had to work a fight scene with "Hardboiled" Haggerty, who was a big, ripped pro wrestler and former AWA tag-team champ with a menacing look so that was going to be tough with that bum shoulder. One of the production guys told me that if I was in pain to go to this hypnotist and he would make the pain go away. So I went to this hypnotist and he tried to hypnotize me. I really tried to cooperate too, but he just couldn't put me under his spell. So I was still in pain and worked a fight scene with Haggerty and he slammed me down onto the cement and I felt every bit of it and then some.

When I returned to LA, I went to Doctors Bob Rosenfeldt and Fred Nikola, who are excellent orthopedic specialists. Doctor Nikola was the team physician for the Raiders football team when they were in Los Angeles. They x-rayed me and found that my shoulder was busted in three parts, but they pointed out that the break was straight and they told me that it would heal in another six weeks and sure enough, it did. After six weeks, I could salute with both hands. I still have a bump in my shoulder from that injury though. You may wonder why that first doctor at the emergency hospital didn't see that, but I'll never know.

Years later, I had a scene with Jackie Chan in the smash hit "Rush Hour." I play a cab driver in a scene where Jackie and Chris Tucker are pointing guns at each other to prove who was boss and I get out of my cab and point a pistol at the both of them. We did some quick dialogue and at the end of the scene, I was still pointing my gun at them and they asked me what I wanted. "I want my three bucks for cab fare," I said and the whole cast and crew broke out laughing. I thought that it was a funny little bit but it still ended up on the cutting room floor as so many of the good scenes do.

Another guy that I have worked with a few times is Burt Reynolds. Burt isn't all business like Clint Eastwood. He's got a lot of stretch in his personality: he can really joke around with you but when it comes to business, he's very serious. He has come up to my cabin a few times to ride motorcycles while his then 10 year old son Quentin wrestled me into submission in my wrestling room (I must have had an off day).

Now Burt told me this story about Hal Needham who directed the Burt Reynolds blockbuster "Smokey and the Bandit" so I don't know if it is true or not because Burt really loves to joke around but it is too good not to repeat.

Before Hal Needham started directing movies, he was a very good stuntman and he and Burt were roomates. As a stuntman, Hal pushed the envelope and he broke just about every bone in his body. He isn't afraid of anything. He was working on this movie and a horse rolled on him and crushed some of his ribs. In the middle of the day he started throwing up so he decided to go to the doctor to get some shots for the pain so he could go back to work. Burt, being a good friend, drove him to the doctor's office.

When Hal was young and single, he was the kind of guy who hit on every woman he came in contact with whether she is good looking or not. So Burt and Hal got into the waiting room at the doctor's office and there is this gorgeous, gorgeous nurse working there. Hal immediately went to work and started hitting on her. He told her who he is and what he does for a living and Burt put him over as being a hell of a macho guy and everything. The nurse was really going for it and she agreed to go out on a date with Needham the next night.

Hal was just dripping with sweat the whole time because he was really hurting but he wasn't going to let that nurse know it. They finally went into the office and the doctor pulled down Hal's pants and told him to put his hands on the wall. The doctor then told the nurse to stand right behind Hal and hold him steady so that he wouldn't move when he stuck the needle in.

While the doctor was preparing the pain shot, Hal turned to the nurse and said, "Okay, We're on for tomorrow night, right?"

"Yes, yes," the nurse replied. She was really on to it.

As the doctor then stuck the needle into Hal Needham's rear end Hal squirted diarrhea all over the beautiful nurse's chest and pressed-white uniform. The young girl bent down in total disgust and Hal turned around and said, "Does that mean that our date's off for tomorrow night?"

Burt was the biggest star in Hollywood for awhile there back in the 1970s and 1980s so I took my wife out to the set of one of his shows that I was working on for him because she really wanted to meet him. When we were driving to the studio I said, "This guy is loose and I mean really loose," but she never believes me. She loses her concentration as soon as I open my mouth.

So we picked up Burt and it was about a ten minute drive to the set and Burt started telling my wife about how he slept with his love who was named Charlie and how Charlie hugged him and kissed him and licked him. Burt went on about how affectionate Charlie was and how he got under the covers with him every night and rubbed against him. Burt was a huge sex symbol to the women back then and my wife was thinking that he might be gay. A lover named Charlie? She struggled to be polite and interested throughout the whole thing. She finally found out later that Charlie was not a man but was Burt's cat. Burt really likes to put people on and most of the stories that I could tell you about him aren't really fit for publication!

Now everybody wants to hear about a couple being happily married for 30 or 40 years but for better or worse life isn't how you want it, it's how it is. I've had a lot of girlfriends and a lot of wives when I was young but unfortunately, I just don't have them now. I'm down to just one woman. There have been some that have passed away and some that have moved on, but I don't bear any ill will towards any of them. I get along with all of my ex-wives (at least the ones that are still alive) and why not? They are all my favorite wives. I loved them all – every last one of them. There's good and bad in all of them, but in their husband, there was only good.

My first wife Olga was a very smart woman and she helped me write my first judo book and she is the mother of my son David. David has a son who is my grandson Jimmy James.

Joyce was my second wife who died suddenly from encephalitis meningitis. It took years after I had lost Joyce for me to even look at other women again, but when I was ready, I married Linda. Now Linda and I never argued. We never fought about anything. Although that might seem like a match made in heaven, after awhile, we grew apart, and Linda moved on, but not before she gave birth to my daughter Monica. Monica is an FBI Agent today and there really isn't a lot that I can say about her line of work other than that I am extremely proud of her. Monica is my daughter and she is the apple of my eye. She is more important in my life than just about anybody. One of the reasons for this is that when she was seven years old she said, "Dad, don't worry about when you get old. I will take care of you and pay all of your bills." Monica, I'm old. I'm old. Monica, I'm old!

After Linda and I had split up, I married Midge in Vegas. As I said before, Midge's real name is Eleanor, but she is a little on the short side (under 5 feet tall) so I used to call her "Midget" and then just Midge. Our first marriage was a complete disaster and it didn't last very long. She thought that she was an equal.

Following Midge, I was married to Billy for 10 years. Billy was the most free-spirited of all of my wives so after awhile, she outgrew me and moved on. After she got rid of me, Billy had started seeing this man named Sylvio, but I called him Silverado because it was more macho. After Silverado and Billy had married, Billy brought him into my judo school to learn self-defense. She wanted a man who could fight her battles for her. He might have been a little bit nervous taking judo lessons from his wife's ex-husband, but we got along fine and Silverado became a fanatic at grappling. He was one of my best students and he came into the dojo three or four times a week and finally became a black belt in my system and ended up earning a second black belt in jiu-jitsu from the Machado brothers (who are fine jiu-jitsu competitors and teachers.) After ten years Billy and Silverado went their separate ways. After their divorce, Silverado asked me what he should do for a living. "It's simple," I told him. "Make your ex-wife happy and give free jiu-jitsu lessons to her next husband."

After Billy and I had been divorced for awhile, and I was still single, Midge (my ex) needed some money. So I loaned her a thousand dollars and said, "You don't have to pay me back. I just don't ever want to see you again."

She said, "Things have been tough, but what can I do for you."

"Nothing," I said, "I'm going on a movie location for a month." Midge told me that she would pick up my mail and my newspaper while I was gone. That seemed fair to me.

I was gone for a month, but when I came back and opened the front door, I found all of my closets filled with her clothes. She had cleaned up my whole house and redecorated everything. "I'm in trouble," I said to myself. "How do I get rid of her?" I went to sit on my favorite comfortable chair and fell on my butt. As I looked up I saw that she had moved my favorite chair to another corner. She had moved in and she just wouldn't leave. There was nothing that I could do about it. I would have kicked her out but she was a good cook, she cleaned, she did laundry and best of all, she was great at doing what married people do.

After Midge had moved back in, she wanted to go to Vegas and get remarried. "I married you once before in Vegas," I told her, "and that was a bad omen. I only get married on Sundays and that's motorcycle day."

I played it up real big in the hopes of avoiding walking down that aisle, but then she said, "Well let's get married on a motorcycle."

She had me dead to rights. "You want to get married on a motorcycle?" I asked. So she wore a beautiful gown and a helmet that was covered with flowers. While the minister said the vows on the lift gate of my truck at 40 miles an hour, I was doing a wheelie with my wife on the back of the bike. Everything was wonderful. I had a great time until I woke up the next day and said, "My God. I'm married." I swore off riding motorcycles for almost a month. Midge and I have been together ever since although at times I think that she talks too much. When I get married again, my next wife will be a deaf-mute and if she begins to talk, I'll break her fingers (Midge, if you're reading this, I'm only joking.)

A mechanic who fixes cars and motorcycles is often called a wrench. Today Midge's on Danny is all grown up and he is my official wrench. He fixes my cars and he even fixes my plumbing and electrical problems at no cost. He's a real jack of all trades. Danny has a son named Daniel Gene, who is my grandson by marriage and is named after me. Danny will do anything for me. He even sticks up for me over his own mother when we get into arguments. When Midge gets mad at me, she says that she isn't going to change my other grandson Jimmy James' diapers. Everybody knows that changing diapers is a woman's job. Anytime she won't change him, I call my wrench Danny and he'll change him and all I can say is that everybody should have a wrench that does it all like I do.

Daniel Gene is seven years old today and he does TV commercials and he is quite successful as a child actor. My son David's kid Jimmy James does nothing but eat, but he is still young yet — he is only three years old, but if show biz truly runs in the family we should be seeing him on the screen any day now.

My son David often takes Jimmy James to my brother Mike and his wife Molly's house. Mike and Molly own a two million-dollar home and they have imported tile floors from Europe and a very elaborate air conditioning system with floor vents in every room and hallway. When Jimmy was two years old, he said to his father, "Somebody pee peed in the air conditioner." David looked down and could clearly see yellow liquid all over one of those vents.

"Was it you?" his father asked.

"No," the two-year old answered. "Uncle Mike and Aunt Molly did it."

CHAPTER 13

THE RESUME

I have never got much work from talent agents and I don't go to too many casting calls because most of the movie jobs that I get, I get from other stuntmen (and sometimes from directors or producers that I've worked for in the past.) Stuntmen hire stuntmen that they know because they have observed their abilities. I do the same thing when I run the stunts on a show. I know who to hire and I know who has the ability to make me look good as a stunt coordinator.

To be a good stunt coordinator you have to know people. If I want a guy to do a top-notch burn stunt, I'll hire the best because I am lucky enough to know them. If want a motorcycle guy to do a crash, a jump or a wheelie, I would hire Gary Davis because he's one of the best at motorcycles. If I want somebody for a fire stunt, then I would hire some one like Perry Barndt who is one of the best. Perry produces "Fear Factor" now and he has set me on fire a few times. He makes his own gel and he's very good at it. If I had to coordinate something with trapeze, I would get Bob Yerkes because he has his own circus trapeze. If I wanted somebody who does martial arts or wrestling, I would get Gene LeBell – he works cheap – hell he is cheap. If I want somebody for a boxing match, I would bring in Jimmy Nickerson because he was the stunt coordinator on "Rocky," "Raging Bull," and "Streets of Gold" and he's hired me a few times as a referee and ring announcer. If I can't find the man or woman or little person, there's always "Wally Crowder's Stunt Players' Directory," which is the bible of the stunt profession, but knowing all of these guys and hiring them for movies makes me look good. They give me jobs and I give them jobs so I have never had to spend that much time dealing with agents and casting people during my movie and TV career.

I went in for this casting interview about two or three years ago and the casting gal looked like she was about 14. I don't do a lot of these interviews because I have been around so long that that isn't the way that I get most of my jobs so going in for interviews isn't one of my strong suits. I went into her office and she asked, "Well what have you done?"

My mind went blank. Here I had done hundreds of movies and television shows, but I just couldn't think of anything. "Well I did 91 'Fall Guys,'" I replied. That was the only show that I had worked on that came to mind.

"Was that a TV series or a movie?" she asked. She was too young to have ever heard of the show.

"Well I did 91 of them," I answered.

"Ninety-one? Well what was it?"

"It was a TV series," I said. If you did 91 of them it was a TV series — it wasn't a movie.

She didn't seem very impressed. "What else have you done?" she asked.

"Well I did 'Raging Bull," I told her. "I had an acting part. I was the ring announcer during a boxing match in the opening scene when a riot broke out and then I came back the next day as a stuntman and played one of the audience members so I was throwing chairs at myself."

She didn't seem to believe me that but it was a true story. I was the ring announcer in one shot ducking out of the way of chairs that were being ripped out of the floor and then the next day I was one of the guys tossing the chairs. There's even shot in the movie that's supposed to be from my point of view of chairs flying at me and I was both the guy ducking them and the one throwing them, which meant that I got two different checks for two different parts.

She looked at me and you could tell that she thought that I was full of it so she asked me what I had done for the third time. By this time, I knew that I wasn't going to get that job. There was just no way so I said, "The Birth of a Nation" which came out in 1915 and had no sound. Even I'm not old enough to have been in that movie — I was only a young child at the time.

"That's nice," she said in an almost patronizing tone. "You're very interesting." When I got up to leave she said, "Next time, bring in a resume."

"A resume?" I said.

"Yes a resume," she explained. "You know, a list of all of the films and TV shows that you have done."

I had a resume years ago but when I got to be fifty or sixty, I figured that I was a little too old to go out and hustle jobs. Like I said, I get most of my jobs from other stunt coordinators or from directors and producers who know me. Ever since that interview though, I've decided to make a list of all of the movies and TV shows that I've been in and to keep track of all of my residuals. When I get a check for a movie or show that I had worked on or a residual, I always put it down on the list. Whenever a movie is on TV, I always check out the stunt guys to see if anyone I know was in it and sometimes I see myself in the movie and I don't even remember making the thing so that goes down on the list too. Now when I go in for an interview I give them a picture of me and a sheet with a few of the movies that I have done and it's well over 500 different movies. I have probably done double that amount but many of them have never shown or never will be shown. You see a lot of times you don't get residuals because they sell the film then somebody else picks it up under a different name. It's all a part of the business and if you do enough movies you are going to work on more than your fair share of those kinds of productions.

Many of the fight scenes in "Raging Bull" were filmed in the Olympic Auditorium. In "Raging Bull" I was in a scene as the ring announcer and Robert DeNiro was playing the boxing champion Jake LaMotta. When I announced that he had lost the fight the riot broke out. Working on that movie was kind of weird. The ring that they were using was 24' by 34' instead of the standard 24' by 24' to accommodate the angle that they were shooting it at. They were also filming it in black and white and this was 1980 and nobody was shooting anything in black and white anymore so I had to ask the director why they weren't shooting it in color like every other movie. The now famous director Martin Scorsese looked at me like I was the dumbest man that he had ever laid eyes upon. He was an artiste. "That's art," he told me and I felt pretty stupid. To show you how little I know, today everybody is saying that "Raging Bull" is one of the ten best movies of all time and it won Robert DeNiro the Academy Award for Best Actor.

Years later I worked on another black and white movie about this incompetent director. The movie was called "Ed Wood." I played a ring announcer in that one too, but when I saw it I thought that it was just a nothing of a movie. Out of all of the directors that they could have made a movie about why did they pick that guy? I will never understand that, but that movie got Martin Landau the Best Supporting Actor Oscar for playing Bela Lugosi! I don't know what it is about these black and white movies, but the next time that somebody offers me a part in a black and white movie, I'm going to take it because then maybe I'll get an Academy Award.

I've worked on a few movies that were the life story of people that I had actually met in real life. One of these movies was called "The One and Only" with Henry Winkler (you know – The Fonz) and it was based on the life of Gorgeous George. They wanted to call the movie "Gorgeous George" but one of his wives threatened to sue them so they had to come up with a different name for it, which was actually for the better because the movie was really only inspired by Gorgeous George Wagner. There really wasn't a whole lot of truth in the movie, but it was still a fun show to work on. Ex-pro-wrestler Count Billy Varga played a referee in the movie and it also bears the distinction of being the great Roddy Piper's big screen debut.

There's a scene in the movie where the Fonz is wrestling using a German gimmick and he wins his matches by hitting his opponents with one of those spiked World War I helmets. Piper was the guy lucky enough to get smacked by that helmet. Before they shot the scene I told Winkler that Roddy was a tough guy and to let him have it and sure enough he did. He really slammed that thing into Roddy's skull and they filmed it over and over again from different angles and they cut it with footage of a train going by to make it look like it was a different match in different cities. Although Roddy only worked a couple of days, he ended up in the movie four or five times and has the lumps to prove it.

Near the end of the movie, I played the world champ in the scene where the Fonz finally gets his title shot. By this time in the movie he's entering the ring in ballet tights and spraying the ring with perfume and the whole bit. We were shooting a scene where we are supposed to shake hands and come out fighting but instead Winkler kissed me right on the lips. That wasn't in the script and I really didn't know what to do. Henry did that for shock effect and he got it and it ended up in the movie.

I also worked on a movie called "Man on the Moon" which starred Jim Carey as Andy Kaufman. Buddy Joe Hooker was the stunt coordinator on that movie and he brought me in to teach some of women how to wrestle and I also played a referee during some of the wrestling scenes. Buddy Joe is one of the biggies as far as stunt coordinators go. He did an incredible car jump in the Burt Reynolds movie "Hooper."

I had worked on a couple of episodes of "Taxi" usually playing a referee in the Tony Danza boxing episodes and I had met Andy Kaufman on the set of that show. One time Andy came up to me at the Olympic and he was a big wrestling fan. He told me that he wanted to learn how to wrestle but he looked a bulimia victim to me. I mean he was just too skinny. I looked at him like he was nuts and said, "What are you are you kidding?"

"No," he said, "I want to be a pro-wrestler."

"For goodness sakes," I told him, "you're a great actor and a darned good comedian – stick with that."

"That's okay," Kaufman said, "I just want to wrestle right now."

Kaufman was strange even back then. I guess that he was always strange. He was very much in his own world and very aggressive but not in a bad way. He had an intensity to him and if he wanted something that's all he seemed to want no matter what it was. I ended up showing him a few moves after the matches were over. A year later, he wrestled some women as a novelty and drew a couple of pretty big houses in the South and he did very well.

Of all of the TV shows that I worked on, I liked "The Fall Guy" the best and that's probably why I mentioned it during that casting interview. If you remember the show, Lee Majors played a stuntman who moonlighted as a bounty hunter. How he had time for both jobs, I'll never know, but since stunts were built into the premise of the show, we got to do a lot of them. We got to do car stuff, motorcycle gags, tickles and tackles, boxing and wrestling, and just about everything else that you can think of. Since there were so many stunts in "The Fall Guy," I managed to work on 91 episodes of it and I got all 91 residuals at one time and I was shocked that I had worked on that many episodes.

Mickey Gilbert ran the stunts on that show and he is, in my opinion, the best stuntman to ever put on stunt pads. Mickey got into the business because he rode horses and did rodeo work. I've seen him work with a trampoline and I've seen him work with fire. I've worked on shows where he's done motorcycle stunts and I've worked on a lot of shows where he did car jumps and he did a lot of those in "The Fall Guy." Now you can say that there's better motorcycle guys or better tumblers, but he is so close to all of them that he is in a class by himself as a stuntman, second unit director and all-around good guy as far as I'm concerned.

There was a boxing episode of "The Fall Guy" and Mickey asked me to help him hire some boxers for the show. My mother and matchmaker Don Chargin were able to help me get world champions Larry Holmes, Archie Moore, Bobby Chacon and Sugar Ray Robinson for the show. They all got more than minimum scale and everybody on that set asked the great "Sugar" Ray for his autograph. Years after he had retired from the ring people still knew that he was maybe the best pound-for-pound best fighter of all time.

Mickey Gilbert still coordinates stunts today. I just worked with him on a movie called "Bruce Almighty" with Jim Carey. When Carey saw me on the set he walked up to me and hugged me because I worked with him on some of his other shows. It's nice to be remembered. Mickey used a lot of older stunt guys who really don't work much anymore for that movie and it was really nice to see some of them. Sometimes it's difficult for the older guys to get jobs although they are still handy and might need the money. In the movies, there are good guys and bad guys and Mickey Gilbert is one of the good guys.

Mickey's three sons are also doing stunts and they're all almost as good as their dad. They're all talented kids showing that the apple doesn't far from the tree.

Everybody on the set of "The Fall Guy" was very nice to work with. Heather Thomas was one of the stars of the show and she had a great personality. She was fun people. I used to have these t-shirts that said things like "Gene's My Friend" or "I Stole This Shirt From Gene LeBell" and she used to wear them all of the time and she teased the stuntmen about it and it really got to them. She would walk around the set and say, "I had a good time sleeping with Gene," and "Gene is so warm and comfortable." It drove the stuntmen nuts because she was a real knockout. They all thought that that I was going with her which, of course, I wasn't. She called the t-shirts that I had given to her "Gene" and that's what she was referring to. She slept in those shirts with my name on them, but of course she never slept with me.

Another show that was fun to work on because it had a lot of stunts was "The Dukes of Hazzard." It had a lot of car crashes, turnovers and motorcycle gags. It was a very fun show. One time when I was working on that show, I was in the backseat of a car and I was supposed to shoot at the Duke boys out the back window and the window was to be blown out as I took my shot. The show's special effects guy seemed a little green to me and I was pretty sure that glass was going to end up all over the place. The way that they were shooting the scene, my face wouldn't be in view of the camera (the audience could only see the gun) so I went to the welding guy and got a pair of safety glasses and put them on. They didn't put in a plexiglass shield to protect me from the explosion and it turned out that the special effects guy put the charges in wrong. When they blew out the back windshield, the glass flew everywhere and I ended up with minor powder burns on my face. Luckily I had the glasses on so my eyes weren't hurt. The special effects guy apologized to me, I cleaned myself up and it wasn't too bad. I was glad that I protected my eyes. You have to watch yourself as a stuntman. I could have been blinded.

In the next scene, I was in that car shooting out the broken back window while stuntman Jerry Summers took the car up a ramp and jumped it. I told the first assistant that there was still glass all over the seats and in the little flat space by the back window. They told me that they were leaving it there for effect. I told them that camera wouldn't even see it and then the first assistant told me, "Don't waste time Gene. Let's get to it. We're losing the light." Losing the light meant that they were running late, but it was still early in the morning. I had a pretty good part with dialogue in that episode so I didn't press too hard.

So we headed down the dirt road to the spot where we were going to jump the car. The car took off and the broken pieces of glass went up on the headliner and what goes up must come down and it came down and sliced the right side of my forehead and face. I bled like a stuck pig. I told the first assistant director, "See I told you it was dangerous." It wasn't him so he didn't care. They were behind and that was in the morning. Later, at ten o'clock at night I was still working but they couldn't see my face. After wrapping up the scene, I finally made it to the emergency hospital. The right side of my face was all swollen and they had to put in several stitches to close those deep cuts.

The next day, we had to shoot the scene where we were going to rob a bank and I had a lot of dialogue, but the entire right side of my face was covered with bruises and stitches. To the show's audience, all of a sudden I would have had bandages all over my face for no reason. You can't do things like that. This was very funny. I cut the medical tape back so that you could only see the left side of my face. I looked sideways into the camera and they filmed the shot from the point-of-view of the guy sitting next to me so you could only see me in profile. I was in the passenger seat. I did my two or three lines of dialogue and I looked back and forth only using my eyes with no head movement whatsoever. My head was stock-still. The show was a bit of a comedy anyway so it was terrific. It took about a week for the swelling to go down and another couple of days for the stitches to come out but then we moved on. Just another day at the office.

What's funny about working on movies is that it gives you the opportunity to go to strange new places that you normally wouldn't get to go to and meet even stranger people in the process. No movie that I worked gave me these kinds of opportunities more than "Lock Up" with Sylvester Stallone. Stallone wanted the movie to have a certain look so it was filmed on location at the Rahwey State Prison in New

Jersey and they actually used some of the inmates as extras. He wanted it to be more gritty and realistic and wanted the audience to see ice on the ground during the outdoor scenes in the prison yard. When you spoke you could see the steam rise out of your mouth. Man it was cold out there.

When we got to the prison the warden told us that we weren't allowed to talk to the inmates. He warned us that the prisoners would get us in trouble and try to get money from us or have us write letters for them. He really went on and on about not talking to the prisoners. I was out in the prison yard with some stunt guys and everyone was saying things like, "These guys are murderers and they cut throats and they'll kill you at the drop of a hat."

A few of the convicts walked by us accompanied by some guards. They stopped and one con looked at me and said, "You know there's 200 people in here that have AIDS."

All of the stunt guys were backing away from the guy. I crossed the line that separated the film crew from general populace, which I shouldn't have done, and I grabbed the con and said, "Two hundred and one!" That inmate jumped back against the wall and all of the stunt guys started laughing.

Later on while we were shooting "Lock Up" one of the stunt guys Matt Johnston and I were talking to this inmate and the guy seemed really normal. We were having just a regular conversation with the guy. He really didn't seem like he belonged in there. After talking to him for awhile, Johnston asked him why he was in there.

"I don't know," he replied, "I can't understand why I'm here."

"Well what were you convicted of," we asked.

"I'm here for murder," he said after a pause. He was very calm about it – very matter of fact. Then he said, "I killed my wife," and he started to sob. He was breaking down and I thought he might have killed his wife by accident in a car crash but then he screamed out, "I cut her heart out. How did I know that she was going to die!?!"

He cut her heart out, how did he know she was going die? The guy then went into major hysterics and I told my buddy, "This guy's a whack job. Let's get the hell out of here!"

I was really impressed by this African American inmate who was giving a speech in the prison auditorium to a bunch of high school kids from bad neighborhoods. He was about 6'7" and 280 pounds and scary looking. The speech was called "Tough Love." The kids were taken out to the prison by the juvenile authorities and this inmate told them what was going to happen to them if they landed themselves in jail. He told them that he was going to make them into his girlfriend. He was a pretty imposing guy and he talked pretty frankly about anal rape. He used a string of the most brutal profanities that I have ever heard and the woman from the juvenile authority didn't even flinch while he said all of this. She must have heard it all before.

That guy was really good. I mean he got in my head so I talked to him after he was done scaring the bejesus out of those kids. "I'm here for murder," he said. "I was guilty and now I am here for the rest of my life."

"I wish that I could start my life all over again," he continued, "but I can't so that's why I want to stop these kids and change their lives." He told me that if he got to just one young boy and kept him from doing something stupid and going to prison, then it was all worth it. That really made an impression on me.

Now I have very little stretch as an actor: I either play drunks (which I have never had a drink in my life) or I play a crazy guy. At least those casting agents get things half right: because I'm not a drunk but as for crazy, I'm just playing myself.

I had a lot of fun working on this wrestling comedy called "Bad Guys" with Ruth Buzzie. She played my wife in it. She probably wouldn't know me if I walked down the street, I'm sure, but she was extremely nice to me on the set. In "Bad Guys," I played a crazed ex-wrestler which should have gotten me that ever elusive Academy Award, but it wasn't filmed in black and white so they passed me up for the nomination again. At least the six people that saw the movie liked it.

"Bad Guys" had a lot of pro wrestlers in it such as Sgt. Slaughter, Jay York, Alexis Smirnoff and Toru Tanaka, but for crowd shots and backgrounds they used non-union waivers instead of union extras because the company was trying to save money. Waivers oftentimes aren't actual actors and they aren't members of the Screen Actor's Guild – they are just people off of the street who get a cold lunch and maybe a small payoff for their trouble, but they do get to be in the movies.

One of these waivers tried to muscle his way into every shot. I saw the rushes and there he was over and over again. He jumped in front of people in every scene so that you would notice him. I knew that we had to get rid of this guy. He was always getting other waivers to take off their costumes so he could put them on and do another scene. He was wrecking the picture. I told the second assistant director (casting director) but he shrugged it off.

I was doing a scene with Ruth Buzzie in the wrestling ring and this guy was on the set so I told him to stay out of the ring and that he wasn't supposed to be near us when we did our dialogue. He said that he would stay out of the shot, but as soon as they started to roll film, he jumped in the ring, cut in front of me and stepped on Ruth Buzzy's foot to get a close-up. I grabbed him and shoved him over to the other side of the ring and said, "Get the hell out of here!"

He looked at me and said, "F— you!"

He took a couple of steps towards me so I picked him up and slammed him down hard and landed on him. He was out cold and they hauled him away to the hospital.

Although they should have given me a hero button for body-slamming that non-union waiver the second assistant was quite upset over it so Eddie Donno, the stunt coordinator, came up to me to try to smooth things over. Eddie is a great stuntman and he's the kind of guy that's always in your corner. He walked up to me and said, "Gene, you've got to calm down. You can't have a temper. You've got to be nice and cool like I am – love, love, love."

I could tell that he was being a little sarcastic but I was hot. "You know what this guy did," I said. "He stepped on Ruth Buzzie and he tried to push me out of the way to be in the shot and he cursed at me!"

Right after Eddie was through talking to me, the next thing that I heard was a heavy thud. I turned around and the second assistant director was out cold and Eddie was shaking his fist. Eddie let the guy have it right between the horns.

I went up to Eddie and put my arm around him and said, "Eddie. You've got to be calm. You can't have a temper."

"You should have seen what that son of a bitch did!" Eddie said

"But you knocked him out," I said jokingly, "I never lose my temper. Love, love, love."

Since I am a professional wrestler a stunt coordinator named Buck McDancer got the bright idea that I would be perfect to double Hulk Hogan on a motorcycle in one movie. Now the problem with this was that Hogan is 6'8" and is 305 pounds of solid muscle while I stand a tad shy of 6 feet tall. He is balding and has platinum blond hair and I have red hair the last time that I looked so I have never really thought of myself as the spitting image of the Hulkster.

When I got to the set of the show where I was doubling Hogan, I decided to swerve (play a joke on) him because I remembered when he wrestled for us at the Olympic Auditorium back in the 1970s. I started telling anybody who would listen that I knew Hulk Hogan and I was going to tear him limb from limb when I got a hold of him. "I'm going to annihilate, mutilate and assassinate that bum! Anybody knows that one stuntman can beat any ten wrestlers any day of the week!" I proclaimed. Word got back to Hogan pretty quickly that some guy was looking to beat him up on the set. Hogan had no idea who it was who was after him. When he finally ran into me, he cracked a big smile and said, "You friggin' SOB," and invited me into his trailer for a drink. I don't drink but I went in there anyway.

Hulk Hogan is one of the biggest grossing guys in pro wrestling history. He's an athlete and he trains hard to keep in shape and look the part. He still has a lot of the old fire horse left in him so keeps on wrestling, but he is just as successful as he ever was. He a seasoned veteran and in the last couple of years he has drawn some pretty big houses for his matches with The Rock and his boss Vince McMahon, Jr. so I don't think that we're going to see Hogan quit anytime soon.

You are only supposed to wrestle until you are 55, but I wrestled until I was well over that on one-shot spot shows, but my pro wrestling career eventually came to an end. I didn't have any big, tear-jerking retirement match or anything like that. There just came a time when I finally earned enough paychecks and residuals as a stuntman that I didn't need to lace up the boots and step into the squared circle anymore. You had to be a superstar to make a decent living wrestling in the United and I wasn't one except maybe in Texas years back. In most territories, I was a main eventer but not always a superstar. My movie and television career eventually eclipsed pro wrestling.

I always wanted to go out undefeated like Rocky Marciano did in boxing. That's why I quit competition judo after I had won the nationals for the second time and that's why I have never really looked back at my professional wrestling career while some guys can never leave the ring. A lot of boxers, wrestlers and martial artists still have it in their hearts to be champions but maybe their reflexes have slowed down just a bit. Sure they are still tough and talented guys, but time has passed them by. Even the great Joe Louis made a comeback because he needed the money and ended up being beaten by Marciano. Louis was knocked out of the ring in that fight and he could only use one arm, but the outcome may have been different if the fight had happened 15 years earlier. Muhammad Ali who, in my opinion, was the greatest heavyweight fighter in my lifetime or anytime also fought beyond his years and he was beaten by Larry Holmes who used to be his sparring partner. Most idols have clay feet if they stay in their chosen game past their prime. You really remember the guys that quit when they're on top. Undefeated people are few and far between.

In the 1980s, the professional wrestling landscape started to change. The system of smaller regional promotions that I had worked for throughout most of my career had started to fade away and the reason for that was Vince McMahon, Jr. and the WWF (known today as the WWE.)

When Vince, Jr. bought his father's East Coast wrestling promotion, he went national with it. The first time that Vince came to Los Angeles and ran in competition with us, he lost money because when he had a show, we'd have one too and our tickets were cheaper because his overhead was higher because he had to fly his talent in. His stars national and ours were local and we had more people coming to our shows. But this was still only temporary because Vince is bar none the PT Barnum of professional wrestling. At first he had stars like Bruno Sammartino and Bob Backlund who had their biggest followings out on the East Coast but later he had Hogan, Andre and even Piper so it was only a matter of time before he outsold us.

Of course it really didn't hurt McMahon that my brother made some pretty bad business decisions along the way in those years. For years, our wrestling show was on KCOP Channel 13, which is a pretty high wattage station in the Los Angeles area. Business was hurting so Mike panicked and kept on running commercials during the wrestling TV show to hype the live shows but you were only allowed so much airtime for advertising back then. He overdid the commercials and thought that he could get away with it because he was the boss. The station warned him verbally and warned him in writing. They told him that he couldn't plug his own shows at his arena. I think that you were allowed a minute and half of commercial time for every half-hour of programming at the time, but he slipped in five minutes of commercials because he was the stage director.

I told my brother Mike that he couldn't get away with over-commercializing on Channel 13 and that the station was going to pull the plug on him and he told me to shut up. Although I liked my brother, he thinks that he's God and wouldn't take advice from anyone. The last show that he had taped for Channel 13 was practically an infomercial and it never did air. In trying to squeeze every last dime out of the wrestling promotion, he had ended up not only costing himself money, but he cost me and a lot of other people money as well. The wrestling show was picked up by Channel 34 and then moved to Channel 52 which was a Spanish language station. We did the announcing in English and Spanish, which may have been a bit ahead of our time but it sure wasn't drawing ratings.

Channel 34 and 52 just didn't have the viewership that Channel 13 did so when Vince McMahon and his WWF started to turn up the heat, the Southern California Promotion couldn't compete any longer. The houses kept getting smaller and smaller.

Today pro wrestling is full of gimmicks. It's for show. Vince McMahon, Jr. has had two male wrestlers get married to each other on his show when they weren't even gay. A lot of people will do anything for money. The WWE has had a lot of other crazy things go on during their shows too. Lou Thesz hated that. He said that it was prostituting wrestling and there's a part of me that agrees with him but I'll tell you something – the bottom line is that these guys are making money. Today there is a guy named Duane Johnson but everybody knows him as The Rock. I wrestled his father and I wrestled his grandfather. He's from Hawaii and his mother was a wrestling promoter there. It's funny now this guy is making millions. He's making more money than anybody's ever come close to making plus he's become a big action star in the movie industry.

I helped coordinate some of the stunts on the pro wrestling episode of this half-hour sitcom called "That 70s Show" and he was on it. He did a little bit of wrestling and he was just getting to be known in the mainstream then. His opponent on that show was Ken Shamrock who is a fine grappler and ultimate fighter. This was two or three years ago and now The Rock gets a lot of money to be in big action movies like "The Scorpion King" and Vince McMahon, who's built him up, gets either a quarter or a third of any check that The Rock gets from outside. It's a loan out so Vince McMahon is making a lot of money, and The Rock is making a lot of money, and pro wrestlers in general are taking home more now than they ever have and you really can't knock that.

The boxing business out of the Olympic Auditorium also started to change around the same time that the wrestling business did. Things started to go badly for my mother Aileen Eaton and attendance started dropping and a lot of people were out of work and the economy was on a downer so I asked her why she didn't just sell out, take the money and travel around the world. The truth was that she would rather be on the phone, losing money and wheeling and dealing for something than retire. I couldn't understand it back then but today when I get a call for a job on a movie, I am right there and ready to take a fall or roll a car or whatever it takes to get the job done. Just like my mother, I would rather be working. If you don't use it, you'll lose it and retirement is not in Gene LeBell's future.

My mother was ultra generous. She loaned a lot of money to old fighters, trainers and managers when she knew that she wasn't going to get it back. I disagreed with a lot of the people that she loaned money to. When I asked her about it she said, "Oh Gene, those people have made so much money for me over the years."

I said, "Yeah, but they earned a paycheck when they fought for you. You don't owe them for the rest of your life." She wouldn't hear it and it was her business. She told me that she could just write it off.

My mother was named to the California State Athletic Commission in 1982 and she worked in boxing until the very end. Even after she had suffered from a stroke, matchmaker Don Chargin came by the house people in the world of boxing, but Don Chargin is one of the best if not the best to ever work in that sport or walk the earth for that matter.

My mother passed away on November 7, 1987. Out of everybody that I have ever met, she had the biggest impact on my life of anybody. Without her I would have never met people like Ed "Strangler" Lewis, Lou Thesz, Vic Christy, wrestling promoter Jules Strongbow, and boxing matchmakers Babe McCoy and Don Chargin who all shaped my life by getting me into both wrestling and boxing. Judo was the only thing that I took up independently of her, but I probably would have never been as good at it if she had never sent me to train with the pro wrestlers at the LA Athletic Club when I was seven years old. Most everything that I have ever accomplished in martial arts, movies and wrestling I owe to her.

My mother may have died but she will never be forgotten. In 2002 she became the only woman to ever be inducted into the Boxing Hall of Fame. I flew out to New York to the Boxing Hall of Fame to accept the award for her. A lot of world champions that had worked for my mother at the Olympic like Marvin Hagler, Ken Norton, and Gene Fullmer were there as well as old-time trainers and managers like Angelo Dundee (Ali's trainer), Lou Duva.

Gene Fullmer talked to me for hours. He told me that Milo Savage was his sparring partner and that he never wanted to fight him because

Savage was exceptionally tough. "Milo would have been a world champion if anyone would have given him a title shot," Gene Fullmer told me. Fullmer had a classic series of fights with Sugar Ray Robinson but he wouldn't fight Milo and he was really impressed that I had in our boxer vs. wrestler match and won.

My mother Aileen Eaton was a boxing promoter for 38 years and she promoted 168 world championship matches during her career. Bob Arum, who is one of the biggest promoters in the business today, said that he learned everything that he ever knew about promoting fights from "a little old redheaded lady in California" referring to my mother.

Today, from the parking lot of the Olympic Auditorium you can see the bigger and more modern Staples Center. It takes up two city blocks and dwarfs the old Olympic in every way. The Staples Center comes fully equipped with the riggings for lighting and pyro that modern audiences have come to expect. It is now the place where you are going to see the superstars of both boxing and wrestling such as the Rock, Hogan, Oscar De La Hoya and Lennox Lewis. The Olympic is still standing but the new owner Steve Needleman has renamed it the Grand Olympic because it is on the corner of Grand and Olympic Streets in Downtown Los Angeles. They still hold independent wrestling shows and amateur boxing matches there, but now my mother's old stomping grounds is mostly used as a location for movies and television shows, which means that I still work there from time to time. As long as I earn a paycheck in this world it seems that I will always do business at the Olympic Auditorium.

CHAPTER 14

PASSING THE TORCH

When you have been around as long as I have and have had a bit of success in your field, people might start calling you a legend. "Legend" isn't a term that I would use lightly. I would reserve it to describe the true greats like Lou Thesz, "Strangler" Lewis, "Sugar" Ray Robinson or Muhammad Ali but a lot of other people throw it around without giving it much thought. So as I'm starting to finish this book, I've had to think, "What does it mean to be a legend?" Well, I'll try to tell you.

When I was narrating wrestling on television in Los Angeles, I was spotted in a public restroom by a fan. He was excited as all get out to see me there, standing over a urinal and relieving myself and he yelled, "Hey! There's 'Judo' Gene LeBell taking a whiz!" I was in a state of shock and I damned near peed down my leg. I had never heard the expression "taking a whiz" used for urinating before so that was a little bit of a vocabulary lesson for me. My son David was there and he was laughing his butt off at the young man's comments. If nobody was there, I would have probably urinated on my kid's pants, but I have an image to protect. Needless to say, the men's room is no place for an autograph session, so I just wanted to do what I had come there for and get the heck out of there. When I was through doing my business, the young man insisted on shaking hands with me but I insisted on going to the sink and washing my hands first.

Years later, in November 2002, I was one of the guests at Gerald Okimura's "Dragon Fest," which is a convention held in Glendale, Calif. every year where a bunch of martial artists, ultimate fighters, and movie actors all gather to meet with the fans, sell their merchandise and sign autographs. David Carradine was there and so were Gokor, Don "The Dragon" Wilson, Bas Rutten, Oleg Taktarov and too many others to really mention. As the day went on, I had to take a whiz. I decided to go to the bathroom upstairs at the venue thinking that it would be less crowded than the ground level bathrooms so that I wouldn't get noticed. So I get up to the upstairs restroom, and there is a big, long line waiting to use the facilities. I had no choice, but to wait my turn like everybody else. As I was waiting to use to use the john, the guy in front of me turned around and recognized me. "You're Gene LeBell," he said. "You're a legend! Cut in front of me line. You're a legend man. You go first."

Now I was embarrassed. "No come on," I said, "You go first."

"No. You're Gene LeBell! You're a legend," he said as he insisted that I take my turn in the toilet ahead of him so I did. You can't fight city hall. Since you can't eat glory or make a house payment with trophies, to me being a legend means that you get to cut ahead in line to take your turn in the bathroom. Sometimes being a legend can be awfully embarrassing.

I have taught martial arts, boxing, judo, grappling and wrestling for a lot of years now. I have taught a lot and I have learned a lot. I have always cross-trained and learned techniques from everybody and have studied many different styles. Everyone who has come into my dojo that is an expert in their art has been like a teacher to me and I am eager to learn from anyone who knows something that I don't. I believe strongly in never knocking other styles of the martial arts because they all have something to offer. They all may have some effective techniques that work in self-defense or in the ring.

There are a lot of people in karate that do have a grappling background but they're not known for it. I have a karate background. I have a boxing background. You don't even hear of me doing judo although I won the US judo nationals a couple of times because people now think of me as being a grappler.

When I turned pro in 1955 the old time pro wrestlers used to call it grappling so I used grappling and I tried to say that grappling was a part of the martial arts because in my opinion it is. At various times though, some people in martial arts argued that grappling (or boxing for that matter) weren't a part of the martial arts. Peoples' perceptions of what is a martial art and what isn't changes with the times and a lot of that has to do with the movies as much as anything. Years ago they used to have this Chinese movie detective named Charlie Chan (who was usually played by a Caucasian actor) and he did these pressure points that made a guy go unconscious and people thought that that was judo. Bruce Lee came in later with his style of kung fu and everything was punching and kicking. Today, after Ultimate Fighting and all of these get tough contests grappling has become more accepted and everybody wants to learn grappling and finishing holds.

I have had the privilege of learning from and teaching some of the best martial artists and fighters of all time and I am very good friends with a lot of them too. Benny "The Jet" Urquedez, who is a world champion kick-boxer and one of the best in his sport ever, taught me some kick-boxing and I taught him some grappling. I taught Bruce Lee judo and finishing holds and he taught me his way of doing kung fu and I still use some of his moves today in the movies as a stuntman. Bill "Superfoot" Wallace is a great full-contact karate man and he is a black belt in judo. He has taught me some of his moves, like how to swing a golf club and in turn I taught him how to do the dance of the seven veils. Joe Lewis is one of the best karate people of all time. He worked out with us and then he wrote an article that said that that the best karate move is a judo choke.

There was this one very successful martial artist, who was good at submission holds, but other martial artists didn't like him because he tried to build himself up by knocking the other fighting styles. He wrote an article in one of the martial arts magazines that knocked Benny "The Jet" Urquedez. He said that one of his students could beat Benny easily and that he would give Benny $100,000 if his guy couldn't.

Now Benny is a warrior. He doesn't have a weak bone in his body and he always goes out to win. He's a real class act and he's the kind of guy that you want as a student because you know that he's a winner. He could have been a champion in judo, wrestling, boxing or any martial art but he competed in full body contact karate and he's an undefeated champion at that. Benny wanted to accept the challenge kind of like the way that I did when I went up against Milo Savage in that boxer vs. wrestler match.

I told Benny that if he accepted this challenge and went into this guy's dojo and fought his guy that it would be anything goes. It was going to be a street fight and on the street you attack a guy's eyes or groin. You pull people by their ears or hair and you do whatever it takes to win. In my fighting system, we call this "the dark side of the moon," which are all of the moves that you use when the ref's back is turned.

So Benny trained with me every day for six weeks and I just showed him what to do when he got in close and I wasn't showing him Queensbury rules. Now, if you've ever gotten a piece of dirt in your eyes, you know how excruciating that is. The nerve endings in the eyes are so close to the brain that the toughest guy in the world is the guy that can gouge the other guy's eye out first. He's the winner. I worked with Benny from every angle. Benny was very fast at snatching a guy's eye from any position – up, down, sideways and from behind. I taught him to snatch the leg and pluck the eyeball, or grab the arm and get that eyeball or go behind and snatch that eyeball. Now the blue eyes taste real good but the brown ones are salty if you should decide to eat them.

After six weeks of training we were about to have the fight but the guy who put up the challenge in the first place told Benny that he had to put up $100,000 too. Benny is a very successful martial artist and world-class fighter but he just couldn't raise that kind of money over night. That's when Bob Wall of "Enter the Dragon" fame stepped in and put up the 100,000 dollars. Bob even offered to put up a million and he has it too, but the fight still stalled and ended up never taking place. I wonder why?

Chuck Norris is one of the most modest guys that you will ever meet. He came down to my school once to work out and he put on a white belt. I saw him do this and I said, "You're a teacher and a champion. Wear your black belt."

He told me that he wouldn't do it out of respect for me. "What if somebody in here wants to learn a spinning back kick?" I said to him. "There is nobody here who is going to be as good at that move as you so when you show somebody that move you are a teacher and you deserve to wear your black belt."

He wouldn't budge on the issue so finally I had to threaten him and said, "Okay, I'll have to sit on you then."

He relented and agreed to wear a black belt but he didn't have one with him so I gave him one of mine. My black belts have my name "Gene LeBell" stitched into them. At the end of the evening after we were done training, he wouldn't give me back the belt with my name on it but I didn't think anything of it. Belts aren't that expensive.

Later on when he was in Texas working on his highly successful TV show "Walker Texas Ranger," he was wearing my belt during a rehearsal and there were some newspaper people around. One of the reporters asked him, "How come you have somebody else's black belt on?"

Bob Wall was there with Chuck and Bob likes to joke around as much as the next guy. They both told the reporter that the only way that you could get somebody else's black belt was to kill them in a death match. The upshot of this is that I'm dead in Texas. I can't go there and that might explain why Chuck only used me on his show once even though the thing ran for six years. Bob and Chuck sent a poster sized picture of the both of them in their gis with big grins on their faces and Chuck is wearing that controversial black belt with my name on it.

For about the last ten years now, we have had the Ultimate Fighting Championships and then later on there was Pride in Japan and also the King of the Cage. In these get tough contests, you have fighters from all of the different martial arts going against each other and to me, I think that this is wonderful. I don't have enough good things to say about it. It proves what is practical on the street. The only bad thing is, is that it proves that there are certain martial arts moves that aren't as practical as some people think they are. In the early days of Ultimate Fighting you would have a guy who's 10th degree in his style and he would go against one of the Gracie kids and get choked out in a matter of minutes. Now the guy was tenth degree and he was top of the line in his discipline, but he would go into his karate pose and get choked out for his trouble.

Now to some that may have been bad for the martial arts and a lot of guys may have been left with their hats in their hands as a result of it, but the get tough contests were a huge victory for cross-training in different styles. When UFC first hit the scene, the fighters with a wrestling or submissions background like Dan Severn, Royce Gracie and Ken Shamrock were beating everybody by using leverage, take-downs and finishing holds on their opponents.

The wrestlers and jiu-jitsu fighters were dominant back then, but later on outstanding fighters like Bas Rutten and Don Frye started to cross-train and added striking to their repertoires as well as wrestling. You then started to see guys getting knocked out by kicks and punches. Today you have to be well versed in a lot of different fighting styles to be a top fighter in mixed martial arts. Guys like Don Frye and Bas Rutten have been very successful in today's get tough contests because they are skilled in boxing, kick-boxing, finishing holds, wrestling and takedowns. You have to have it all to take it all and you can't just train in one style anymore – you have to train in all of them.

John Perretti was the matchmaker for the Ultimate Fighting Championships and he was very good at it. He hired me to judge some of the fights and he even named his son Lucca LeBell Perretti after me. Perretti once had a fighter that was an Olympic gold medallist in American freestyle wrestling who he was trying to build but the wrestler didn't know any finishing holds because they aren't allowed in his sport. Perretti wanted to make sure that the guy won so he wanted me to teach him some submissions. I called the wrestler on the phone and told him that I wanted to teach him some finishing holds. "Look I've beaten the best in the world," he told me. "What do I need finishing holds for?" I just shrugged my shoulders and hung up the phone, but in his next fight, he ended up tapping out to a leg lock in something like 46 seconds.

After his victory, the winner was very excited. I showed him my stopwatch, which was stopped at 46 seconds – the time that it had taken him to beat an Olympic champion. He kept on grabbing my hand to look at the time on my watch. Finally, I handed it to him and said, "The watch is yours. Take it." It was a brand new stopwatch, but I couldn't see myself hanging onto it at that point. The fighter thanked me by saying that he would never wind it again as he walked away from me while staring at the watch and firmly grasping it with both hands.

All of this is similar to an ongoing argument that I have had over the years with various law enforcement agencies. Sometimes I will be asked to sit in on their training courses and they will have some sergeant instruct the class and he will show the cadets a series of moves and have them drill on it. I have always argued that unless you spar and do the moves for real, that you won't have any way of knowing which moves work and which ones don't. A lot of these young officers learn a few moves out of context and will end up on their backside if they every go up against some real tough guy out on the streets.

I think that police officers should do a lot of sparring. They should practice how to disarm a guy with a club or a knife so that they will know what to do if they get in a real situation. They should practice how to duck, how to tackle, how to go behind, how to kick, how to punch, how to bite, how to gouge. Now then you are probably never going to use any of this, but you should be qualified. If you are going to get out on the streets where anything can happen, you should get your hands dirty while you are training. In law enforcement, the dangers are very real, and sparring as though you were in a real life or death situation is the best way that I know how to prepare yourself.

I believe a good student can be better than his teacher because he adds his creative genius to the techniques. That's why we now have better radios, better televisions and better planes. One person started the idea and then other people improved on it. I learned different martial arts and I added them to my style. I learned wrestling from the great pros. I learned how to box at the Main St. Gym from world champions. I studied judo from the great judo instructors from Japan and Europe, and I learned kendo and other Japanese martial arts in Japan. I took the moves that were practical from many different styles and integrated them into my system. As for the dance routines, they are useful for exercise and movie choreography, but I would never attempt them on the street. I call my system Gene LeBell's Grappling World (just like the book) and it is made up of the practical moves from many different arts. In my system I take moves from many different arts and combine them into one practical art, but I always credit other teachers and systems for the moves that I have borrowed because you should always give credit where credit is due.

Gokor Chivichyan is the best student that I have ever had and I jokingly nicknamed him "The Armenian Assassin," because of the way that he easily dominates his opponents. Gokor and I are cut from the same cloth. He is the same kind of fanatical competitor that I am and he is an outstanding teacher so I am passing the torch to him. I push him at the seminars as my number one student because he does everything that I do and he is very good at it. Now our students do our system, which is heavily based on cross training in different styles and techniques. If I didn't have Gokor, the Gene LeBell system would die. We both do judo throws and grappling with and without a gi. We do all the good stuff and the dark side of the moon and all of it's allowed at our school. Now at a lot of jiu-jitsu schools heel-hooks are a no-no – they aren't allowed. If you go to a judo school and you do a leg lock or a neck crank or a body squeeze that's also a no-no. When I teach, I want the guys to know everything and Gokor does also. I want students to put on boxing gloves and learn how to bob and weave and throw hooks and jabs. I want them to learn how throw good karate kicks and also how to wrestle and apply finishing holds. That way when our students go up against a karate fighter or a boxer or a wrestler they will know what to do. They will know what the guys who train under different systems and styles can come up with.

I first met Gokor when he was 16 years old and he came into the judo class at Los Angeles City College. Hayward Nishioka was the head of the athletic department. He had me come to the college to teach the judo classes. He told me to try teaching there for a year and I ended up staying there for 17 years total and that's where I met Gokor. Gokor is Armenian and he had just emigrated from Europe to the United States when he came into my judo class. He was already very well trained in judo and Russian Sambo fighting, but he always wore a gi. I had him take the gi off and work on all of the grappling moves without relying on the handles that a judo suit provides. I taught him to beat a guy with what he doesn't know and how to use that old dark side of the moon. If the shoe fits wear it. If you have to fight dirty, always remember it's the final score that counts and 100 years from now, nobody will know the difference. A win is a win.

While I was teaching at LA City College, there was this one student who kept on trying to break into the teachers' room. The guy was a dead ringer for Charles Manson – I mean he was the spitting image of the guy if you know what I mean plus he had a bad attitude. I caught him trying to break into the instructors' room. I said, "You don't belong in here. You're not a teacher. This is a teacher's room." He told me that Hayward Nishioka said that it was okay for him to be back there but when I asked Hayward about it, he said that he had done no such thing.

I caught him the next day and he got really sarcastic with me. I really wanted to drop kick him into the nickel seats but I decided not to out of respect for Hayward. I might be a sadistic bastard but I'm not a bully. Later on, the guy got on the mat during class and he was sarcastic with me again so I threw him around a bit and choked him unconscious and set him in the corner. I was talking to the class while he was out and said, "You know if a guy has an attitude, this doesn't hurt him one bit but it sure keeps him quiet." Some people laughed and the others just stared.

When class was over, I took a shower and left the guy there but after he came too, I guess that he called the police. Gokor talked to the police and told them that the Manson lookalike broke into the coaches' room and that "Sensei Gene gave him a judo lesson and that's a fact." You have to be in trouble to find out who your friends are and Gokor has always been in my corner as I am in his and he is family to me.

There was another time at LA City College when this guy came in and said, "I want to wrestle that old man over there – or does he wrestle?" He was pointing at me.

I acted like I was hard of hearing and said, "What did you say?"

"Yeah old man do you want to wrestle?" he asked.

"Yes I do," I replied, "I will wrestle you but only if you take it easy on me. I have only been working out for a couple of months." Little did he know I was putting him on big time.

I got on the mat with him and threw him around and when he started to squeak, I wouldn't let him up. I had him pinned and I was applying some pressure with a hold and I said, "Please try not to throw up on the mat because that would be bad." A couple of the students there were just laughing and having a good time. It wasn't that I was good, it was that he thought that he was better than he was and he was very arrogant about it. Maybe I shouldn't admit it but it felt really good to stretch a guy who has an attitude.

At the school we are at now, I call that an attitude adjustment and Gokor does too. If a guy comes in with a chip on his shoulder you just knock it off of him. The way to do it is to make sure that he remembers it. The only way that I know to improve his memory is to humiliate him and make him experience pain. Sometimes it's fun being a teacher.

When you are a teacher you can take kids that might have been gang members who might do graffiti on the walls and don't have the opportunity to have a vocation or avocation and put them in a dojo where they can learn some respect and self-discipline. It keeps them off of the streets and they might just learn a little more than judo in the process. They might learn how to be a considerate human being.

In Gokor's and my school, if somebody doesn't treat you with respect you stretch them. A guy can go to high school and tell the teacher to screw off but he can't do it in my class. If he does it, I usually wouldn't give him a chance to get off of the mat. If he got off of the mat, he would either come back with a different attitude or he wouldn't come back at all. If he doesn't come back, then you don't want him around anyway because he would probably be that bad apple that would ruin the whole class.

I get a big thrill out of people that say that they would have been a hoodlum if they didn't come to the dojo and learn that other people have feelings too. It feels good to know that you have taught them respect. You teach them that a guy who doesn't think of the future doesn't have one and to try to get as much of an education as possible. When I teach the young kids, I say, "If you finish the third grade you'll be making a dollar an hour. If you finish the eighth grade you'll be making 3 dollars and hour. If you finish the 10th grade or 12th grade you'll be making five to ten dollars an hour. If you graduate college you'll be making 50 dollars an hour." I tell them that the more education that they get, the more money they are going to make which means that they have a better car, a better house and a better lifestyle. The more education you get the better human being you are going to be. I really believe that and I get a kick out of it when I am able to pass that on to a bunch of kids who might never have heard that from anybody else.

When I teach a class, I like to tease and joke but everyone who knows me knows that I'm teasing. In class, I will put a painful finishing hold on somebody and ask them, "Who's the best looking?" They will always reply "You are," but everybody knows better. It's all a joke. I don't try to make anybody feel bad. When I tease in the class it's because I want to make people enjoy themselves. I'll hug them or something like that just to let them know that I care and it's all in fun. I like to make a person feel good. I've been to a lot of martial arts schools where many instructors put themselves on such a pedestal like they're a policeman or a commanding officer in the military. People come into those schools and they're afraid to sign up because they are intimidated. When somebody comes into Gokor's and my school, I might joke around and say, "Why aren't you on the mat, you're late!"

It might be the first time that they are there and they haven't signed up. They might not even know me, but if they have their gear I tell them to suit up and get on the mat. I give them special attention to make them feel good. After the class is over I go up to them and tell them, "Well you can sign up but I don't want you to because I never did like you anyway." They laugh and most of the time if they say, "Hey I've had a good time. Where do I sign up?" If my school is too far from where they live, I ask them where they live and I'll send them to another dojo. If they want to learn karate I send them to Benny or I might send them to the Armenian Martial Arts Coalition (who are friends of Gokor's) or the Machados (they are excellent teachers) if they live closer to those schools.

When I give seminars, I ask if there are any volunteers who want to be choked out. If someone does volunteer, I give them a patch that says, "I WAS CHOKED OUT BY GENE LeBELL," which most people wear on their judo jackets with pride. To add a little levity after I have put somebody to sleep, I will go through their wallet and pull out a picture and say, "Well here's a picture of my wife and my girlfriend!" The audience gets a big laugh out of this. If the guy has a couple of bucks in his wallet, I'll take that and stuff it into my gi while he's sleeping. After that, I wake the guy up and the whole audience starts screaming, "He's got your money!" I shush them and tell them to be quiet and usually the guy that has just been choked out doesn't know what is happening. Of course, after we all go back and fourth with this for a bit, I give the guy his money back. It's the same shtick that I used to do in pro wrestling in Texas back in the 1950s when I took challengers out of the audience. In the seminars, it's all a big joke as long as they learn something and the audience really enjoys this routine.

Today I have this dojo with Gokor. It's called Hayastan, which in means Armenian in Armenian. He calls it our dojo, but it's really his dojo. I don't get paid. I don't have to pay the rent. I just get people to come on in there. I never took a penny in all these years. I just teach because I love people. I've had many teachers that devoted a lot of time to teaching me and as I get older, now it's my time to return the favor.

When Gokor first opened the school, he asked me if I would teach for him. I said that I would teach there for a month free if he got a shower. I joked around and called them the dirty Armenians because they didn't have a shower in their dojo. "You put in the shower and I will teach there for free for a month," I said. Gokor came over to my house a couple of weeks later and asked me to come with him to his school. I walked into his school and found a newly installed shower with hot and cold running water and there was a big sign on the shower door that said, "Gene LeBell Only."

I started to teach there on Monday nights for a month. Now 15 years have passed and I'm still there. You know how those Armenian calendars are. I hope to be there for many more years. The school is my home and the students are my family.

Gokor has always treated me with respect. If I'm carrying something he grabs it away from me and carries it. I didn't teach him that. That was bred into him. His whole family is the same way. He has a beautiful wife named Noreen and two sons. His oldest son Arthur is the Junior National Judo Champion many times over and we are all very proud of him. When he grows up, he'll be a champion also. As for the second son Karren, who is quite a bit younger, he is not a judo champion but he's got a fighting spirit – he bit me twice last week.

Gokor is a marvelous athlete but he's a fanatic's fanatic in grappling but he also makes sacrifices for his family. For example, he's taking classes to be a real estate agent. He studies all phases of computers and he's good at it. God forbid something happens to him where he can't teach or work out which is his first love, he has a backup to take care of his family. He sleeps very little because he's always on the road doing one thing or another to make extra money to give his family a better life.

One of the things that Gokor has learned from me is that when you are no longer competing in judo or any of the martial arts, your students become like family to you. I am as proud as I can be when our students make a good showing in competition. When my students do well, it's like my grandkids are doing well. There are people who say, "That's Hayastan Dojo or that's Gene LeBell and Gokor's Grappling guys – you know they're going to come out on top." That really makes me feel good when I hear people say that. It makes me feel like my life has not been wasted. As long as my students and their students live, I will live on and so will my system.

CHAPTER 15

STATE AID

Now I have worn a lot of hats during my life. I have been a judo champion – eight years undefeated, winning 2,000 fights – professional wrestler, grappling teacher, TV pro-wrestling commentator, author, movie actor, and stuntman and I have been lucky enough to achieve some level of success in all of these endeavors. Most people consider themselves highly fortunate to make it in just one vocation and that's with a lot of hard work. Of course, I realize this, but maybe I don't always realize it enough and that could be why Noelle Kim, who runs my website (www.genelebell.com if you're interested) put together the Gene LeBell Celebrity Roast, which was held on April 14, 2003 at the Anoush Restaurant in Glendale, Calif. For those of you who don't know, a celebrity roast is a Hollywood tradition where a bunch of people who know you and have worked with you all gather to get up in front of an audience and dish dirt on you and insult you in the worst ways possible. It is all in good fun, unless, of course, you are the guy getting the dirt thrown at you.

Now Noelle is also a talented producer as well as being good with computers so she did a heck of a job in putting this thing together. It was attended by too many movie stars, directors, professional wrestlers, martial artists, stuntmen, friends and family members (with 200 people turned away at the door) to really mention every one of them by name. Actors, martial artists and pro wrestlers like Chuck Norris, Roddy Piper, Bob Wall, Joe Don Baker, Bill McKinney (he made Ned Beatty squeal like a pig in "Deliverance"), Branscombe Richmond, James Lew, Perry King, Nicholas Worth, Bruce Buffer, John Saxon, Hank Garrett and even Anne Francis came to either say nice things about me or let me have it. Such legendary stuntmen as Terry Leonard, Mickey Gilbert, Eddie Donno, Gary Davis, Vince Deadrick, Sr., Joey Bucaro, Bobby Hoy, Jimmy Nickerson, Roy Clarke, Loren Janes, Wally Crowder and many others also attended to either roast me or see me get roasted.

The Anoush Restaurant serves Armenian food and boasts a pretty spacious dining hall and after the show, the owner told me that his venue was filled to capacity. Of course my roast was held at an Armenian restaurant because Gokor had something to say about it. Liquor flowed freely and I hear that there was some excellent food served there but I never had a chance to try any of it. After the roast was over I was mobbed by a line of people that wanted my autograph or to have their picture taken with me. One voluptuous woman even sat on my lap to have her picture taken with me and she wouldn't get up so I never got to have my dinner. That's one of the sacrifices that you have to make. My wife was dancing at the time and didn't notice, so I am here to tell the story.

Now there is a lot of competition in the stunt world and the martial arts world and people end up disliking each other over it. There are different stunt associations and independent stuntmen all competing for the same pool of jobs, glory and recognition. All of this gave Noelle fits when she was making out the seating chart for the roast. In the end, everybody had a good time, which had nothing to do with me – I think that it was because the wine flowed freely. For me, the best-remembered thing about the roast was the next day when the men sobered up and called their best friends and said, "You'll never believe who I had dinner with last night!" To me, that's what the roast was all about – love they neighbor.

I first met Noelle Kim about a few years ago when her boyfriend, now husband Steve Kim became one of the better students at Gokor's and my grappling school along with Karo, Manvel, and Romeo. Steve is South Korean but I refer to him as the "North Korean fighter pilot." When he first started training with me, he was very shy and serious and this drove him nuts, but since then, he has loosened up quite a bit and now jokes around with the best of them in two languages.

About four years ago, Noelle found this Website that lists all of the unclaimed money that is owed to people. She checked for my name on it and found that Disney owed me 75 dollars for some job that I had done for them. I called up Disney and sure enough, they owed me money. They told me that they had lost my address.

When Noelle showed me the Website so I could see that Disney owed me 75 bucks, I noticed that there were also a lot of Lebells listed on the site that lived in Southern California. All of them spelled their name with a small "b" in the middle instead of the capital "B" that I spell my name with so I thought that they were no relation to me. Now I hadn't seen anybody from the LeBell side of my family since my father died from an accident when I was six years old. I decided to attempt to get a hold of some of these other Lebells. At the very least I would be helping people track down some money that was owed to them and, who knows, maybe I would get lucky and find some long lost cousins.

I tried to get a hold of these people, but I had trouble tracking down phone numbers for them. I found one number and called it and it turned out to be a fax line, so I wrote them a note that said something like, "I found your name on this website and if this is you, these people owe you money. By the way, I could possibly be a relative of yours. If I am, my name is Gene LeBell. If we're not related, have a nice day." I put my phone number and contact information on the fax and sent it off.

I didn't think anything of it but later on in the day I got a call. I answered the phone and the voice on the other end of the line said, "Hello Gene, this is Malca LeBell." A million things go through your mind in a half a second and that left me at a rare loss for words. "I'm your cousin," she continued. "I'm Doctor Malca LeBell." She then told me that she was a psychiatrist at UCLA for 20 years plus.

For years and years, relatives from my father's side of the family called the Olympic Auditorium and they asked to speak to my brother Mike or me. My brother always got the calls and I never did. He sarcastically told them that he wasn't interested in talking to them and then he hung up on them.

When I heard that these long-lost LeBells had called, I told Mike that I wanted to talk to them. "Get their number," I said, "I want to call them back. That's my father's side of the family. I want to get to know them. I want to find out more about who I am."

"To hell with them," Mike answered. "They're losers. They're on state aid and we have the Olympic Auditorium and all they want is our money."

"If they want money, I will give them money," I said to my brother. These people were relatives after all, and if they were down and out, I wanted to help them. They called four or five or six times or maybe more over a period of years. Every time that they called, Mike told me that they ate at the midnight mission and they were all on state aid. He said that they were nothing but trash and they wanted to rip us off, but I just wanted to meet them and help them out if they needed help because they were my family.

As I talked to Malca, she said, "Either you or your brother told us that you didn't want to talk to us." I explained that they had talked to my brother and that he had always told me, "those losers called again."

"Well he was probably right about us being losers," she said modestly. She then told me that the family was having a small get-together at the Marina in a couple of weeks and if I wanted to, I could go there and meet the rest of the family.

I was all excited to finally meet my dad's side of the family. I only have one suit and it didn't really fit me too well because I had put on a few pounds so I spent that two weeks starving myself just to fit into my suit. I wasn't expecting too much because all of these people were on state aid you see. They were probably only going to have a modest little wienie roast with some Costco potato salad, but I still wanted to look my best for the occasion.

Two weeks passed and I went to the Marina with my wife Midge and all of these people that don't have any money and were on state aid, had rented out the whole Marina for their little get together. Among these welfare recipients were four lawyers, a judge, and four doctors. One of my cousins walked up to me and said, "I'm Don. I guess that I must have talked to your brother and not you." Don had tried to contact my brother over the phone, but Mike always told him that he didn't have time to talk to him.

"Well I apologize," I said, "but that wasn't me talking. I've wanted to get a hold of you for years."

Don hosts many of the family members and he brings them to New

York for a two week vacation, but he must do it with food stamps because my brother said that he's on state aid. He had just tried to contact us all of these years to get a piece of the Olympic Auditorium, but the property value of the Olympic is probably what Don pays for a telephone bill each month.

The party was a birthday celebration for my cousin Allen who is married to Betty and they are both lawyers. It was Allen's 80th birthday and this guy was still as sharp as a tack. He didn't exhibit any signs of senility. I hope that I am that together when I am 80 years old – heck I wish that I was that together now. Everybody on my father's side of the family was very intelligent and they all had a nice sense of humor, which was how I remembered my dad. He was a doctor and he made everybody laugh and have a good time.

Now for dinner these people on state aid served steak, fish, lobster, chicken and just about everything else that you could think of. Once the servers took one plate away, they put another plate in front of you and each entree was better than the last, but I tried not to eat too much. Earlier, when I walked into the Marina I spotted this glass case that you could see through with the dessert in it. Our dessert was shaped like roses and made out of chocolate with a big strawberry on top and ice cream all around and the whole thing was about eight or nine inches high. I love strawberries so I wanted to save a lot of room for dessert.

After the servers had taken away the last entree and before they served that wonderful looking dessert, Allen, the guest of honor, got up to speak. I was starving because I didn't eat and I was just waiting for that dessert, but I still wanted to hear what my long-lost cousin had to say. "I appreciate you people coming from all over to celebrate my 80th birthday with me," he said, "but most of all I appreciate finally meeting my long lost cousin Gene." He talked for a couple of minutes about me and then people started coming up to me and asking for my autograph probably because they have seen me on TV or in the movies. There were maybe 90 or 100 people there at the gathering and it seemed that most of them wanted my autograph. Now this is the sad part of the story because while I was busy signing autographs, they started serving those deserts. I was looking around and I saw that the waiter started to deliver the dessert but all of these people were pulling at me to sign these autographs.

When I was finally done signing napkins or whatever people had put in front of me, I saw the server walking away with the dessert cart and I didn't get one. "Hey come back here," I shouted. I spent the whole night waiting for my chocolate, strawberries and ice cream and I had to have it.

I started to get up and go after that ice cream and my wife Midge the Mean told me to sit down. I looked at her with desperation and said, "I'm going to get my ice cream if I have to eat it in the kitchen!"

"You'll do no such thing! Show some class," she said and she made me sit down. I never did get that dessert.

It really hurt not getting any dessert but the main reason that I was there was to find out more about my dad and my family in general. I had always been kept in the dark about my father and I felt that I didn't really even know who I was or where I had come from because of it. My brother had this picture of my Dad and I always wanted to make a copy of it, but he would never let me borrow it. Mike always said no and he was always on some kind of a power trip not only with me, but also with most people.

At this party at the Marina, everybody told me that if I wanted to know more about my dad that I had to talk to Betty who was Allen's wife. It turned out that she had been very close to my father.

I went to their house to talk to Betty and learn more about my dad. Now you've got to understand that they were both on state aid and they didn't have any money, but they had a cottage on Rockingham with a six-car garage and a house to match. I told Midge that we must have had the wrong house but I knocked on the door and this lady opened the door and she was 80 but looked much younger than her years. "I'm your cousin Betty," she said as she welcomed us into her house. "Gene, I've been waiting to meet you all of my life."

We went into her kitchen, which was a fully loaded, gourmet affair and the room was about as big as my entire cabin in the mountains. I asked her to tell me about my grandfather. "He used to tell me great stories when I was five," I said. "He told me how he won World

War I all by himself and how a town in France called LeBell was named after him and he was French so that made me French."

"First of all he had help winning World War I," Betty answered, "and he was not born in France at all. He was born near the Volga River in Russia and he was a Russian Jew."

I spent my whole life telling everybody that I was French, and I believed it, but it turned out that I was Russian all along. I later told this to my Armenian-Russian student and partner Gokor and he said, "I knew that there was something that I liked about you!"

After Betty told me about my grandfather, she started to tell me about my father. "You've got to understand when I was a teenager," she said, "the most important person in my life was your dad. He used to have all of these musical instruments and he taught me how to play them. He gave me some of his instruments. When he got divorced!"

"Got divorced?" I interrupted. I had never heard that he and my mom had gotten a divorce before. This was news to me.

"Didn't you know?" she asked.

"Know what?" I answered.

"That your mother and father were divorced." In 1939, people didn't get divorced – it was embarrassing, but my mother and father did get divorced. Everything in my whole life began to add up all of a sudden. I now understood why my mother prevented me from seeing my grandmother and grandfather after my dad had died and why my dad had never seemed to be around the house all that much when I was a kid. It was a big disgrace for a woman to be a divorcee in 1939, but being a widow didn't have the same stigma and that was why my mother didn't really talk too much about my father when I had asked about him.

After all was revealed to me, Betty told me that she had my father's accordion and all of these other instruments that used to belong to him and that after he had died, my mother came and took them from her except for one guitar, which she hid underneath her bed. "I still have this guitar," Betty told me and then she had me come into the front room to see it.

I walked into her front room and it looked like a museum. There were all of these paintings on the walls that were done hundreds of years ago by famous artists. How they could afford such art treasures on state aid, I will never know. They must have been from second hand stores or something. They also had a piano that was as big as an entire dance floor and on the wall among all of those expensive paintings hung an oversized Spanish guitar that looked out of place. I looked up at it and Betty said, "Yes, that's the guitar that I was talking about. Your father gave it to me and I loved and respected him. That was my Uncle Murray."

Midge looked at the guitar and said, "Go touch it because your dad used to play it."

I was embarrassed. You don't just go into other people's houses and touch other people's belongings so I whispered to Midge that I didn't want to touch it, but then Betty also told me to go and touch it because it really meant a lot to my father. That guitar was a big part of his life.

I finally weakened and decided to touch the guitar and make Betty and Midge happy. They weren't going to leave me alone until I touched the thing so I reached up and touched it and all of a sudden a feeling shot through my arm and down my body. It was a feeling of tremendous well being. I looked around like somebody had pushed the special effects button. I looked at Midge and she was talking to Betty and then they both were looking at me. "Your father will be very happy that you touched his guitar," Betty said. "It really meant a lot to him."

I didn't really know what to make of any of this. I thought that maybe I wasn't getting enough sleep lately, but on the way home I told Midge what had happened. I thought that she would take it all as a big joke because I always tease her. The next day she called Betty and told her about it and Betty said, "Yes, I knew that would happen." She told Midge that my father was happy and that he could finally rest in peace.

While my brother wouldn't let me borrow that one picture of my father to make a copy of it, Betty had 26 photos of my dad. Before she had met me, she was about to throw them away, but something stopped her from doing it. A couple of weeks after I went to her house, she hunted up those pictures and gave them to me and among them was a picture of me when I was three years old hanging from my dad's fingers and I am laughing and smiling. Many of those pictures now hang on my walls. My brother told me that all of my cousins were on state aid to put them down. But contrary to what my brother had told me, my cousins are all millionaires and now that I have met them, I am also a millionaire.

Throughout my entire life, my brother used to chew me out and told me that he paid for the grass, flowers and a tombstone at my father's gravesite. I always offered to help him pay for it but he said, "No I'll do it myself. I want it done right."

I then asked where my father was buried. I never knew where my father's grave was but my brother always said, "Well I know but you don't." My brother did tell me that my father's grave was all by itself off to the side of the cemetery and was covered with grass and was marked by a big grave stone that he had personally paid for out of his own pocket.

After I met my long-lost cousins and aunts and uncles, they decided to visit my father's grave to show it to me. I went there and it was in an old Jewish cemetery and there was no grass there at all. It was all cement and my father's grave wasn't off to the side but he was buried next to my grandmother and grandfather. Gray tombstones marked my grandparents' graves, but my dad's grave marker was pink. I've wrestled in pink for years as a joke. Did my father have anything to do with that? I was told that my dad's brother Frank had paid for the stones and my brother knew nothing about it. It was done before my brother was old enough to ride a bicycle. There wasn't even a place for all of the flowers that my brother had told me that he had bought. In other words my brother had been fibbing to me for years.

I took pictures of my father's grave. One of the pictures came back and there was a light rising out of it. It was probably just how I took the picture, but I couldn't help but think that my father was trying to tell me something that day at his graveside as I snapped that picture. I knew what he wanted to tell me. He wanted to say that he loved me, and I finally had the opportunity to tell him that I have always loved him and I always will. No man ever dies until he is forgotten and I will never forget my father.

I've have had a lot of ups and downs in my life but I've enjoyed the ride and I wouldn't trade my life for anything. I've been to the bottom of the barrel and the top of the mountain. I've had disappointments and I've had things that went wrong that were out of my control. Sometimes I've cried, but everyone has so live with it. I have broken bread with movie stars, sports heroes, governors, generals and even a president. I have been to Mecca and I've played with the Gods. Tomorrow will come if you like or not. I'll be on that train. It is often said in the Bible that the Lord giveth the Lord taketh away. In my case, the Lord giveth my family back to me.

God Bless

Your Friend,
Gene LeBell

Message from Roddy Piper

I started in the sport of professional wrestling when I was 15 years old. I was 167 pounds. I was an amateur wrestling champion and I was a very scared little boy that had already been living on the street by that time for two years. The first wrestling match that I had was against a man named Larry Henning who beat me in 10 seconds. That match certainly didn't help my confidence, but it did introduce me to what would later become my savior and my dream come true. After that match, I kept trying and I wrestled every night. At 18 years old, I came to Los Angeles to the Olympic Auditorium. I was 170 pounds, I wore a kilt and I played the bagpipes, so you can imagine how intimidated and mixed-up a young man in that position in his life could be.

The first time that I saw Gene LeBell, I had never heard of him. It was one Friday n night and I had wrestled at the Olympic Auditorium. My opponent was much larger than I was and he beat me up pretty good. To him I was just a young, punk kid and he was a main event wrestler and he thought that I didn't warrant any respect at all because of my size.

The locker rooms at the Olympic Auditorium could be described as a modern-day Roman gladiator setting. After that match, I headed back to those locker rooms and I was as humiliated as I had been in my whole life and there stood this man with bright red hair. It was Gene LeBell. He looked at me and walked with me into that gladiator's locker room and he sat me down and put his arm around me. When he sat me down, I looked into his eyes and I could tell that I was safe. I don't know how – it was just the way that he looked at me and the confidence that just exuded from him. I instantaneously wanted to be this man. He was my savior.

As I got to know Gene LeBell, which was about 20 choke holds later, I found out that this kind, warm gentleman that took me under his wing only because he hates a bully, was also the toughest man in the world. I remember one time I was up against this very large man and before the match, Gene just came by and told me, "When you go to lock up, don't lock up. Grab him by the pecks, up under the arms, squeeze hard and as he starts pushing you back, switch and he'll go down hard." I turned and looked at the 250 pound black gentleman across the ring from me and I thought that I was going to die, but doggone it, it worked. I did what Gene told me to do, and that guy fell hard. It was on the job training.

Six or seven months after Gene had taken me under his wing, my wrestling career was recognised throughout our sport for the first time. Gene had given me my first big break. As I look at the wrestling industry in hindsight, I believe that I would be dead had it not been for the warm heart and the exceptional perception of Gene LeBell. Gene is the dad that I never had and he is the ultimate positive force in my life. If I could just be half the man that he is, I would be happy for the rest of my life.

Roddy Piper
May 24, 2003

Gene LeBell Filmography

Following is the most complete listing to date of Gene LeBell's film and television credits. Due to the nature of Hollywood stunt work where the stuntman shows up to the location or sound stage does his job and leaves, Gene Lebell is often unaware of many of the films that he has worked on. This is a constantly expanding list because, as stated in in a previous chapter, Gene often discovers films that he has worked on by either spotting himself on television or by receiving residual checks for his work. In many of these movies and TV shows, Gene appears on screen and has lines, but in so many others, he is the unknown stuntman who is rolling a car, crashing a motorcycle or falling off of a building. Keep in mind that Gene LeBell is still working in motion pictures and television today and that this list does not include his numerous appearances as both a pro wrestler and color commentator on TV wrestling shows in the Los Angeles as well as other wrestling territories.

FILM

3 Ninjas Knuckle Up (1995)
4 From Texas (1963)
4th Tenor, The (2002)
7 Women (1966)
99 and 44/100% Dead (1974)
A Fine Mess (1986)
A Matter of Wife and Death (1976)
Airplane (1980)
Ali (2001)
Alien Nation (1988)
Alligator II: The Mutation (1991)
Almost an Angel (1990)
Almost Summer (1978)
Americathon (1979)
Animal Factory (2000)
Another 48 Hours (1990)
Another You (1991)
Any Which Way You Can (1980)
Army of Darkness (1993)
Article 99 (1992)
As Good as it Gets (1997)
At Long Last Love (1975)
Bad Guys (1986)
Bad News Bears go to Japan, The (1978)
Ballistic (1995)
Bandits (2001)
Batman and Robin (aka: Batman 4; 1997)
Batman Forever (1995)
Batman Returns (1992)
Battle for the Planet of the Apes (1973)
Beast Master (1982)
Beneath the Planet of the Apes (1970)
Best of the Best II (1993)

Best of the West (1981)
Big Brawl, The (1980)
Big Bus, The (1976)
Bitter Harvest
Black Samson (1974)
Black Sunday (1977)
Blacula (1972)
Blind Date (1987)
Bloodfist IV: Die Trying (1992)
Blown Away (1994)
Blue Hawaii (1961)
Blue Thunder (1983)
Bronco Billy (1980)
Bruce Almighty (2003)
Buck Rogers in the 25th Century (1979)
Burke's Law (1963)
Busting Loose (1977)
Cade's County (1971)
California Split (1974)
Camp Nowhere (1994)
Challenge, The
Childish Things (1969)
CIA II: Target Alexa (1994)
City Heat (1984)
City Limits (1985)
Cleopatra Jones (1973)
Code Name: Zebra (1984)
Conflict of Interest
Conquest of the Planet of the Apes (1972)
Cover Up
Crazy like a Fox
D.A.R.Y.L. (1985)
Dalton
Dante's Peak (1997)
Darkman (1990)

Day of the Locust, The (1975)
Dead Heat (1988)
Dead Men Don't Wear Plaid (1982)
Death Warrant (1Deuces Wild (2002)
990)
Deathwish 4: The Crackdown (1987)
Devlin Connection, The (1982)
Dick Tracy (1990)
Die Hard 2 (1990)
Die Trying
Don't Just Stand There! (1968)
Double Tap (1997)
Down and Dirty
Dude, Where's My Car? (2000)
Dutch (1991)
Earthquake (1974)
Ed Wood (1994)
Eishied (1979)
End of Days (1999)
Every Which Way But Loose (1978)
Eye of the Tiger (1986)
Eyes of an Angel (1991)
Fletch (1985)
Fifth Floor, The (1978)
Flesh and Blood
Fletch Lives (1989)
Flintstones (1994)
Foolin' Around (1980)
Fortune Dane (1986)
Freebie and the Bean (1974)
Freeway (1988)
Fresh
Gambler, The
Gangster Chronicles, The (1981)
Ghost of Baxley Hall
Going Ape! (1981)
Golden Child, The (1986)
Goldie and the Boxer (1979)
Gone Fishin' (1997)
Gotcha! (1985)
Hagan
Hammer (1972)
Happiest Millionaire, The (1967)
Hard Justice (1995)
Hard Times (1975)
Hard to Kill (1990)
Heart Like a Wheel (1983)
Hell Up in Harlem (1973)
Hidden, The (1987)
Honey, I Blew Up the Kids (1992)
Hook (1991)
I Wanna Hold Your Hand (1978)
Independence Day (1996)
Inside Moves (1980)
Internal Affairs (1990)
Jackass: The Movie (2002)
Jerk, The (1979)
Jig Saw John

Jingle All the Way (1996)
Johnny Dangerously (1984)
Judge and Jury (1996)
Jury Duty (1995)
Kickboxer 2: The Road Back (1991)
Killer Elite, The (1975)
King Kong (with Jessica Lange; 1976)
L.A. Confidential (1997)
Last Boy Scout, The (1991)
Last Precinct, The (1986)
Lethal Weapon 4 (1998)
Let's Do It Again (1975)
Liar Liar (1997)
Live Wire (1992)
Lock Up (1989)
Loose Cannons (1990)
Losin' It (1983)
Lost Boys, The (1987)
Lou Grant (1977)
Mac and Me (1988)
Mad Bull (1977)
Major Payne (1995)
Man & Machine
Man on the Moon (1999)
Manhunter (1986)
Marlowe (1968)
Meet Wally Sparks (1997)
Melinda (1972)
Men at Work (1990)
Miami Shootout
Micki & Maude (1984)
Million Dollar Mystery (1987)
Mom & Dad Save the World (1992)
Money Train (1995)
Morning After, The (1986)
My Giant (1998)
Mystery Men (1999)
Naked Gun 33 1/3: The Final Insult, The (1994)
Naked Gun: From the Files of Police Squad!,
The (1988)
Newsies - 1992
Night and the City (1992)
Night Force (1987)
No Holds Barred (1989)
No Way Back (1976)
Nothing To Loose
Nowhere to Run (1993)
Number One With a Bullet (1987)
Nut House, The (1992)
One and Only, The (1978)
Other World, The (1976)
Out For Justice (1991)
P.K. and the Kid (1987)
Paradise (1991)
Patriot Games (1992)
Planet of the Apes (1968)
Presidio, The (1988)
Pretender, The (1996)

Prize Fighter, The (1979)
Problem Child (1990)
Problem Child 2 (1991)
Quest, The (1996)
Raging Bull (1980)
Rapid Fire (1992)
Rat Race (2001)
Remo Williams: The Adventure Begins (1985)
Remote Control (1987)
Resurrection Blvd. (2000)
Robocop (1987)
Robocop 2 (1990)
Rocky (1976)
Rocky IV (1985)
Runaway Train (1985)
Running Man, The (1987)
Rush Hour (1998)
Sandlot, The (1993)
Savage Land (1994)
Shakes the Clown (1992)
Skokie (1981)
Slaughter's Big Rip-Off (1973)
Sledgehammer(1983)
Smokey Bites the Dust (1981)
Split, The (1968)
Steel Frontier (1995)
Strange Days (1995)
Streets of Gold (1986)
Surviving the Game (1994)
Tango and Cash (1989)
There Was a Crooked Man (1970)
They call me Bruce? (1992)
They Came From Outer Space (1990)
Three on a Couch (1966)
Total Recall (1990)
Towering Inferno,The (1974)
Trancers II (1991)
Tyson (1995)
US Marshalls (1998)
Vegas Vacation (1997)
Wackiest Ship in the Army, The (1965)
Walking Tall (1973)
Waterworld (1995)
Welcome to 18 (1986)
When the Whistle Blows (1980)
White Dog (1982)
Wild Pair, The (1987)

TELEVISION

A Team (1983)
Adventures of Briso Country, Jr.
Adventures of Ozzie & Harriett, The (1952)
Aloha Paradise (1981)
Amen (1986)
Barbary Coast (1975)
Barretta (1978)

Batman (1966)
Battlestar Galactica (1978)
Baywatch (1989)
Beverly Hillbillies, The
Big Valley, The (1965)
Bionic Woman, The (1976)
Charlie's Angels (1976)
CHiPs (1977)
Code Red
Dating Game, The (1965)
Dempsy (1983)
Drew Carey Show, The
Diagnosis Murder
Dirty Tricks
Dukes of Hazard, The (1979)
Eddie Capra Mysteries, The (1978)
Entertainment Today
F.B.I., The (1965)
Fall Guy, The (1981)
Family Matters (1989)
Fantasy Island (1978)
Flash, The
Full House (1987)
Future Cop
Gemini Man
General Hospital (1963)
Get Christie Love (1974)
Greatest American Hero, The (1981)
Green Hornet, The (1966)
Guardian, The (2003)
Hardcastle and McCormick (1983)
Hart to Hart (1979)
Heart of the City (1986)
Hell Hath No Fury (1991)
High Performance (1983)
Highway to Heaven
Hollywood Beat (1985)
Honey West (1965)
I Spy (1965)
Jack Benny Show, The (1960)
Jag (1995)
I Spy (1965)
Incredible Hulk, The (1977)
Joe Forrester (1975)
John Larroquette Show, The (1993)
Knight Rider (1982)
Kolchak: The Night Stalker (1974)
Kung Fu (1972)
Land of the Giants
Laverne & Shirley (1976)
Little House on the Prairie (1974)
Lois and Clark: The New Adventures of Superman (1993)
MacGyver (1985)
Maggie
Magnum PI (1980)
MaGruder & Loud (1985)
Major Dad (1989)

Malcolm in the Middle (2000)
Man From Atlantis, The (1977)
MANTIS
Married... With Children (1987)
Master, The
Matlock (1986)
Matt Houston (1982)
Melrose Place
Mission: Impossible (1966)
Misfits of Science (1985)
Munsters, The (1964)
Murder, She Wrote (1984)
New Maverick, The (1978)
Perfect Strangers (1986)
Police Squad! (1982)
Police Story (1973)
Quantum Leap (1989)
Quincy (1976)
Remmington Steele (1982)
Riptide (1984)
Rockford Files, The (1974)
Running Delilah (1994)
Sabrina, the Teenage Witch (1996)
Simon and Simon (1981)
Six Million Dollar Man, The (1974)
Stand, The (1994)
Starsky and Hutch (1975)
Super Fan Show
Taxi (1978)
Tenspeed and Brown Shoe (1980)
That 70's Show (1998)
T.H.E. Cat (1966)
The Strip (1999)
Tonight Show with Jay Leno (1992)
Trial and Error (1988)
Vega$ (1978)
Voyage to the Bottom of the Sea (1961)
Walker, Texas Ranger (1993)
Wild Wild West, The (1965)
X-Files, The (1993)